# RICH HABITS POOR HABITS

## LEARN THE DAILY HABITS THAT SEPARATE THE RICH AND THE POOR

2ND EDITION

TOM CORLEY & MICHAEL YARDNEY

Published by:
Wilkinson Publishing Pty Ltd
PO Box 24135
Level 4, 2 Collins Street
Melbourne, Vic 3001
Ph: 03 9654 5446
www.wilkinsonpublishing.com.au


First Print December 2016
First reprint May 2017
Second reprint August 2018
This edition printed 2021

A catalogue record for this book is available from the National Library of Australia

Planned date of publication: 07-2021
Title: Rich Habits Poor Habits
ISBN(s): 9781925927641 : Printed - Paperback

Internal design by Spike Creative Pty Ltd
Ph: (03) 9427 9500
spikecreative.com.au

Printed and bound in Australia by Griffin, a part of Ovato.

# NOTE TO READER

This publication contains the opinions and ideas of the authors. It is sold with the understanding that neither the author nor the publisher is engaged in rendering legal, tax, investment, insurance, financial, accounting, or other professional advice or services in this publication. If the reader requires such advice or services, a competent professional should be consulted. Relevant laws and regulations vary from state to state and from country to country and are subject to constant revision and amendment.

Any opinions, conclusions or recommendations set forth in this book are subject to change without notice.

The strategies outlined in this book may not be suitable for every individual and are not guaranteed or warranted to produce any particular results. Past performance may not be a reliable indicator of future performance.

This book has been written without taking into account the objectives, financial situation or needs of any specific person who may read this book, which means that before acting on the information in this book, the reader should seek appropriate professional or financial advice.

No warranty is made with respect to the accuracy or completeness of the information contained herein, and both the author and publisher specifically disclaim any responsibility for any liability, loss or risk, personal or otherwise which is incurred as a consequence, directly or indirectly, of the use and application of any of the contents within this book.

# ACKNOWLEDGEMENTS

MICHAEL YARDNEY

This book, like almost everything else in my life, is the result of a team effort.

Firstly, I must thank Tom Corley, without whose efforts this book would never have been conceived or completed. Thank you for your friendship, support, insights and the many long days and nights spent in the original conception of this book and for allowing me the privilege of being your co author.

To my wife Pam — thank you for encouraging me, supporting me in every way and putting up with all my late nights and weekends on the computer. She endures my almost fanatical attitude to business and investment, and continually encourages me through all the good times and through all the things I still need to learn. I am humbled by her love and devotion, which I try hard to match, but never quite succeed.

Special thanks go to my family for their love and encouragement. This includes my four children, Pam's two children and the 11 grandchildren they have blessed us with.

Further thanks to my business partners and fellow directors at Metropole including Mark Creedon who's been my "unreasonable friend" and business coach for years, as well as Ken Raiss, Kate Forbes, Brett Warren, Greg Hankinson, Leanne Jopson and my son Bryce Yardney.

And this book would not have been possible without the skills of Nicola McDougall, our brilliant and supportive editor who took our words, notes and scribbles and made sense from them, crafting them into the manuscript for the first edition.

Over the years I have read almost every book about wealth creation, success and investment ever written. I have learned a lot along the way and there are many ideas sprinkled throughout this book that I have learned from others. I guess I had to learn everything from someone at one stage, so I am sorry I cannot acknowledge everyone – I really can't remember where I first came across many of my strategies.

Where I recollect first hearing about an idea I try to give credit where it is due, but if I have omitted mentioning your name, please excuse me as I shamelessly acknowledge borrowing other people's good ideas picked up from observation or from conversation, books, blogs, CDs, DVDs and seminars. As knowledge about becoming rich and successful isn't one individual's sole domain and there are really no secrets, I can only assume that these people also learned from other people's ideas, books, blogs, CDs, DVDs and seminars.

Over the years I have learned from the many successes, and particularly from some of the failures, of the over 2,000 property investors I have personally mentored through my 12-month mentorship program.

I must thank Michael Wilkinson from Wilkinson Publishing for having faith in me way back in 2006 and publishing my first book. Michael has become a friend and mentor and continues to encourage me to write.

And finally to you, the reader — thank you for choosing to invest in this book. Please take advantage of the information we have to offer by using it to obtain the success you deserve.

# CONTENTS

# SECTION ONE

# WHY WE CAN TEACH YOU TO BE RICH

*Tom Corley and Michael Yardney*

# INTRODUCTION

The rich are getting richer — but are you?

Study after study shows that while the rich are getting richer, the middle class are working harder and longer than they did a decade ago, but have less to go around each week.

And what's happening to the poor?

They're growing in numbers and they're hurting. And their numbers are swelling as we are slowly losing a middle-class — but the poor don't get much attention. Yet the growing ranks of the financial have-nots is a bad sign for our economy.

In the old days miners took canaries down into the mines with them to warn of impending danger. When the canary keeled over, the miners ran realising the atmosphere was becoming a threat to their lives. Today the poor are the canary for our society, warning of impending dangerous conditions to our economies and lives. Just look at the social and political unrest around the world.

It may not seem fair, but the fact is the "income gap" is increasing and the economic turmoil and Coronavirus-induced recession only accentuated this, with most financial experts seeing this trend continuing with no end in sight. One of the realities of life is that, despite living the best of times in some of the richest countries in the world, most people today are struggling financially. And the gap between the wealthy and the average person only seems to be getting wider.

So, this has led many people to ask, "Why do the rich keep getting richer?"

Most of the time, it's not because of luck. It's not because of the family they were born into and it's not because they won the lottery.

***Wealthy people simply do things differently.*** They think differently, they act differently and they have different habits.

But succeeding today is harder than ever, despite the plethora of information available online, in podcasts and in the many get rich books. The problem is, much of the time, we've been lied to. We've been told that you need a good education and then work hard — that's simply not true!

Those who've succeeded in business, entrepreneurship and investing have come to realise they need Rich Habits — they are your foundation for building your wealth.

So our goal in writing this book is to teach you these Rich Habits and reassure you that wherever you are in your financial life today, you too can become rich.

But to become rich you'll have to do things differently. You'll have to think differently. You'll have to behave differently. And you'll have to develop different habits — Rich Habits.

What we're going to show you has worked for us and countless others, so there is no reason why you can't achieve your financial dreams if you're willing to take the time to learn how to attain them.

However, this is not a book about money, investing, real estate or stocks — there are plenty of good books out there on these topics — in fact, Michael has written a number of them that you can find at www.MichaelYardneyBooks.com.au.

Instead this is a book about modelling the way rich people feel, think, act and behave. It is a book about developing Rich Habits (the habits most rich people exhibit) and deleting Poor Habits.

But don't misunderstand us — we believe that talking about getting rich is really a discussion about what's important to you in achieving a fulfilling life.

This will mean different things to each and every reader, but if you're honest with yourself, in Western societies, money is seen as the number one benchmark of success — not only do we want to keep up with the Joneses, many of us want to have a bigger and better house and car than they do, too.

And even if you don't aspire to riches or a big home or a fast car, if like many people you live in fear because your wallet is empty, we'd like you to have the satisfaction in life of knowing that you're financially secure.

## Can this book really make me rich?

We bet that when you picked up this book you wondered, "Can this book really make me rich?"

The truthful answer is — possibly.

There are only two ways to learn what you need to know about becoming rich. You can learn from *your own* mistakes and experiences or you can learn from the mistakes and experiences *of others*. The first way is too hard, too expensive and too demoralising.

The second method — learning from the experiences of others — is by far the cheapest and easiest, yet it is also the least used.

Imagine if we offered you two books:

1. Here's one with all the mistakes you could make;
2. And here's another one with all the ways to do it right.

Which one would you choose?

Interestingly, most people choose to try and learn to do things on their own, however you can greatly accelerate your growth and progress towards financial success by systematically copying the rich and successful people who have gone before you.

Now we're not talking about how they invest or what businesses they run, even though this is important to understand. We're suggesting you look a level higher to understand their daily habits and what they do from the moment they get up until the moment they go to bed. We want you to get inside their heads and discover how they feel and how they think because this determines their actions, their habits and their results.

Of course, there is nothing new about this.

The concept of modelling successful people has been used by the top performers in every field from music to sports to business. All people at the top of their field today began by learning from the best at some stage.

Once you do the things the rich and successful people do, once you think like they do, once you act like they do, once you adopt their Rich Habits, you will begin to feel like they feel — you will feel rich and you will start to get the same results that they do, and you will become rich.

## Oh no — this is not a metaphysical book is it?

Don't worry this is not a metaphysical book — it's not full of "rah-rah" feel good stuff. It is based on scientific evidence — in particular Tom's five-year study of the rich and the poor.

You will learn that the rich are not very different from the poor. There've simply learned to do things in a different way from the majority. We'll show you that if you do what other successful rich people do over and over again, you'll eventually get the same results.

That's because financial success is not a matter of luck, it's simply the result of the law of cause and effect — if you initiate the causes you will get the effect.

Both of us have independently studied the rich and wealthy and how they became that way.

While we were on opposite sides of the world — Tom in the United States and Michael in Australia — we both came to similar conclusions.

As a CPA, Tom saw how some of his clients were so much more successful than others, so he set about studying 233 rich people and 128 poor people over five years and analysed the results from 144 individual questions, which totalled nearly 52,000 answers!

For many years Michael studied rich and successful people who were being mentored by some of the most successful business people in the world. He spent hundreds of thousands of dollars on personal development education, coaching and mentoring himself. Michael grew his own national business and a multimillion-dollar property portfolio and then went on to educate more successful property investors in Australia than anyone else. Michael and his team have been involved in more than $4 billion worth of property transactions and he has personally mentored over 2,500 investors, business people and entrepreneurs over the past two decades.

Not surprisingly, both Tom and Michael came to similar conclusions. They realised that becoming rich and successful had little to do with education, race, background or age. Yet it had a lot to do with the way people think, the way people act and their habits.

Their learnings confirmed what Wallace Wattles wrote many years ago in his book *The Science of Getting Rich*, which was **your thoughts lead to feelings — your feelings lead to your actions — and your actions lead to results.**

***Your outside world is a reflection of your inner world*** — your thoughts, your feelings, your actions and your habits.

So, while this is a book about getting rich, it is not a book about investing money in stocks or real estate. Instead, Tom and Michael will share the biggest secret of getting rich — you have to think like the rich and act like the rich if you want to join the rich.

## It couldn't be as simple as that could it?

Yes, but while it's simple, it's not easy. And that's not a play on words. That's why most people don't become rich, but it's also the reason why those who understand the principles we are going to share do become rich.

And that's why you can become rich!

You'll learn how important your financial conditioning is to the habits you practice.

We'll show you that the best way to solve your financial problems is to change the way you think, which will lead to a change in habits — start thinking like rich people, rather than the way that middle-class or poor people do.

You're not going to change a situation with the same old thinking.

There's an old saying, "Give a person a fish feed him for a day. Teach a person to fish and you feed him for life".

That's what our intention is in this book.

If you don't change your way of thinking, all the financial advice — in fact all the money in the world — won't make you rich. We know this may be a little hard to believe, but please bear with us and we'll explain why we believe this wholeheartedly.

## How long will it take me to get rich?

It will probably take a little longer than you'd like and the lessons we'll share most likely will be very different to what you're expecting.

As we studied the biggest differences between our wealthy clients and the average person, we came to realise that their success had very little to do with their backgrounds, education, nationality, investment vehicles or starting capital. Instead it has a lot to do with how they think — in fact, 80 per cent of the reason for their success was their mindset.

Now this may not be what you initially want to hear. You're probably hoping for us to show you how to make a killing in the stock market, how to unearth the next property hotspot, or how to start a business that will be a goldmine.

Imagine for a moment that somebody was willing to give you a million dollars in cash or alternatively, they offered to teach you how to create the mindset of a millionaire. Which would you prefer? We believe that most people would take the cash and run, rather than learn how to change themselves.

So ask yourself: which option would you choose?

If you really understand that you would be better off changing your mindset, that's one of the many concepts we'll be sharing with you and you'll discover that ***your world will change when you change.*** The exciting thing is that the faster you work on transforming yourself, the faster you'll be able to start creating the things you want.

## No judgment

In this book we use the words wealthy or rich and poor or average to differentiate between those who have achieved financial freedom and the vast majority who never quite make it beyond the nine-to-five grind and continue to live just within or, in many cases, beyond their true financial means.

We realise that in Australia and America (where we each live) there are few really poor people — we tend to have the rich and the middle-class.

When we use these terms we're trying to make a distinction and we're **definitely not making a judgment** about the "wealthy" or the "poor" and whether one socio-economic group is better than the other.

This is not a social analysis or commentary. We're just suggesting that most people want to become rich or at least financially well off, in fact most people we deal with want to become financially independent. They are not happy with mediocrity or struggling for a wage.

We also want to make it clear that when we're talking about rich or poor, wealthy or hard working, we're not putting a value on the person, because truthfully there is no way to do that — all of us are priceless. What we're saying is that from a financial standpoint, some of us are doing better than others.

Also, throughout his book we're going to use the words "wealthy", "rich" and "successful" interchangeably, just for convenience, even though our definition of wealth is much more than having money.

To be truly wealthy you need money plus your health; money plus friends and family to enjoy it with; money plus time to enjoy it; money plus the ability to keep growing; money plus spirituality (and this will mean different things to different people); and money plus the ability to contribute to society and your community.

And finally, just to make things clear…

## This book is not about making money

"Making money" suggests that you obtain wealth through, or in proportion to, your efforts or your hard work. Instead we're going to show you why the rich keep getting richer, and while they do work hard, it's much more than that. They keep getting richer because of:

**1. Their Mindset**

So we'll be discussing their thoughts, attitudes and beliefs about wealth. There is a way of thinking that makes you magnetic to wealth and there is a way of thinking that repels wealth, and this, obviously, is how most people think. But we won't stop there — unfortunately you can't just "Think and Grow Rich".

**2. Their Behaviours**

***THE RICH DO CERTAIN THINGS IN A CERTAIN WAY*** that make them attract money. They have Rich Habits. They work in jobs or are self-employed or run a business. The rich invest in shares or real estate like many others, but the point we're trying to make is they not only do certain things, they do them in a certain way — a different way to most people. Then, of course, there are certain habits the rich have that the average person does not.

**3. Their Knowledge**

The rich are financially fluent, which places them in the right position to attract wealth.

## A word of warning!

A lot of what you're about to read in this book is initially going to be hard to accept, because it goes against your teachings or what you read in the day-to-day media, so you may be tempted to reject it. It may even make you feel uncomfortable.

To avoid having wasted the price of this book, and more importantly to avoid missing out on having your share of the wealth that is out there just waiting to be shared, please be patient and prepared to consider ideas and suggestions that at first may seem wrong and unreasonable to you.

As you read on there are two things that could get in the way of you learning the valuable lessons within these covers.

Firstly, you could think *"I already know that"* and the second inhibiting thought may be, *"This is all too much, I don't understand it. I'll never get there anyway so I may as well give up now"*.

Beware: these are both excuses that your mind uses to keep you in your comfort zone.

If at any point you feel overwhelmed, simply say to yourself: *"I don't need to get it all in the first reading"*, just read through initially to grasp the main points and then re-read the sections that don't make sense the first time.

Are you up to it?

When you hear your mind saying, *"I already know that"* — maybe you do. Or maybe you should look at it afresh. Is there a new angle that you haven't considered before? How can you apply the new information that you have learned?

Change can be difficult, but if you put in the effort to transform your thoughts and feelings about money and your relationship with it, you will come out richer in mind, spirit and, yes, in money itself!

To encourage you, in the next two chapters we're going to briefly describe our "qualifications" to assure you that you should take our suggestions seriously.

We hope this rather long introduction has set the scene for the exciting journey we are about to share together.

We're about to show you a way of approaching financial independence that is quite unique. We've seen people in serious debt use these wealth-building strategies to break out of the rat race and we've also seen what many would consider already rich people grow their wealth exponentially. Wherever you are starting from, these strategies will give you the edge in the years ahead.

However, as you earn more money, you will realise that money doesn't bring you happiness. It may give you some short-term satisfaction, especially if you are financially insecure. But as you work your way up the Wealth Pyramid (a concept we'll explain shortly), you'll find that relationships and contributions will mean more to you than money.

Money by itself is empty and meaningless — you have to give it a meaning. Money can be earned, grown, invested, fought over, won, lost, watched over, exchanged, given away or buried. But the nicest thing you can do with money is share it.

Contribution has become an important part of life for both of us as well as our families. Every dollar we have shared with someone less able to gain prosperity has doubled in value — maybe not as cold hard cash but in myriad other ways.

So, are you ready to learn the habits and the mindsets of the rich?

# CHAPTER 1
# WHO IS TOM CORLEY?

Why do so few succeed in life?
Why are some people rich and other people poor?
What specific things are the rich doing every day that the rest of us aren't?

Few ever find out the answers to these questions during their lifetime. Unfortunately, how to be successful in life is not a subject that is taught in our schools. We are all in the same boat, attempting through trial and error to figure it out on our own.

I understand the difference between being rich and poor because at age nine my family went from being multimillionaires to broke in just one night. As an adult, for five years, I observed and documented the daily activities of 233 wealthy people and 128 people struggling with poverty.

I discovered there is an immense difference between the habits of the wealthy, particularly self-made millionaires, and the poor.

You see... I grew up in a very religious family. Every Sunday we attended mass. Every Saturday was confession. I said the rosary every night before I went to sleep.

At a very early age I truly believed my calling in life was the priesthood. But things changed and, instead, I became a certified public accountant (CPA). Most CPAs I know are very moral and honest individuals.
I suppose those not cut out for the priesthood become CPAs!

One of the things my mother would often recite to me was a biblical scripture in Matthew 19:24:
*It is easier for a camel to pass through the eye of a needle than for a rich man to enter the kingdom of God.*

As a result, I grew up convinced that the pursuit and acquisition of wealth was a mortal sin and saw all wealthy individuals as sinners. That all changed in 2009, after completing my analysis of my five-year study on the daily habits of the rich and poor. That study opened my eyes. I learned that wealthy individuals were not bad people. So many of them had devoted their time and money funding and running charitable organisations that helped poor people, disabled people, homeless people and those otherwise cast aside by society.

Rich people, I found, were among the finest human beings to walk the earth.

No, it's not a sin to pursue and acquire wealth. In fact, I have come to believe that those who pursue and realise their dreams, and become wealthy in the process, are actually closer to God than those who sit in condemnation of them.

So, don't let ignorant ideologies hold you back from the pursuit of success. Unshackle yourself from them. Those who embrace the notion that the pursuit and acquisition of wealth is bad, are, in my opinion, the real sinners.

During my research I identified more than 300 daily activities that separated the "haves" from the "have-nots". The culmination of this research can be found in my #1 bestselling book, *Rich Habits: The Daily Success Habits of Wealthy Individuals.*

I'm also a certified financial planner (CFP) and hold a master's degree in taxation. As president of Cerefice and Company, CPAs, I head one of the premier financial firms in New Jersey.

Between 2004 and 2009 I devoted five years of my life to studying the daily activities of more than 350 rich and poor people to find out what the rich and the poor do from the time they wake up in the morning to the time they put their head on the pillow at night.

Thanks to my research, I was able to uncover exactly what the rich are doing right and what the poor are doing wrong. I incorporated what I learned into the "Rich Habits Program" which is designed to provide timely, easy-to-follow guidance on achieving unlimited personal and financial success.

***Wealth is not just a by-product of random luck***, advanced formal education, a superior work ethic or inheritance.

Success is a foolproof process. Within these pages is the 21st century blueprint for financial success and happiness!

The genesis of my research began when a struggling client came to my office seeking advice. The client's business was growing however he had difficulty in making ends meet, particularly at payroll time. In sheer desperation, he asked, "What am I doing wrong?"

For months I analysed his business, his expenses, processes, labour rates and industry comparative data. I even sought advice from a "rich" client in the same industry, with a similar level of gross revenues and whose business shared comparable demographics. After all of that work the only thing I had to show for my efforts was that my client was taking a salary that was about $40,000 more a year than my "rich" client.

At a lunch meeting with my struggling client, some weeks later, I confessed that the only variable that stood out was that slightly higher salary.

The client was not happy. I was not happy. We sat in silence at our table for some time. In an effort to break the uncomfortable silence I asked my client what he did for fun. That seemed to break the ice, as there was an immediate shift in my client's demeanour.

The client leaned in, eyeing the other tables at the restaurant and said ever-so-quietly, "On Wednesday nights I get a couple of ladies of the night, a few bottles of wine and..."

The client, in response to my obvious look of shock, stopped mid-sentence. "I'm sorry," he said. "I shouldn't have shared that with you. I talk way too much sometimes."

I assured him that I was an Irish Catholic boy from New York raised in a family of eight. I told him that growing up in my family we looked at laws as mere obstacles to be overcome. There was very little I had not seen in my life.

My shock was not from moral indignation, but from the realisation that I had been asking my client all the wrong questions these past few months. I went on to ask him how much he spent on those Wednesday nights and how long he had been doing this. He confessed that when he got divorced some 10 years ago he adopted this Wednesday night habit.

He thought for a moment about what it cost and guessed those nights ran to about $500.

I did some quick math and determined that those Wednesday nights were costing him about $25,000 a year. I further determined that over the course of 10 years this one habit cost him about $350,000. This $350,000 was almost exactly what he owed on his company's line of credit that the bank had shut down. His additional $40,000 in salary was being used to fund his Wednesday night trysts. Worse, he was funding it with his line of credit!

That one habit ended up putting my client into bankruptcy.

The epiphany I had was that there was much more to financial success and failure than meets the eye. ***The devil was in the details.***

The only way to uncover those details was to ask the right questions. I eventually came up with what I now call my "20-questions list".

This list is actually 144 questions, grouped into 20 categories. I asked these 144 questions to 233 rich people and 128 poor people over a five-year period. If you do the math, that's 51,984 questions. Of the 233 rich people, 177 were self-made millionaires; 31 per cent came from poverty and 45 per cent from the middle-class. It took me five years to complete my research and analyse the data.

The data I gathered from these 51,984 questions makes it clear that there is a difference the size of the Grand Canyon in the way rich people and poor people live their daily lives. This one client unknowingly took me down a path toward the discovery of the secret to financial success and that secret is our habits!

***Our habits***, good or bad, ***determine the financial circumstances of our lives***. Those habits that lead to financial success I call the Rich Habits. Those habits that drag us down into poverty I call Poor Habits.

If you would like the list of questions plus the details of my research findings, please register your copy of this book at www.RichHabitsPoorHabits.com and you'll be able to get all the details plus more in the bonus section.

If you're one of the tens and tens of thousands of readers of my first book *Rich Habits*, I promise this new and improved, expanded edition will blow you away. It includes all of my most recent research as well as insights from Michael Yardney to help you think and live like the rich. Thanks for picking up a copy of our book. Your life is about to change!

# CHAPTER 2
# WHO IS MICHAEL YARDNEY?

Of course you're not going to listen to just anyone telling you how to get rich, are you? At least, I'd hope not! So this is an introduction to who I am and why I'm qualified to share this information with you; but don't let that stop you from reading this section! I merely want to explain how I learned about wealth creation and to show you that if I can do it, so can you.

I also want to help you understand a little about the things that influenced me over the years, because if you're going to take advice from someone in wealth creation, it's only right that you should ask: "Why should I listen to you?" It's important that you know that they know what they're talking about and have a long-term, verifiable track record.

You see... I've read most books on finance and personal investment and many of them were written by authors who were not what most of us would call "rich". If they haven't achieved true financial independence themselves, what makes them think they can show you how to do it? Most of them believe in the "fake it 'til I make it" philosophy and some have done well during the last few years, but many have done well for the wrong reasons — a rising tide lifts all ships.

While I'm Australasia's most published author on the psychology of success and wealth creation, I'm not a theorist — I bought my first investment property in the early 1970s for $18,000 and proceeded to turn a $2,000 personal loan into a very, very substantial multimillion-dollar property portfolio... in my spare time.

Today I am CEO of the Metropole Group of Companies, with a team of wealth and property professionals across our offices in the three biggest capital cities in Australia — Melbourne, Sydney and Brisbane. Together we have bought, sold, negotiated and project managed over $4 billion-worth of property transactions to create wealth for our clients (and ourselves) and we currently manage over $2 billion of clients' property assets. And even though I'm not licensed to give financial advice, my Metropole Group of Companies includes a high end Wealth Advisory firm as well as a financial planning company.

I've written nine bestselling books, I've once again been voted Australia's leading property investment adviser and I'm frequently quoted in newspapers, magazines and on the radio.

My www.PropertyUpdate.com.au blog has been voted the #1 property blog in the world for the last five years and last year alone had more than 2.5 million individual readers. The Michael Yardney Podcast has had over 2 million downloads and I have been voted one of Australia's top 50 Influential Thought Leaders.

Over the past 15 years I've personally mentored more than 2,500 property investors, entrepreneurs and business people and I have made a lot of money for myself and for others. But I have also lost money making foolish decisions at times through what seemed to be prudent decisions that caught me out when economic circumstances changed unexpectedly.

I have a beautiful wife, Pam, who was also one of the founding partners in my business until she retired. Together we have six children and 11 grandchildren. We own a very substantial property and share portfolio, live in a beautiful penthouse apartment, have many good friends and enjoy a life we could have only dreamed of when we were growing up.

I tell you these things not to brag — I don't need to — and just in case you wondered, life wasn't always this way or this good…

The son of working-class parents, I came to Australia at the age of three when my family settled in Melbourne. My recollections of my childhood include my parents arguing at the end of each month when it came time to pay the bills. I remember hearing them discussing who would get paid that month and who wouldn't. I remember them struggling to put a few shillings (this was before dollars and cents) aside each week to save up to have some money to spend at Christmas.

Interestingly, while both my parents worked as employees (my father was too afraid to take the "risk" of running his own business), almost all of their friends owned their own businesses and were considerably wealthier than we were. It seemed to me that we were the poorest family in the street and I definitely felt the poorest amongst our friends.

My friends' parents all owned cars — mine couldn't afford one for many years. My friends and their parents went on summer holidays — for many years we did not. And my friends' parents owned investment properties — mine didn't when I was young.

So, while my friends' parents owned their own businesses and invested in property to grow their wealth, I remember my father's financial plan.

Every Saturday morning he would sit at the kitchen table smoking his cigarettes, drinking his black coffee and daydreaming. He would make a list of how he would spend the winnings when his lottery numbers would come up. Of course, he never won the big jackpot. But occasionally he won a small prize, just enough to encourage him to buy a few more lottery tickets in the hope of getting the big one the following weekend.

Of course, the lottery is not a financial plan... but it was the only way my father could see himself escaping the rat race.

I learned a lot of very beneficial things from my parents who tried to instil good moral values in me. They wanted me to have a better life than they did. They strongly encouraged me to get a good education, get a secure job, buy a house and pay it off.

On the other hand when I visited my friends, I heard their parents give them very different advice. They said things like, "If you want to get on in Australia," (the "lucky country" as they would call it, as most were European migrants) "you need to go into business and earn money which you should then invest in property — that's the true path to real wealth."

Through my friends' parents I learned you couldn't count on the lottery or your boss to make you rich. I knew from an early age that I wanted to be rich and I soon realised that if I was going to get rich it was up to me!

## What makes people rich and powerful?

I don't remember exactly when I decided that I wanted to become rich, but I know I was pretty young. At an early age, I determined that I did not want to struggle when I grew up like my parents had. I didn't want to fight with my wife about money and which bills we could pay and which we could not.

Apart from seeing how my friends' parents did it and learning what I could from them by endlessly asking questions, I studied rich and successful people because I wanted to be like them. I read all I could to find out what it was that caused certain men and women to succeed in everything that they did, while others of equal intelligence failed. I wanted to know what it was that set the rich and super successful apart from the rest.

As I studied these people I found that they did not necessarily have a higher education — there were many examples of rich and successful people who didn't go to university; in fact, many didn't finish school at all. They didn't necessarily have more resources; many came from poor or migrant backgrounds — so I looked for common threads.

What I found was that many had made their fortunes in real estate. And those that had made their money in other industries seemed to have invested their money in property.

Now you may say that not all successful people are rich and not all rich people are successful, and you would be right. We've all read of rich people who lead miserable lonely lives or don't lead a balanced life to enjoy the pleasures that family and friends can bring.

It took me many years to learn that to be truly wealthy you need to a lot more than money. But remember I was still young and naive and I wanted to have it all! This led to an unbalanced life and at times, more problems than I care to discuss.

Looking back now, I can see that because of my early childhood experiences I was tainted and angry. I was angry that we were poor and I felt that I had missed out on many things my friends enjoyed. So for the first half of my life I chased money. I desperately wanted to be "rich" and I went about trying to "prove" myself to the world.

Interestingly, as the size of my real estate portfolio grew, it wasn't enough. The anger didn't really go away and I still wanted more. It was many years later that I realised that if what drives you to want money is fear, or anger, or the need to prove yourself, money won't help you. When you get the money, the fear doesn't go away. The anger doesn't disappear. ***The money doesn't make you a different person.***

Chasing money in an unhealthy way led to a very unbalanced life and this, amongst other things, led to me sabotaging the first half of my life and this broke up my marriage and ruined my early career. I paid the price for my actions and it made me a very different but much better person.

I came to understand what was really important to me. Over time I realised that there has to be a more significant reason to have money. I then set about building the Metropole business and this became the focus of many years of hard work for Pam and I. But it wasn't until I found a real purpose for the money that I became truly wealthy.

I'm sorry to say that it took too many years to realise that the true purpose of money for me (and I accept that it will be different for every reader of this book) was contribution.

For many years now I have enjoyed giving back to the community in a number of ways. I have dedicated myself to educating property investors through my blogs, writings, webcasts and podcasts. Pam and I donate to many charities — not only money, but also time and energy.

Yes, I've had my challenges in life (mostly self-inflicted) and I've hit rock-bottom, but I got up again, learned from my mistakes and moved forward.

## Why are some people so much more successful than others?

I conducted seminars on wealth creation for almost 20 years and I found something very interesting.

I would present to an audience with a few hundred people but only a small group — maybe about one or two per cent of the attendees — would take action and did something to grow their wealth and protect their financial future. And guess what the rest did? You're right, nothing at all.

As an educator, this disappointed me as I wanted to be good at my job. So I started running longer seminars, sometimes over two or three days. I brought in guest speakers and I taught people even more material about how to become rich.

And guess what happened?

One or two per cent of the attendees would take action and do something to grow their wealth and protect their financial future. And the vast majority of attendees at my seminars said they really enjoyed them but went home and took no action.

This made me wonder, why do some people take all the available knowledge and can immediately apply it to improve their situation and become rich, while others struggle to make even the most basic changes? What separated the ones who succeeded from the ones who did not?

Albert Einstein made an interesting observation: *"We can't solve problems by using the same thinking we used when we created them."*

From my experience working with thousands of ordinary people I've discovered where many get stuck along the road to getting rich. As Einstein suggested, there are levels of thinking that got them there and continue to keep them there.

As I speak at these seminars people ask the same questions: *"Why does success seem to come so easily to some people, while others have to struggle?"* and *"How do I build the financial freedom I've always wanted?"*

If you ask these people, "What does money mean to you?", they'll generally say "freedom". When asked what freedom means to them they'll say things like: *"I can live my life in my own way"* or *"I can order in a restaurant without having to look on the right-hand column of the menu"* or *"I can buy things for my family without worrying about the price."*

One of my aims in this book is to show you the road to riches and at the same time open your eyes to the fact that the way you have thought about money and most of the ways you've behaved around money (your money habits) for most of your life is most likely flawed and this has been holding you back.

It's not your fault... most of what you were taught about money was probably taught to you by people who were not wealthy, and our educational system has failed you. But ***now is the time to educate yourself*** — to learn how to become rich by understanding how the rich think, feel and behave and then by doing what the rich do. To learn about their Rich Habits.

## Why am I still working?

Recently a prospective client asked me: "Michael, now that your candles cost more than your birthday cake, why are you still working?"

I know others have wondered — is this guy really financially independent? If so, why is he sitting here across the table from me wanting to show me how to become financially independent?

I'd like to answer these questions for you because there are some instructive lessons in the answers for anyone who wants to develop financial freedom.

Firstly, the answer to the second question is — yes, I am truly financially independent, having built a very substantial real estate and share portfolio over the years. But I think the biggest lesson for you will come out of my answer to the question of why I am still working.

Let me explain with a little story…

I remember reading that Ringo Starr (the famous Beatle) was doing a multi-city tour of America at the age of 75, turning up at one city performing, leaving, on to the next place.

I repeat — he was 75 years old and still on tour.

I suppose this should be reassuring — it suggests that years from now I might still somehow or other get up on stage and deliver my seminars.

Over the years I've worked hard so that I now don't need to work for financial reasons, but I think I will still enjoy doing it when I'm 75, just like Ringo does. As far as I know, Ringo has no unmet financial needs. He's still touring largely because he has nothing better to do for which he has comparable enthusiasm.

Why successful people stay at it long after they need to reveals why they became so successful in the first place.

I guess what I'm trying to say, because many people don't seem to understand, is the reason so many business people, entrepreneurs and investors became so successful and rich is the enthusiasm they had in their job to begin with.

This is the main reason why I'm still working.

I still get an intense buzz putting deals together, developing training programs, writing my blogs and books, educating investors and more importantly seeing clients become financially independent and successful.

You see… I spend all day talking about property while drinking coffee and dealing with nice people.

Why wouldn't I still be working?

And to be honest I am still clearly, unashamedly, intensely enthusiastic about making and multiplying money. I enjoy passing it on and helping future generations, including my children and grandchildren as well as also contributing significantly to charity.

I am very grateful for what I have and believe it's my obligation to repay the world, and that's in part why I spend so much time writing, educating and podcasting.

These activities are clearly the least financially profitable of all that I do, but they are the most rewarding.

## Why would a rich person waste time writing a book helping others to get rich?

Now that's the type of question asked by a poor person with a scarcity mentality. I'll explain why in a moment, but the reason I took the time to write this book with my friend Tom Corley is because I enjoy writing about the topic of the psychology of success, a topic I've been studying closely for almost 35 years.

I've been mentoring successful investors for almost two decades and writing about wealth creation in major online and hard copy publications for the past 20 years. I'm proud that many recognise me as a leading expert in the field and I'm pleased to share my knowledge. In fact, ***I see it as my obligation to share my knowledge*** and give back to the world that has given me so much.

Of course, it helps that I've got the time and freedom to do what I please because I've built substantial wealth that gives me the ability to work at what I want to do when I want to do it.

Now back to that comment I made about scarcity a moment ago…

If you buy an investment property does that stop me buying one? No!

If you grow a substantial stock portfolio, does it stop me building one? No!

The fact is that wealthy people come from an abundant mindset, and while some poor people would ask why would I share my "secrets" (coming from an scarcity mindset) ***I believe anyone of reasonable intelligence*** can become rich, given sufficient motivation, the right mentorship and application, and if they do so, it not only helps them but it helps the economy as well as society.

By the way… I'm not doing it for the money. Writing a book is not a very good way to get rich. However, I get paid handsomely by many readers of my books who send me emails about their successes from the lessons they've learned from me and, to me, this is worth more than any royalties this book will ever bring.

One more thing: mentoring (advising, training and educating) is one of the secret habits of most rich and successful business people. When most people think of mentoring, they invariably view it as one-sided: an apprentice learning from the master, but there's a lot more to mentoring than that.

It's not just paying it forward and giving back. There's a selfish component to it. I've found that by training others to do what I do and helping them excel in life, I multiply my own chances for success. Mentoring creates a cycle of exponential success, making not only the student wealthy but making the mentor's life more meaningful — no one loses.

So thank you for allowing me to take you on the journey to your financial freedom.

Here's all I ask of you… please read the book, then register your copy so you can use the resources we have waiting for you at our free website www.RichHabitsPoorhabits.com and take action. That's it. You won't become rich overnight, but I know that it can transform your financial future.

# CHAPTER 3
# WHY WE WANT YOU TO BECOME RICH

We assume that most people who pick up this book have decided that they want to turn their life around. They want to stop struggling to pay their debts, they want more time and money to do all of the things they have been dreaming of for a long time and, most probably, they want to become rich. Are we right?

Well, in order to achieve these goals, you are going to have to change.

You are in your current financial situation (whatever it may be) because of how you have handled your money to date. If you want to be somewhere else, logically you are going to have to do things differently. But for most people making a change in the way they do things (especially with money) is a scary prospect. It transforms the known to the unknown and means relinquishing old thoughts and habits that can be hard to break.

Sometimes fear can be good.

The world has experienced some challenging times recently, hasn't it? Currently many people are worried about the economic climate, concerned about social unrest, their job and financial security. When you're afraid that things could get worse, afraid you could lose money or your job, it could prompt you to accept change when you might otherwise shy away from it and continue down the same dead-end path.

To become wealthy you are going to need to discard many of your old ways (which probably haven't really worked too well for you up 'til now anyway) and adopt new ideas and strategies.

In other words, you have to CHANGE. Importantly, you also need to take control of your financial affairs yourself.

The problem is many people will find that fear takes over and clouds their judgment when it comes to deciding how to think about money or what to do with their money. Some will even be paralysed by their fears and choose to remain in the past.

***If we can change what we believe, we can change what we do.*** If you keep thinking in this new way, if you keep doing new things, you'll develop new habits. However, if you keep doing what you've always done with regards to money, it's likely that you are going to fall behind and find that you are not left with many choices.

You only have to turn on the TV, open the newspaper or browse your iPad to realise we are living in interesting and, for many, fearful times. Yet there's a lot the average person can do to build and protect their financial security even in the challenging times we're living in today.

We've found that the same events that have made many feel uncertain about their financial future could, on the other hand, produce some of the best opportunities for you to realise your own financial independence.

Having said that, there has been a great deal of talk by economists, social analysts, some politicians and the media about our need to lower our expectations and shrink our lifestyles to cope in the current economy. They see the rich getting richer and want them to share more of their money with the rest of the country.

This may be valid advice for those who are prepared to accept governance by circumstance; but lowering our expectations doesn't make sense. As long as there is money, wealth and riches out there it is your right to attract it and acquire it by combining the right thinking, strategies, behaviours and habits that we'll share with you in this book.

And there will be opportunities aplenty since we're living in a very exciting financial era — a time of fast change brought about by globalisation of many markets and changing technology.

We believe we're living at the best time in history, a time when it's easier to become wealthy than any time before. In the 1900s you needed substantial money to become rich, to become an industrialist or a businessperson. Today, many people have become rich using "intellectual property" or investing in plain old real estate.

In fact, more people have become wealthy in the past 20 years than at any other time in human history — which may make you wonder why you haven't become rich.

The problem is just because it's easier doesn't mean everyone is doing it. They're not. Tom spent five years studying the rich and the poor, and found that ***only around four per cent of the poor ever become rich.***

Fortunately, there are a few shortcuts to financial freedom and we're going to share them with you.

Having said that, if getting rich was easy everyone would be wealthy. Each year more and more reports are released suggesting very few of us will have enough savings, superannuation or investments to comfortably retire on. And with medical advances meaning that we are all going to live longer, many of us will be forced to work longer in order to fund our retirement.

## So why do we want you to become rich?

There is a saying that we believe to be true: "Any problem that money can solve is not a problem."

We've also heard it said that "the state of your wallet plays with the state of your mind". That is, when you have money problems you're likely to also have more stress.

Now that's not to say that the rich don't have problems — they do. But Tom's study found that being rich eliminates 67 per cent of life's major problems. That's a pretty big percentage.

So, let's look at the common problems we all run into and how the rich eliminate many of them. We'll also look at the Wealth Pyramid so you can better understand where you sit and where you want to be.

### 1. Financial problems

While the poor worry and lose sleep about money (well… actually the lack of it) and many of their relationship problems are due to lack of money, the type of financial problems the rich have involve managing their money and investments.

One hundred per cent of the rich in Tom's study owned their home and 84 per cent had no mortgage.

### 2. Health problems

According to Tom's research data, 76 per cent of the rich do about 30 minutes of cardio exercise every day. The science on the health benefits of cardio exercise is clear — it improves your health and extends your life.

OK, you may be thinking, what about cancer? Surely money can't prevent that!

You're right — cancer is fairly democratic in that it plagues the rich and the poor alike, however, studies indicate that a poor diet increases the incidence of cancer.

According to Tom's research, ***the rich and the poor have very different diets***. The rich ate significantly less junk food, consumed significantly less alcohol, avoided fast food restaurants and consumed far less sugar than the poor did.

On top of all of this, the rich have the financial means to secure the best medical care in the event that something does go wrong.

### 3. Family problems

Now some bad news… Rich or poor, we can't control family problems. Having a family means you will deal with a whole host of family issues.

### 4. Neighbour problems

The rich have the luxury to pick their neighbours by choosing the neighbourhood where they live. And in general, they reside in more spacious accommodation, rather than right next to their neighbours.

### 5. Homeownership problems

Not only can the rich choose where they live and how they live, if things go wrong with their home, the rich have the money to fix it immediately.

When it comes to major repairs, the only issue for the rich is how fast the electrician, plumber or carpenter can get the job done. There are no financial concerns for the rich when something goes wrong with their home.

### 6. Car problems

Similarly, the rich can own whatever car they want, and if something goes wrong with their car, they can afford to get it towed to a repair shop or simply buy a new one.

### 7. Addiction problems

Drugs are a blight on society that not even the rich can escape.

The big difference is that the rich have the financial resources to secure the best care in dealing with addiction problems and can afford to send themselves, their spouse or their children to the best and most effective drug rehabilitation centres.

### 8. Job problems

According to Tom's data, 86 per cent of the rich like or love what they do for a living and because of this they do a better job. They have no fear of being fired because they either own their own business (51 per cent of the rich in his study owned their own business) or they were a decision-maker where they work (91 per cent in his study were decision-makers), which means they do the firing.

### 9. Relationship problems

According to Tom's data, relationships are the currency of the wealthy.

***The rich surround themselves with other like-minded people*** who share their goals, dreams, thinking, morality and virtues. They devote an enormous amount of time to managing their successful relationships and they make a habit of avoiding toxic relationships.

### 10. Death and disability problems

Of course, death or disability can happen to anyone at any time, rich or poor.

### 11. Time management problems

Sixty-five per cent of the rich have at least three sources of income to manage. As a result, they are constantly pressed for time in managing those activities. Plus, because more than 90 per cent of the rich are decision-makers where they work, responsibility follows decision-makers wherever they go, even on vacations.

This means unless they learn the right strategies to focus their energies, time management is a problem for the rich.

**12. Weather problems**

Do we need to even address this? Weather affects everyone, rich or poor.

## Here's another reason we want you to be rich — you'll live longer.

Yes — ***the rich really do live longer*** according to a report published in 2016 by the Brookings Institute, which confirmed other previous studies and showed that the more money you have, the healthier you are and the longer you live.

The study found that on average, a rich man born in the US in 1920 could expect to live about six years longer than a poor man born in the same year.

For those born in 1940 this gap had more than doubled. Among rich and poor men born in 1940, the difference in life expectancy was 12 years.

This same trend was also seen with women's life expectancies. The gap between rich and poor women widened from 3.7 years for women born in 1920 to 10.1 years for those born in 1940.

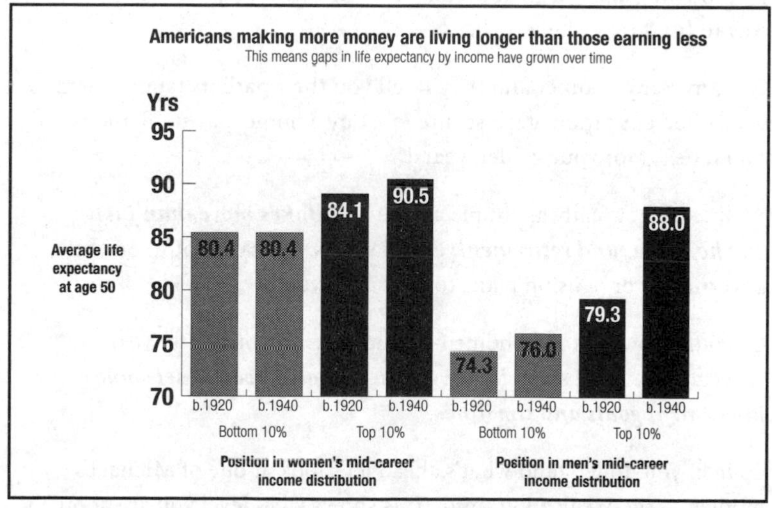


*Source: Brookings.edu*

In trying to find out why the rich live longer, the researchers examined variables such as smoking, obesity, education, nutrition and exercise, but were unable to find a definitive cause for the growing disparity.

While access to better health care is an obvious reason, people with higher incomes also benefit from better living conditions and tend be more focused on the future, which probably also helps them make healthier choices.

The poor are also far more likely to be stressed, worried, sad and angry than the rich.

So, while money can't buy you happiness, it can buy you a better chance at a considerably longer life. I guess it could be said that… poverty kills you.

## The Wealth Pyramid

Now let's move on to considering where you currently are on the Wealth Pyramid.

Not too long ago the great dream of home ownership was considered a way to fund retirement.

Ask any Baby Boomer and they'll tell you their parents taught them to get a good education, get a secure job, buy a home, pay it off and voila! You'll be set for your golden years!

Well… it's not really as simple as that — ***it takes more than just one house to fund retirement***, especially as you can't count on the government or pension plans to look after you.

Of course, owning your home free and clear in your latter years is certainly a good start, ***however you will also need to set some investment goals and timelines***.

To help you understand what's ahead let's look at one of Michael's models — the Wealth Pyramid. This shows what level you are at on your way to financial independence and what the key focus areas and leverage points are to speed up your journey.

It allows you to take stock of where you are now and where you want to be.

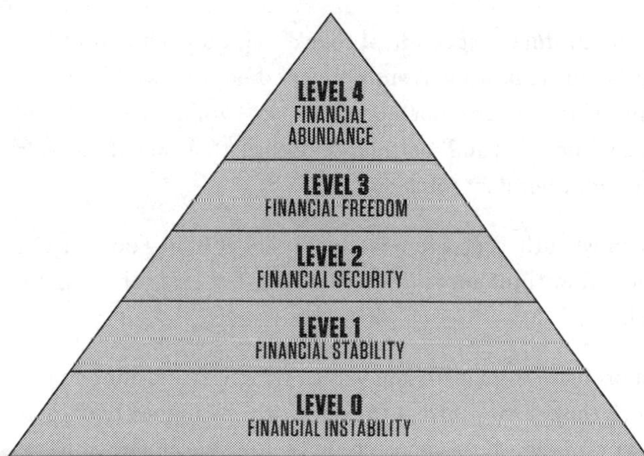


Like all pyramids it has a wide base and tapers towards the top — in other words, most people are at the lower levels of the wealth spectrum and fewer reach the top.

Hopefully the knowledge and skills you'll learn from this book will help you work your way up the pyramid, but the solutions you'll need to move from one level to the next will vary depending on where you are on the pyramid. Unfortunately, most people don't really have any wealth and therefore are stuck at the first level.

**Wealth Level 0 — Financial Instability**

Since most people live from one pay day to the next, they're what's called financially unstable.

If they lose their job, or if they have an emergency (you know how these keep cropping up — an illness, the car breaks down, the refrigerator packs up), they have no financial reserves to cope.

Since they have no spare financial capacity, the only way to deal with these burdens is for people at Level 0 to borrow more (and get further into debt) and this only creates more financial hardship. They live their lives with their heads buried in the sand, not really conscious about money and their spending habits.

***If they have money, they'll spend it,*** if they don't, they'll borrow it because their favourite pastime is shopping and buying "stuff" they don't really need. This means much of what they own has debt attached to it. They keep doing this and fooling themselves that they'll just work harder and pay off their debt some day.

If you ask them what their problem is, they'll tell you they don't make enough money. They think more money will solve their problems. But that's not right.

Their biggest problem is their money habits, which has nothing to do with how much they earn. It's what they do with the money they earn. As they move on in their lives and earn more, they just spend more. Today, they can't survive on the type of income they would have only dreamed they could achieve five years ago.

There are many high-income earners who fall into this category because they spend as much, or more, than they make. Sure some people at Level 0 Wealth can look rich — they may even have big homes or fancy cars, but they also have huge loans that they struggle to repay.

Unfortunately they often argue with their spouses about money, being in financial denial and justifying why they bought this or that.

Level 0 Wealth can really be divided into two subgroups:

1. *Casualties* — We call those at the lowest level of the pyramid this because they're casualties of the money game. Each month they seem to find themselves in a worse place than they were the month before — getting themselves deeper and deeper in debt, usually through credit cards. They're paying high interest rates today to use tomorrow's money now. Of course they blame others for their problems — it's never their "fault".

They've often read books about budgeting or been told the trick of cutting up credit cards, but that just doesn't work. They don't know how to "do" money. Then half a level up the pyramid are the...

2. *Survivors* — these are the employees, self-employed or even business people who seem to make just enough money each month to have nothing. And, if by accident, they end up with some money in the bank they spend it or take a holiday. They are just surviving.

While the fact is that at Level 0 people simply live beyond their means, the real cause of their problems is denial of this fact. Unless they are prepared to change, their financial future is bleak.

The fundamental key to getting out of this level is mindset, education and taking financial responsibility.

**Wealth Level 1 — Financial Stability**

This is the most basic level of wealth and gives you some level of financial security or stability, which is when:

1. You have accumulated sufficient liquid assets (such as money in an offset account, line of credit or savings) to cover your current living expenses for a minimum of six months.

2. You have private medical insurance and some life insurance to protect you and your family's lifestyle should you become permanently ill, disabled, unable to work or if worst comes to worst — you suddenly die.

At this level you will have the peace of mind that should any unexpected challenges come your way, such as retrenchment, a business failure, illness or disability, you and your family's lifestyle will not be unduly compromised. You will have adequate time to look for new sources of income to put you back on track.

The problem at this level is that your cash flow is being controlled by others — your boss who pays your salary or your clients who pay for your services. This means you're still on a treadmill and you don't have the ability to increase your cash flow without working more and that has its limits. Sure you've got a bit of a financial buffer, but if you stop working for a while you slip back to Level 0.

If you're at Level 1 your goal should be to move more of your cash flow into assets and build a "Cash Machine" of investments so your income does not depend on you putting in more effort.

Before we move on, however, let's explain a little more about what a Cash Machine actually is.

Way back in the early 1980s Michael's business partner at the time, Brian, came up to him and said, "Michael — I'd like a Cash Machine!"

"What?" he responded.

Brian explained, "You know, a Cash Machine. I'd like to come to work in the morning, flick the switch and the machine would start working and churn out money. At the end of the day I'd flick off the switch and go home to my family and then come back tomorrow and flick on the switch once more. And the machine would again start working and churn out more money."

As you can imagine Michael replied: "Sure, I'd like a Cash Machine, too." Who wouldn't want one?

And even though at the time it seemed like a rather absurd pipe-dream, over the years Michael actually created exactly that — a substantial property investment portfolio.

It has allowed him the opportunity to take two extended holidays per year with his family, to work because he wants to work not because he has to work, and the ability to contribute back to the community, charities and family.

We guess you also want a Cash Machine, don't you? And why not? If you invest wisely over time you will be able to build your own substantial asset base that will become your Cash Machine.

This will take time, effort, moving out of your comfort zone and a little risk, and it has nothing to do with how much you earn in your day job. We've seen many people who earn hundreds of thousands of dollars a year, yet by spending most of it on a flashy lifestyle they fail to become wealthy.

Having said that, we've also seen successful investors build a substantial property investment or share portfolio while working at what some would call menial day jobs, earning relatively little in their pay packet. In other words, their job becomes something they choose to do, not something they have to do for their primary source of income. Yes, to build our own Cash Machine.

At this level ***your biggest leverage comes from investing in yourself*** and becoming financially savvy, building a solid base of financial and investment skills upon which you can grow your financial future, as well as beginning to build a network of peers you can make your journey with.

You'll also have to choose the first investment vehicle you are committed to master and become a devoted student, learning all you can about this niche wealth vehicle. Michael clearly has a view that the best place for most people to start is residential real estate investing.

In making the decision on which wealth vehicle to go after, you must cultivate the discipline to say no to the pull of other "great opportunities" and methods. We've made more money by saying no to second-rate investment opportunities than we've made by saying yes to them.

Then very carefully choose who you'll study with. Contrary to popular belief, the most expensive education isn't graduate school, like an MBA. The most expensive education is one based on a flawed models and incorrect information. The hardest form of learning is unwinding all the wrong, mistaken, and flawed things you "learned" from unqualified teachers. So ***CHOOSE TO LEARN FROM THE BEST***. It will save you years of frustration following defective models.

## Wealth Level 2 — Financial Security

You achieve financial security when you have accumulated sufficient assets to generate enough passive income to cover your most basic expenses. These would include the following:

- Your home mortgage and all home-related expenses such as your utilities, rates and taxes.
- All your tax payments plus the interest payments on your loans and debts.
- Your car expenses.
- Your grocery bills and minimal living expenses.
- Any insurance premiums including medical, life, disability and your house.

When you reach this level of financial security you will be able to stop working and still be able to maintain a simple, basic lifestyle. Of course you'll want more than that.

At Level 2 you will be an investor focused on building your net worth by owning assets that appreciate in value.

At the advanced stage of Level 2 you are beginning to make the transition from capital gains investing to investing for passive, residual cash flow. This means you've got to master a whole new skill-set.

You'll also have to radically upgrade your advisor network and peer group. Being the big fish in a small pond no longer serves you. You need to begin playing with people better than yourself.

## Wealth Level 3 — Financial Freedom

You know you have achieved financial freedom when you have accumulated sufficient assets to generate enough passive income to pay for the lifestyle you desire (not necessarily your current lifestyle) and all of your expenses, without ever having to work again.

Having first built a substantial asset base (of properties, shares or businesses), now you are using your assets to create cash flow, which doesn't mean you won't go to work again, but you will now be able to make the choices you want because you have freedom.

At Level 3 your focus should be on stabilising your passive income streams and fine-tuning your estate planning and asset protection. Now is also a great time to grow your service to the world by finding ways to expand your contribution.

Level 3 is NOT about "retirement", it's about regeneration and contribution.

**Wealth Level 4 — Financial Abundance**

A small group of people around the world achieve financial abundance when their Cash Machine of investments works overtime. Not only are they free of financial pressures, but they have so much surplus income after paying for their lifestyle, all of their expenses and their contributions to the community (often through charity work or donations) that their asset base just keeps growing and growing.

A couple of last thoughts about the Wealth Pyramid. There is nothing new about this hierarchy of wealth — it's always been there and we're all part of it. Complaining about where you are won't help however — ***your level of wealth is your choice***. Despite that, most people get stuck at a particular level and never achieve investment success.

The main question you need to ask yourself is this: "Are you planning on getting rich by adopting Rich Habits or are you planning on being poor?"

So, we hope that you now better understand why we want you to become rich. Being rich gives you choices. It allows you to lead a better, more fulfilling life — one that is wealthy in every possible respect.

# SECTION TWO

# HOW TO DEVELOP A RICH MINDSET

*Michael Yardney*

# CHAPTER 4
# YOU CONTROL YOUR OWN FINANCIAL DESTINY

I hope you realise that by many measures you're already rich.

We know true wealth is much more than how much money you've got in the bank or how many properties you own, but in this chapter let's talk a little about money.

Each year Credit Suisse produces a Global Wealth Report showing how money is distributed around the world.

According to the 2020 Credit Suisse report, global household wealth has remained 'unscathed' despite the global COVID-19 pandemic. It revealed that the top one per cent of households globally own 43 per cent of all personal wealth, while the bottom 50 per cent own only one per cent.

That top-tier one per cent amounts to 52 million people who are all millionaires in net wealth (after debt). Within this elite fraction are 175,000 ultra-wealthy people (those with over $50 million in net wealth), or 0.1 per cent, who in turn own 25 per cent of the world's wealth.

Australians have the second highest median wealth in the world, and we have a very low percentage of poor people.

Prior to the COVID-19 pandemic, the wealth of the average Australian household surged past $1 million and this was not materially changed by the short, sharp recession Australia experienced in 2020. But the gap between the rich and the average Australian only widened, with low-income families not seeing any increase in their net worth for more than a decade.

And in Australia it has a lot to do with property.

The fact is ***Australia's wealth is heavily skewed towards property ownership***. It's the investment vehicle that more average Australians use to develop their wealth than any other asset class.

Simply owning their own home over a period of 10 years or more has made money for an incredible number of people. Over this period many homes doubled in value, which meant that many homeowners saw their household wealth increase substantially. And it's much the same in many of the world's big capital cities.

But another group discovered how to profit in ways other than just owing their own home. They became real estate investors and bought additional properties. They took their financial future into their own hands.

## How the rich differ from the average person

If you study how the wealthy have achieved financial freedom you will realise it has very little to do with how they earn a living, and much more to do with their mindset (how they think about wealth) and their habits (how they behave).

When it comes to how people make their money we can all be placed in one of four categories: Employees, Self-employed, Investors and Business Owners.

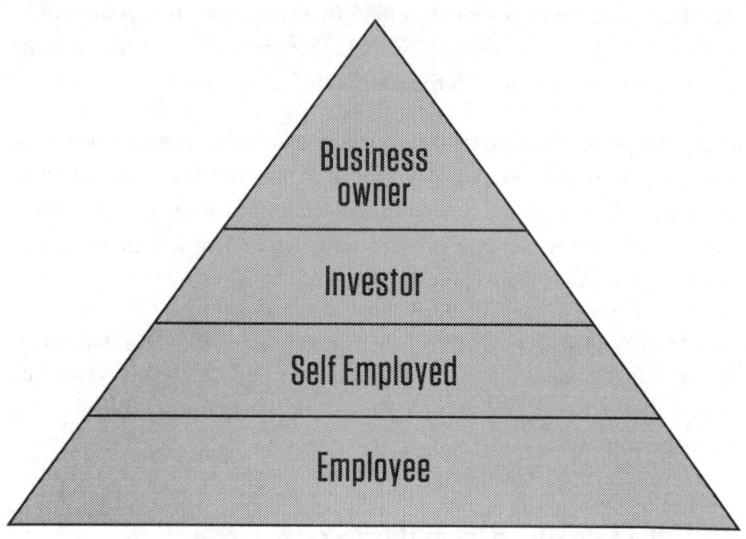


In his *Rich Dad, Poor Dad* series of books, Robert Kiyosaki suggests that we all fit into one of four categories when it comes to how we earn our income.

**1. Employees — have a job** and receive an income from their employer, trading their hours for dollars; however before they even see their money the government takes its share in taxes (because its smart like that).

You're probably thinking, "Of course they do, isn't that what happens to everyone?" Interestingly that's not always the case — some investors and business owners only pay tax on what's left over after their bills are paid.

**2. The Self-Employed — own a job** and are typically small business owners or professionals who work hard and expect to get paid for their efforts.

In reality, though, they have swapped one boss for hundreds — called customers or clients and are still swapping time for money. If they take time off or fall sick, they simply don't get paid.

**3. Investor — money works for them.** Unlike employees and self-employed people who trade time for money, ***investors make money with their money.*** Some build a sufficiently large investment portfolio so they don't have to work, because their money works for them.

Regardless of how you make your money today, if you hope to become rich in the future you'll ultimately have to become an investor.

Obviously you won't become a full-time investor overnight, but you can start moving in that direction by establishing your own property investment business. Done correctly, income-earning residential real estate can be your vehicle for getting out of the rat race!

There are also many tax advantages available to property investors in Australia. One of the reasons the rich get richer is because, in some cases, they can make millions and legally pay very little tax because they build their asset base, not their income.

For example, if you own a $1 million investment property portfolio that increases in value by seven per cent, your asset base will have increased by $70,000, yet in Australia no tax is payable on this capital gain. You could then ***borrow against the increased value of your assets*** and use this money to reinvest or live off.

**4. The Business Owner — owns a system and people work for them.** The true business owner not only doesn't have to do the work, he doesn't even have to be at work every day.

Why?

Because he or she has a system and has hired people to do it all for him or her, along with qualified supervisors to manage his team.

The true business owner asks, "Why do it yourself when you can employ someone to do it for you?"

One of the best ways to earn more and work less is by owning a business, because the tax system favours business owners who understand finance, tax and the law (I have previously written a book about this topic).

As a businessperson you could own a McDonald's franchise and have a group of teenagers serving Big Macs or you could have a portfolio of investment properties working hard for you.

## Can you see the difference?

As an employee you would have to pay for many of life's pleasures (such as a new car) with after-tax dollars, whereas a business owner can pay for his new car with before-tax dollars as long as it's used for business and meets certain requirements. They can even pay for things like movie tickets and holidays with before-tax dollars if they qualify as legitimate business expenses.

## Does that mean I'm going to have to set up a business?

I'm not advocating that you open up a conventional business; I believe it's just too hard to make money that way as most small businesses go broke in the first five years.

However, I've seen some investors become very rich by growing a multimillion-dollar real estate portfolio and treating it like a business. They get the right type of finance, set up the correct ownership and asset protection structures and know how to use the taxation system to their advantage.

In fact, owning income-producing residential real estate is just like owning a business because your tenants go to work or run their businesses to earn a living. They then pay you for the use of your property to live in. This puts you in a position whereby you can profit from the efforts of other people — think about that!

These people get up every day, get dressed and go to work. You don't have to supervise them, pay their tax or worry about paying for vacations or sick leave. Yet every month you get a portion of their income in the form of the rent they pay for the use of your property. The more of these people you "employ", the more income you receive.

Now, before you get all moralistic, understand that this is not a bad thing if it's done fairly and with a genuine concern for others. You should not feel guilty if you position yourself to profit from the earnings and efforts of others, as long as you are providing fair value to the relationship.

Best of all, you can set up your property investment business while you're still an employee; that's what I did and what every wealthy property investor I know has done. ***They built their portfolio one property at a time***, while living off the income from their day job.

They started with one property, then leveraged off its capital growth to invest in another and another until one day they found themselves with a true property investment business that gave them financial freedom.

But that's not what most people do. Let's look at how many of us go about becoming rich and what works and what doesn't…

## Linear versus passive income

Employees and the self-employed trade their time and labour for dollars, while investors and business people send their money out to get a job.

You see… not all incomes are created equal; some streams are linear and some are recurring. The question that determines whether your income streams are linear or recurring is: *how many times do you get paid for every hour that you work?*

If you answer only once, your income is linear. Income streams from your salary are linear — you get paid only once for your effort. But with recurring income, you work hard once and get paid over and again for the same effort. It unleashes a steady flow of income for months or even years.

This is also the way property investors make their income; they work hard to develop capital to invest in property, which then goes on working for them by bringing in rent and appreciating in value.

Employees and the self-employed struggle financially because they work for money. The problem with working for money is that you have to work harder, longer or charge more for your services and we all have a finite amount of time and energy.

One of the reasons the rich keep getting richer is that they get their money to work for them in order to acquire more assets. By building a significant asset base they end up getting all the income that they need.

Setting up your own property investment business and creating investment income means that instead of just meeting your financial needs, you'll begin to make your own financial choices.

You won't be able to quit your day job immediately, but as your investment income increases, your dependence on your day job will decrease and ultimately, your investment income can liberate you from needing to work at all.

## Assets, not income, creates wealth

It is difficult to get rich from your wages — if you're in the time-for-money economy and get paid by the hour you can only earn so much each hour and you can only work so many hours a day. But no matter how hard you work, or how much you get paid, it's just too hard to make your millions that way.

The reality is that most ***multimillionaires are either investors or business-owners***, not employees. They recognise that while income (cash flow) is important, it's their assets that create real wealth. This is because, if invested wisely, their assets grow and generate an income.

When you buy a property you put down a deposit — this is your money or asset. When the property increases in value and your loan remains the same, your asset (your capital) grows in value. This is called capital gain or capital growth. The great thing about this capital gain is that it is yours and you don't have to pay tax on it unless you sell your property (in Australia you pay capital gains tax or CGT only when you sell an asset).

Unfortunately, most people don't get past the income stage. They don't get their money growing and working for them.

I hope you're beginning to understand that you control your own financial destiny. We'll show you how to take control of it later in this book, but let's first explore a few important wealth concepts.

# CHAPTER 5
# SOME IMPORTANT WEALTH CONCEPTS

While this book is about getting rich, it's not a book about investing or making money. There are many books that will guide you in these concepts, in fact, I've written a number of bestsellers in this field (www.MichaelYardneyBooks.com.au).

This book is about understanding how the things the rich do every day (their Rich Habits) make them rich. However, in this chapter I'm going to share two models I have created to explain how the rich progress along the path to financial freedom. These models, together with the Wealth Pyramid outlined in Chapter 3, allow you to know where you are heading financially, what stage you are along the way and what the key focus areas and leverage points are that you can use to fast track your journey.

This will help you understand what you have to learn, what you need to do and how you need to think to end up where you want to be.

But before we dive into these concepts, I want to mention a few final things about the Wealth Pyramid.

Have you noticed how many people are keen to follow the dream of opening their own business, yet remain in their job? Have you met somebody who was a great employee but when they moved on to run their own business they found it wasn't making money — they couldn't even afford to take a holiday?

This is because as we progress along life's journey we all hit a ceiling, no matter how hard we try. We just can't move up to the next level.

It's a bit like driving your car stuck in second gear. Putting your foot on the accelerator just won't get you going any faster — all that happens is the engine revs louder.

***Moving to the next level requires doing things differently*** — Tom would say it requires you to develop different habits. And doing things differently first requires thinking differently.

The good news is that everyone can move up the Wealth Pyramid. Understanding where you are empowers you to ensure you do what you need to do to get to the next level. But this never happens by accident, you have to earn your way up through personal development and upgrading your mindset.

If per chance you do get a windfall and your money outgrows your level of development, such as when you receive an inheritance or you win the lottery (which is really a tax for those who can't do math), statistics suggest you'll lose it within a few years unless you work on yourself and turn up your financial thermostat.

Those at the top do not behave the way they do as a luxury or because they can afford to; they can afford to because of the behavioural choices and habits they made daily as they worked their way to the top.

When I see a new client or mentor a new member of my Mentorship program I can predict with great accuracy where that person will be end up on the Wealth Pyramid in the future. I can forecast the level of success and wealth they'll achieve merely by observing their habits, their behaviour and their language about money.

You will get to understand how I can do this when I later explain how the rich think very differently to the average person and, of course, it helps that I've engaged in some counterproductive and destructive behaviours myself in the past and that I've since learned to think like a rich person. Obviously it also helps that I've had intimate involvement with hundreds of individuals who have risen from poverty to significant wealth and success including building substantial property portfolios.

Now that you have a better understanding of the Wealth Pyramid, let's look at…

## The Wealth Quadrant

When you look around and see some people enjoying their riches while others are struggling just to pay the monthly mortgage, it becomes painfully clear that while some people have lots of cash flow (income), others don't. And while some have substantial assets, others do not. ***Then there are those people who just appear to have it all*** — the enviable income plus a substantial asset base!

If you want to become financially independent what should you be aiming to have more of? And how do you balance income against assets?

Essentially, when it comes to wealth, we all fall into one of the following four quadrants:

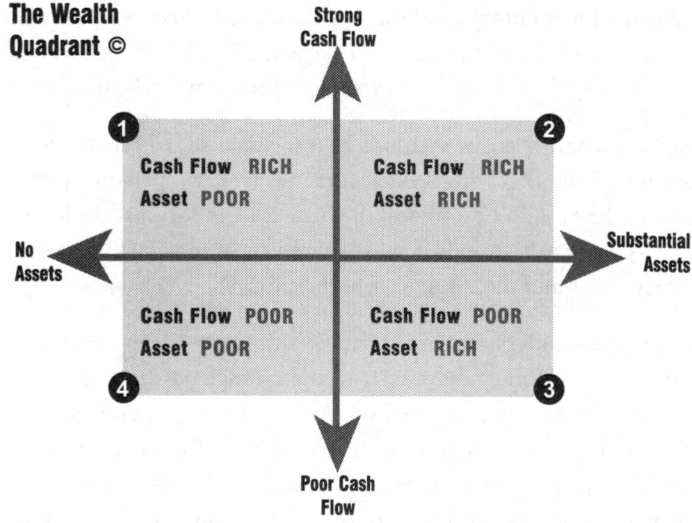

Clearly you don't want to be in ***quadrant 4*** with no assets and poor cash flow, but sadly that's where many people are because they have taken on bad debt and are struggling to make ends meet. They're at Level 0 on the Wealth Pyramid.

Those in ***quadrant 3*** often own their own home (sometimes without any debt), but lack the cash flow to enjoy life.

Others in this quadrant are highly-geared property investors with negative cash flow, who often live month to month because they haven't established the proper financial buffers. These investors usually have little (if any) cash behind them should they have to make up a shortfall in their mortgage commitments and tend to shudder at the thought of rising interest rates, which could decimate what little cash flow they have.

Sitting in ***quadrant 1*** are people who earn a good income, but don't own any appreciating assets. They often look wealthy, drive an expensive car and live in a fancy house; however they tend to have few assets and are totally dependent on their well paying job to support their lifestyle.

When you look at the 4 quadrants you'll undoubtedly want to be in ***quadrant 2***, where you have a substantial asset base that generates cash flow.

Yet I see many people trying to get cash flow the hard way. They either get themselves another job, try to make a go of network marketing or make hard work out of investing by attempting strategies such as trading, flipping or leasing out their properties room by room in an effort to increase their cash flow.

## They are building the wrong sort of income!

The secret of ***the wealthy*** isn't necessarily that they have more money; rather they ***have more assets that produce passive recurring income.*** This is what provides them with time freedom. Because their income is passive and recurring, they can spend time on anything they want.

When you view people's lives through the filter of passively earned recurring income, you find that many people aren't as wealthy as they first appear. Doctors and dentists don't earn recurring income from their work; their income potential is capped by the number of patients they can see and they have to be there for every one of them. That's linear income.

The same is true for most highly paid professionals; they don't enjoy the power of recurring income either. They may appear to have money, but they're on a treadmill just like other workers.

What percentage of your income is recurring?

If you're smart, you will start to develop a stream of passively earned recurring income. This will eventually give you the time freedom to do what you want, when you want.

One way you can do this is to buy an investment property and, whether you're working or not, the rental income will continue to come in and over the years the property's value will increase.

To achieve Level 3 Wealth and have sufficient recurring income to pay for the lifestyle you enjoy while covering all of your debts, you will obviously need to buy more than just one investment property. You'll need to build a property investment business — one that manages your multimillion-dollar property portfolio so that your passive income is substantial.

Essentially, to become financially independent you are going to need to get another job — but not for you. You need to get a job for your money where it will be working hard for you, making passive income.

## Assets, not income, create wealth

While passive income (cash flow) is important in becoming financially free, what I'm trying to explain is that it's your assets that create real wealth; because, if invested wisely, your assets grow and income flows from them.

Unfortunately, most people don't get past the income stage. They don't manage to make their money work for them and, quite simply, ***you can't save your way to wealth with income.***

Becoming rich involves four stages:

1. Educating yourself.
2. Building your asset base — by taking on debt and owning real estate or shares.
3. Lowering your debt levels and transitioning into the cash flow stage of your investment career.
4. Living off your Cash Machine.

One of the reason most people don't get rich is they invest for cash flow — not asset (capital) growth. I know this message is very, very different to what you'll hear from others, yet it's the way the wealthy all around the world do it. Investing for cash flow is the reason most investors get stuck at Level 2 Wealth. Cash flow gets you through life, but asset growth gets you out of the rat race. You'll see this theme runs throughout this book and I know it will be hard for some to swallow, but the results speak for themselves.

Now let's look at another of my models:

## The 5 Levels of Investing

These don't exactly correlate with the Levels of Wealth on the Wealth Pyramid, but as I explain them to you, the relationship between what level of investor you are and your level of wealth will become clearer.

Remember — this has nothing to do with your level of income.

I've seen many people who earn hundreds of thousands of dollars a year, yet by spending most of it on a flashy lifestyle they fail to graduate up the Wealth Pyramid. Having said that, I've also seen successful investors build a substantial property investment business or own a substantial portfolio of stocks while working at what some would call menial day jobs, earning relatively little in their pay packet. In other words, their job becomes something they choose to do, not something they have to do for their primary source of income.

In Chapter 5 I explained that if you want to become rich you're going to have to become a businessperson or an investor. In fact all rich people I know are investors, so let's look at the five levels of investors I've come across:

## Level 0 — The Spender

Level 0 are not really investors — they tend to be spenders and borrowers and as a result, end up with a high level of debt. They spend everything they earn and often more. Their money runs out before the month does. They usually survive from pay packet to pay packet, using credit cards and store credit where they can.

They're at Level 0 on the Wealth Pyramid. The Level 0 investor lives for today. If they have some money they spend it, if they don't have money they borrow it.

These are the people who, when they need some cash, go to the ATM and pay a fee to collect an advance on their own money and then pay interest on it. Their solution to financial issues that arise is to spend their way out of it or to take on more debt.

Do you know any Level 0 investors? A large part of our adult population falls into this category and they will never become wealthy unless they do something radically different.

## Level 1 — The Saver

The vast majority of people who are not spenders will generally be what I call savers. Their main investment is their home, which they aim to pay off over time. Sometimes they save a little, squirreling away a few dollars of what's left over after paying tax but in general they save to consume, not to invest.

***Savers tend to be afraid of financial matters*** and are generally unwilling to take risks. They're following the plan their parents and grandparents followed — get a steady job, buy a house, pay it off and save a nest egg for retirement. The problem is savings, or even owning your home outright, doesn't make you rich.

What usually happens is that they work hard over their lifetime, diligently save or pay off their home and are left with what will be a modest, most likely old and tired house.

Savers are what I would call financially illiterate. They need to focus their efforts on building a solid base of financial and investment skills, upon which they can grow their financial future. They will get the most leverage by investing in themselves and getting a quality financial education and beginning to build a network of peers that they can make the journey with.

## Level 2 — The Passive Investor

Level 2 investors have become aware of the need to invest. They realise their superannuation won't get them through retirement, so they start learning about investment and begin accumulating assets.

While they are generally intelligent people, they are still what I would call financially illiterate — they don't really understand the rules of money. But remember, it's not their fault — nobody taught them. If anything, ***their parents taught them old fashioned, out-dated concepts about money.***

Rather than taking responsibility for their financial education themselves, Level 2 investors tend to look for answers to their investment needs from outside sources or "experts". This makes them easy prey for the newest "get rich quick scheme" advertised in magazines or the latest flash-in-the-pan investment strategies spruiked by telemarketers.

Instead, they should refine their financial and investing education and focus their efforts on choosing a specific wealth vehicle that they are going to master. They must unlearn the flawed, incorrect and misguided lessons they have learned about money and wealth from unqualified teachers.

## Level 3 — The Active Investor

Level 3 investors realise that they must take responsibility for their financial future and become actively involved in their investment decisions. They become financially literate by building a knowledge base of investment strategies and techniques. They are starting to get their money working for them.

***These investors actively participate in the management of their investments*** and concentrate on building their net worth. Their main focus is on growing their asset base.

As this is the asset accumulation stage of their investment life, these investors have in general moved to high-growth, low-yield investments to grow their wealth. This is where residential real estate really shines — it's the best asset class I know for growing your wealth safely.

Level 3 investors usually leverage the time and expertise of a network of industry professionals as they realise that they can't do it all themselves. They also upgrade their network of advisors and peers, often joining a Mastermind group of like-minded people (more on this in chapter 42).

## Level 4 — The Professional Investor

A very small group of investors move to the top rung of the ladder and become a Level 4 "professional" investor who has built, and now manages, a true investment business.

A Level 4 investor's property investment business has a substantial asset base that generates sufficient recurring passive income to pay for their lifestyle costs, plus they keep growing their investment portfolio whether they work in a real job or not.

They are well-educated, financially fluent, comfortable with the language of money and understand how the game is played. They understand the "system" of finance, tax and the law and use them to their advantage.

These investors tend to concentrate on optimising the performance of their properties, whilst at the same time minimising their risks. While they are still accumulating assets, they are now more interested in cash flow that will allow them to gain the most out of life.

Rather than investing what is left after they have spent their money, they have the correct tax structures in place that enables them to spend what is left over after their money-making investment machine ploughs more cash back into further investments.

They have a finance strategy and financial buffers to buy themselves time and see themselves through the ups and downs of the economic and property cycles. And they understand the law as it relates to property, so they don't make the mistakes many beginning investors do.

These professional investors don't hand control of their investments over to others; they retain control while employing a proficient team of accountants, finance brokers, property managers, solicitors and property strategists who have great systems that achieve repeated and consistent results, which are reliable and predictable.

This gives Level 4 investors the freedom to choose whether they get up in the morning and go to work or not. Many still continue working because they enjoy it, like I do, but now they go to work because they choose to, not because they have to. Others find the time to contribute more to their community or to charities.

Neither the state of the economy nor the stage of the property cycle seems to affect the professional investor who makes money in good economic times and bad.

***Level 4 investors rarely stop educating themselves.*** They read, still attend seminars and surround themselves with a team of advisors and mentors. They're prepared to pay for solid advice — not only to increase their wealth but also to protect their assets from opportunistic family members, lawsuits and the government.

You will find that Level 4 investors personally own very little in their own names. But even though they "own nothing", they control everything through companies and trusts. By controlling the legal entities that own their assets, these investors gain considerable legal tax benefits and asset protection.

And a final point about Level 4 investors is that they teach their financial knowledge to their children and pass on their family fortune to future generations as their companies and trusts endure after they have departed this life.

## The asset growth first, then income stage

The first stage in becoming financially free is to educate yourself; the next stage is that of asset accumulation — your job as a Level 3 investor is to build a sufficiently large asset base to fuel your Cash Machine.

Then, only when you have grown a substantial asset base can you transition into the cash flow (income) stage of your life as a Level 4 investor. Sure you need income (cash flow) to service your debts as a Level 3 investor, but your focus must be on asset growth rather than income growth.

## What is your Level of Wealth?

Now it's time for some home truths… How far up the Wealth Pyramid are you? Where do you currently sit in this hierarchy of investors?

Everyone starts at the bottom — at Level 0 — but not everyone makes it to Level 4. In fact, few do. But you can once you understand why the rich keep getting richer.

Remember, this assessment of your current level of wealth has nothing to do with your income. You can be a "low income" earner when it comes to your day job, but still be a Level 3 investor and have financial security. Likewise, you can be considered "rich" by working income standards yet still be at Level 0 Wealth, spending every dollar that you earn.

What I want you to understand is the pay packet that you work for every day has nothing to do with what level of wealth you are and in fact is one of the worst predictors of wealth.

I've come across many clients who earn substantial incomes yet still don't "have" anything.

I know Bob, my doctor, has earned hundreds of thousands of dollars a year for the past 35 years. He's almost 70 now, but still lives in a rented house, drives an old battered car and continues to feel like he's on a treadmill. Every day he goes to his medical practice to see patients and at the end of the month, he just manages to pay the bills (remember the Level 0 casualty we discussed?).

I have spoken to him about this number of times. The trouble is, every time he earns money, he seems to spend it. He has never managed to put anything aside in the way of savings or investments, or even as an emergency fund. He said to me a while ago that his car broke down and needed major repairs and even that created some degree of financial hardship for him.

The story of someone like Bob, who probably earns more than $300,000 a year, may sound strange to you. But if you're like most people, despite working for around 40 years, and having earned up to millions of dollars in their lifetime, very few people become financially free. In fact, ***most retire just above broke***.

So, the question isn't really can you make a few million dollars but are you able to *keep* a few million dollars? If you're like Bob, in fact if you're like many people, you're going to find it difficult to save and easy to spend.

I asked Bob why he still rents; why despite his income he hasn't managed to save up a deposit for his own home and he told me the following story: each new year he makes a resolution and says to his wife, "This year we're going to take $1,000 out of every week's pay and put it aside for the future." (Maybe $1,000 each week is so much you couldn't even imagine having that amount to save from your wages but that's okay, just follow the story and you'll soon see my point.)

He hoped by putting this money into a savings account it would give them a deposit to finally purchase their own home. When I asked him why that didn't happen he told me, "Life keeps getting in the way."

Somebody got sick, or he needed a new TV, or his car broke down. You know what it's like — there are always unexpected expenses.

So he asked me, "How do I do it? How can I do it? What am I doing wrong?"

I explained to him that if he wanted to save but didn't make a firm commitment to pay himself first, it wouldn't work. I suggested he do exactly what the government does.

"What do you mean?" he said.

I explained that every time we get paid, the government automatically takes out small amounts of money in the form of taxes. I guess they do it that way because they know that if they didn't take it then, it would be really hard to get it out of us any other time. Therefore, Bob should similarly set aside a small, pre-determined portion of his wage each and every time he got paid. He should take at least 10 per cent of his wage and put it into a form of savings account before doing anything else with a cent of his money.

Now Bob had heard this before but had just left it very late to change old habits and make a start. You can probably guess what Bob thought when he heard this theory many years ago — "How much difference could 10 per cent of my pay packet really make? How much could I really gain from that?"

We've all heard of the power of putting a small amount of money aside to secure our future, so why doesn't everybody do it? We've all heard of the idea that we should pay ourselves first, yet most of us don't. Although many of us make an attempt, we want to put some money aside to save for a rainy day or we want to invest, why doesn't it seem to happen as we plan?

I've spoken to so many people who've told me the same thing; no matter how hard they try, they just never manage to get ahead. They run out of money before the month is over and regardless of how much they earn, they only ever seem to have enough just to pay the bills and scrape by.

The scary thing is I hear the same story from people making $45,000 a year as I do from people making more than $200,000 a year. Just think of my friend Dr Bob, who earns over $300,000 a year and is still constantly broke.

"That can't be possible," you might think, "If I made that kind of money I'd be rich by now."

But would you? Or would you find more to spend it on? The simple fact is that because Dr Bob does what most people do, spending all the money he makes and then some, and he has no investments and nothing set aside for a rainy day, the fight to get ahead has never worked for him.

**The basis of success in moving up the Wealth Pyramid is to:**

1. **Live below your means so that you have money left over; and,**
2. **Convert your earned income into assets which will generate passive income.**

Since there is no amount of money you cannot outspend, ***managing your money is essential to building wealth***.

To build on this topic, we'll now take a look at a topic that I have much interest in and have written about many times before — it's how to develop a rich mindset.

# CHAPTER 6
# DEVELOPING THE MINDSET OF THE RICH

A few years ago two of my children cornered me and said: *"Dad, how do the wealthy get rich? What's the biggest difference between all those successful businesspeople entrepreneurs and investors that you have dealt with and the average person?"*

Since I have a substantial real estate portfolio and head a company that helps clients become wealthy through property investment I guess they expected me to say something like — "they own properties and shares and businesses".

But I explained that the big difference between the rich and the poor has to do with mindset. Sure they have some financial know-how that helped them become richer, happier and more prosperous than most people, but underlying this is the way they think, which leads to the way they feel which leads to their actions, which gives them their results.

You've probably heard plenty about the importance of "mindset" to your success and wealth. I talk about it too in my books, blogs and seminars.

But what I mean by mindset and what other people mean by mindset are often two very different things.

Most people think of mindset as something like "having a positive attitude". Now there is nothing wrong with that, ***but a positive attitude alone will NOT produce wealth and success*** in your life.

Neither will just focusing on what you want... no matter how hard. You can't just "Think and Get Rich".

You see, when I talk about mindset I mean the specific beliefs and attitudes that make it possible to truly become rich.

It's the difference between theory and reality.

The typical version of a "wealthy mindset" will make you feel good... until you realise you are no better off than you were before. My version helps you achieve financial freedom.

So what's the big difference between the Rich and the Poor?

While many would say it is knowledge, as I just explained, I don't think that's right. Sure they possess a level of financial fluency that the average person doesn't, yet knowledge alone doesn't guarantee success when investing. Rather, it's the way they think — it's their mindset.

Just as there are "outer" laws of money — the ones that regulate how it's made and exchanged — there are "inner" rules as well. These consist of your beliefs about money and getting rich.

Having mentored well over 2,500 mentees over the past two decades and worked with hundreds of multi-millionaire clients I've come to the conclusion that most rich people think along similar lines, and that they think vastly different thoughts than the poor or middle class do.

I've also come to realise that most people have an attitude towards money and a general mindset that simply won't allow them to reach the next level of wealth. ***The way they think is the greatest roadblock*** on their journey to financial freedom. This would suggest that if you re-program your inner dialogue to reflect the way rich people think, you will be moving in their right direction to achieving your own financial success.

Now don't worry… I'm not going to get all metaphysical on you, but please be open to consider this suggestion. It's the basis of a lot of this book, so if you're not prepared to consider this line of thinking you may as well stop reading now and return this book to the shelf, or if you've already bought it, gift it to a friend. You'll be doing him or her a favour.

Now it's not just what you think that makes you rich. It's also what you do — your behaviour, the actions you take or choose not to take.

Interestingly, 40 per cent of all of your daily activities are habits, which means 40 per cent of the time you're on autopilot, every day. And these habits — the way you run your life — are the reason you're rich, poor or stuck in the middle-class. They are the reason you live in the house of your dreams or in a hovel.

I'll explain this in much more detail, but for the moment be open to the idea that…

***Your mindset determines the level of your success.***

It's that simple — but that profound.

The fact is: for you to change your life, you must change your way of thinking. The good news is that you can create new beliefs at any time to support and actually accelerate your success.

Just stop and consider this for a moment…

It's probably true that much of what you have been taught about money and wealth creation has come from people who don't possess real wealth themselves. Additionally, much of what you have read from so-called "experts" is probably the words of people who don't have substantial wealth either. And it's likely that many of the people you associate with — your work colleagues, friends and peers who give you opinions on "money" — are not themselves rich.

What this means is that your present belief systems about money and wealth creation are based entirely on what you have learned from well meaning, but "un-wealthy" sources.

In contrast, what you'll learn from me in this book comes from a source that has "been there and done that". I have accumulated substantial wealth throughout my lifetime, and just as importantly, I have retained it; plus, I've paid a huge learning fee along the way as I've made more than my fair share of mistakes and learned from them.

But rather than putting my feet up and taking it easy, I've chosen to share my strategies and what I've learnt with people like you who strive to become rich but just haven't been given the correct education to enable that goal to be realised.

And just to reassure you that little more, I have gained much of the information and insights I'm sharing from my own peer group and mentors... who are also very wealthy. By now you should know that I am not a theorist.

The problem today is that with a very low barrier to entry, it's easy to have a platform and can look like an expert, even if you haven't achieved that yourself. The average person can go put up a blog, start a Facebook page or group, put up some cool YouTube videos and start spouting off things that they heard about how to be rich.

But that's a problem for those needing assistance and advice but don't know what to look for. This low barrier of entry, which makes it so easy for people to put stuff out there, unfortunately has led to a lot of people putting bad ideas out there.

Let these empty theorists have their say. This is your cue to smile politely, and then find an advisor who has taken that critical 30 foot or 10 metre walk. Your real estate investing and your 'future you' will thank you for it.

So, if some of the things I discuss in this section don't contradict or conflict with your current belief systems, something would be very wrong. I want to challenge your inner dialogue and start the process of re-wiring your mindset for success.

If you want to move your way up from wherever you are now to the top of the Wealth Pyramid, ***you are going to have to think and act like a rich person***, which means you will have to change your way of thinking about wealth.

## So what determines how we think about wealth?

It's our internal programming in our mind that sets the financial thermostat, which we all have inside of us, that in turn determines the level of wealth we are comfortable aspiring to and possessing.

What level is your financial thermostat set for?

Some people have their thermostats set for millions of dollars, while others settle for thousands. As I'm sure you'd agree, the average person has their financial thermostat set very low indeed.

The problem is, if your financial thermostat is set for a low level, then the way you think and the way you behave will keep you poor. Even if you have all the information at hand, and know all the necessary steps to take in order to generate wealth, emotions like fear and doubt will hold you back.

Our misconceptions about money create our unconscious responses, negative emotions and self-sabotaging behaviours around building wealth. If someone was walking around with the belief that "rich people are greedy" or "money is the root of all evil" how motivated would they be towards building wealth?

Not very, right?

The problem is we don't know we are holding onto certain beliefs that manifest into our circumstances, so we're driving around with one foot on the accelerator (driving us towards our financial goals) and one on the brake (holding us back — keeping us in our financial comfort zone).

We've all heard of people who have suddenly come into money, such as lottery winners, and frivolously squandered it because they just couldn't handle it. This is because the settings of their financial thermostat take control and will usually ensure that ***their wealth shrinks back to the amount they can handle***.

I'm sure that if you took all the money in the world and divided it equally amongst everybody, it would soon be back in the same pockets it was before. After all, it's very difficult to keep something that has not been obtained through personal development.

Of course, this means that most people will never become rich. They'll never acquire the wealth they truly deserve because their financial thermostat, which was programmed to a low level when they were children, will hold them back forever.

## Back to the question — what is your financial thermostat set for?

If you really want to know what level your financial thermostat is set for I'll tell you. It's set for exactly the amount of wealth you now have. If it was set for more you'd already have it!

Now you're probably thinking: "Michael, that's not fair — I'm not rich because I didn't get a good education. If I had a better education, I'd have a better job and I'd be rich." Or "Michael, that's not fair — you don't understand I have two children to bring up and school fees to pay." Or "That's not fair — I'm only in my 20s — I haven't had time to get rich yet."

I could answer all these excuses now, but instead at least be prepared to consider the notion that your inner financial thermostat is set to the level of wealth you now have.

## How was your financial thermostat set?

Let's face it: we are not born knowing how to "do money". We are all programmed by our parents, teachers, culture, religion, and peer group. This means that in general we have been programmed by un-wealthy people. Because people's beliefs and feelings about money are strong, they taught us well. We developed strong inner laws. But even though these beliefs are strong, they can be changed.

The patterns we learn as a child are not broken until we understand them, decide to change them, and then with intent, make whatever effort is necessary to create a new pattern of behaviour instead. Our current beliefs were created in three ways: by the things we heard, by what we saw and by the specific incidents we experienced as a child.

Take a minute to think about what you were taught about money. It's only by first acknowledging your current mindset that you'll be able to alter it for the better.

## What did you hear from your parents about money and rich people?

Were your parents fond of using expressions like: "Money doesn't grow on trees" or "Money is the root of all evil"? Maybe they told you that rich people are greedy and selfish or that money won't make you happy or it's just not that important anyway. Sound at all familiar?

The well-meaning adults who said these things to us were our "wealth educators", but it's worth noting that they were not wealthy educators with a wealthy mindset. If they were, they certainly wouldn't have spoken about money that way!

We also learn a lot about how to behave in all areas of our lives by modelling our parents' behaviour. So how did your parents behave when it came to money? Did they argue about it like mine did? Did one struggle to save or did they spend freely? Were they effective at managing money or was one or both of them far more adept at shopping?

It's interesting how many of us end up becoming so much like one or both of our parents in the arena of money. Then there are others who tend to rebel and become the opposite of our parents (like I did), often because they spent their childhood struggling with feelings of anger and frustration.

Your experiences around money as a child also affect how you are programmed.

Think about it. Did money represent happiness in your household or was it the cause of unpleasant arguments and tension? Was money ever used as a substitute for love or as a form of bribery?

For most of us, the subconscious programming we received as a child was, and continues to be, disempowering. Limiting wealth beliefs were instilled in us by what we saw, heard and experienced, and at the time they seemed very true, but they are no longer relevant to us today.

If your experiences were like mine, the people who taught you about money had the best intentions. They wanted you to succeed financially.

Unfortunately, since they had never been taught about how money really works themselves, all they could pass on was their own belief systems, which were more often than not based on scarcity rather than the abundant thoughts required to feel (and become) truly wealthy.

The end result is often a raft of disempowering beliefs about money, wealth and the rich that work at a subconscious level. But ***your beliefs can be the impetus that drives you to succeed*** or the stumbling block that steals your power away from you.

In order to turn your life around and become rich, you must first recognise and acknowledge the negative or limiting wealth beliefs that are holding you back from reaching your true potential. Then you must set about changing them.

## How do you know when your beliefs are sabotaging you?

Sometimes we don't know that we're holding onto certain beliefs until they manifest as our circumstances — our problems and frustrations.

So look for patterns in your life.

Are you annoyed that your bank balance never seems to rise beyond a certain number? Does your investment income or your business seem to hit a wall or plateau cyclically? Are you not putting money aside to invest, even though you know you should?

Non-supportive beliefs about money can create unconscious responses, negative emotions and self-sabotaging behaviours around wealth building. Psychologists would say that "perception is projection" your experience is a direct reflection of your consciousness.

But you can choose to think differently and you can make that choice right now. People at Level 4 on the Wealth Pyramid are people who've learned to change their internal programming.

When you realise where many of your thoughts and beliefs about money originate from, you can accept that you are not entirely at fault for being held back in your quest to achieve financial freedom. But once you have this awareness, it becomes your responsibility to reprogram your mindset and belief systems. You owe it to yourself.

***Initially you must change how you think about yourself.*** Begin to see yourself as a wealthy person, as one who attracts and creates wealth in their life. This will involve changing that ingrained internal dialogue, or overcoming negative "self-talk" that has developed as a result of past experiences.

Then you may need to change your way of thinking about your future. You need to truly believe that you are in control of your life and your own destiny. You need to acknowledge that you are the pilot of your life's fate and not just a passenger going along for the ride. This means that your tomorrow will be directly determined by the decisions you make, and the actions that you take, today.

Maybe now is a good time for you to examine your current way of thinking and how you developed it — warts and all?

Ask yourself: "What do I believe about money?"

This can be a little confronting, but you need to take some steps outside of your comfort zone. Don't listen to your inner voice that has been holding you back. It's only natural that the "old you" will protest loudly with more negative thoughts and beliefs.

The reason this is an important process is because, despite now being exposed to all the ideas and concepts in this book, your thinking and your beliefs are the critical factors that will determine the level of your future success. Your mindset is the ultimate determinant of whether you make it to the top of the Wealth Pyramid and when all is said and done, your income can only grow to the extent you do.

So who are you? How do you think? What are your beliefs, what are your habits and traits? How do you feel about yourself? How confident are you in yourself? How much do you trust others? Do you truly feel you deserve wealth?

Regardless of the size of their winnings, since most lottery winners eventually return to their original financial state — which is the amount they can comfortably handle — it just proves that the majority of people simply don't have the internal capacity to create and hold onto large amounts of money.

On the other hand, if self-made millionaires lose their money through business glitches or misfortune, they usually make it all back (with interest) in no time. Take Donald Trump for instance; he was worth billions before losing everything in the early 1990s. In fact, he owed the banks a fortune, but in just a couple of years, he'd managed to gain it all back... and more.

Why does this happen?

There is one important ingredient these self-made millionaires never lose, regardless of their financial wins and losses, and that's their millionaire mindset.

The bottom line is that if you want to become wealthy you'll need the right mindset. ***Essentially you have to develop a "prosperity consciousness".*** You must become financially successful in your mind, long before you achieve it in reality.

Revising your mind's "money files" is the critical first step on your road to riches.

## Your beliefs about money

Your thoughts about money (in fact about everything) come from the "files of information" in the storage cabinets of your mind and these were put there by your past experiences and programming — which means that your past conditioning determines your current thoughts.

So are your beliefs true? Not necessarily, they are an aspect of your overall perspective on life, which is based solely on your past.

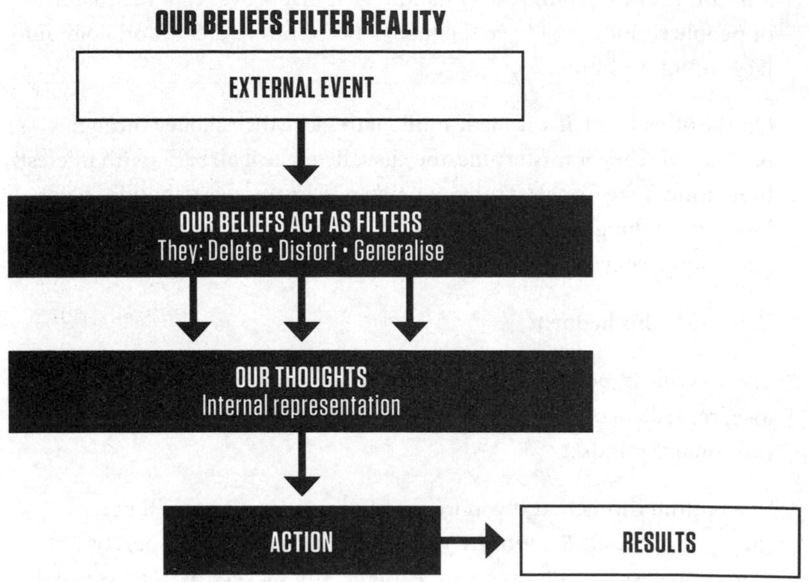


The fact is, though, that your beliefs colour your perception of everything; they filter everything that comes your way. The problem is that over time you grow accustomed to these filters and forget you even have them. Once this occurs, you believe the way in which you see things is the way things really are.

In other words, your belief system is your personal pair of tinted glasses. Everyone walks around with them on, in varying shades depending on their own internal belief filters. These glasses colour how people see the world and often makes reality into whatever it means to them at any given time. So, while one person looks through their rose-coloured glasses and sees opportunity and good fortune, another might look through their murky grey-tinted specs and see misfortune and hard times ahead.

That means that no one sees the world as it truly is, instead ***we see the world as we are*** — through our tinted glasses that we forgot we're wearing. So our beliefs about money can either be supportive or non supportive of our success. They can be empowering or disempowering when it comes to our achievements and happiness.

So, we all walk around with these files in our mind in which we retain attitudes and belief systems that have been supportive and helped us survive and have allowed us to achieve what we have achieved to date.

But we also have several beliefs or attitudes that undermine our pursuit of creating abundant wealth and happiness. We all possess these thoughts to a greater or lesser extent.

Unfortunately, for most of us, a whole section of our mind is devoted to mixed messages about money and wealth. The fundamental problem with mixed messages is that they tend to create mixed results and that's why some of us struggle. In the confusion of the internal banter, many people take one step forward, only to take two steps back, followed by two steps forward and one step back.

Another problem is that ***most of us never review the way we think about money and wealth*** — we go through life without questioning the beliefs we were raised with as children. We never revise our map of life to reflect who we are today and who we want to be tomorrow.

Yet what you believe about money will determine how you see the world and the experiences you have with it.

Like a self-fulfilling prophecy, your beliefs around money will result in what you encounter. If you believe that money only comes from hard work, when you want money what are you going to do? You're going to work hard. That means you'll earn money from hard work, which validates your initial belief.

We will always act (or fail to act) in accordance with our dominant beliefs. And those actions are what create our results.

If you believe you don't have the experience to start your own business, then you'll never start one, which means you'll never have the experience to start your own business.

See how it works?

If you don't believe that real estate would be a great investment, for example, you wouldn't try it and you'd probably never make any profits through property, which means real estate would not be a good investment for you.

See how powerful your unconscious internal dialogue is?

You act based on these files in your mind. When you decide whether or not to do something, your actions will be based on what makes sense to you — on what is logical in your mind. So, you'll make decisions based on the information that's in those files. And if the decisions you want to make are about money or wealth, you will dig down into these files and your decisions may or may not be supportive to you, as they are based on the files currently stored in your head.

For example, if I gave you the opportunity to buy a 20-unit apartment building and you had to make a decision on whether to invest in this property or not, what will that decision be based on? Where will it originate from? That's right... from the beliefs stored in your mind. That's really all you can draw on.

So, while I might look at this apartment building and see a great investment opportunity, all you might see is risk and the chance of losing money. And in light of that perception, your response of, "Thanks, but no thanks," would seem perfectly logical to you. Of course, it would be illogical to me as I have a different set of beliefs. I have updated my beliefs over the years as I have worked my way up to become a Level 4 investor.

That's why you are currently severely limited by the internal files you have stored away to date. And that's why in order for you to reach Level 4, you have to learn to think differently about money and wealth.

Still not convinced? Well, let's look at…

## The Importance of Beliefs

It's said that our subconscious makes up 5/6ths of our brain. The subconscious never sleeps and controls every bodily function, including our breathing, blood flow and metabolism without any conscious direction on our part. It is the seat of our emotions and memory.

Our brain is constantly bombarded with millions of bits of information but in our subconscious there's a section called the Reticular Activating System (RAS) that acts as a data filter.

What's this got to do with becoming rich?

Well, I'm going to explain that in detail in the next chapter but in short: our beliefs direct our subconscious to manifest what we think about and believe in. If we believe, without any doubts, that we are going to become rich and successful, our subconscious makes it happen.

***The rich and the poor have very different beliefs.*** These beliefs are a major contributing factor in their wealth or poverty because their RAS only allows in what data the subconscious has been programmed to allow in. Some of this programming is old programming; hardwired into our brains through millions of years of evolution and some of it is the programming hardwired into our brains by our parents, environment and our self-talk.

## What about the Law of Attraction?

So, does all this stuff about beliefs have something to do with the Law of Attraction, which is often quoted by those in the motivational world?

The answer is — not in the slightest! The Law of Attraction promotes the notion that our thoughts have the power to attract, and what we think about the most is what we become.

***"Think it and it will come to you" is complete rubbish!***

You can't just think about it long enough and money will come walking through your door in bucket loads. You can't just do what you enjoy doing and think good thoughts and manifest wealth. I've never seen a bag of money fall on anyone's head while they sat manifesting money.

No — the real secret (which isn't even a secret as far as I'm concerned) to becoming successful and wealthy is that you can't just think your way to a fortune; you need to take action and provide a product or service that adds value for people.

The crucial bit many motivational speakers omit is the need to take action. I mean, would the concept be so appealing if you had to actually do something about your life? Sure the rich think differently to the average person, but they don't attract money just by thinking about it. It's also because of how they behave — their actions.

Concepts like the Law of Attraction or the book *The Secret*, which was based on it, imply that there is one secret. It panders to people's lust for a magic pill — an easy cure. Sure, thoughts matter. There is abundant evidence that your view of the world and your attitudes about yourself, money, family relationships, health and so forth all impact on your experiences.

But you have to take action. If you think about it, all action and all behaviour starts with a thought, which lead to habits that differentiate the rich from the poor.

So, in the next section, Tom will take you through his Rich Habits Program as well as the results from his five-year study of the rich and the poor. It's extraordinary reading, which can make the difference between a wealthy life and a substandard one in my opinion. Before then, though, let's consider why I think most people will never become rich.

# CHAPTER 7
# RICH THINKING – HOW YOUR RETICULAR ACTIVATING SYSTEM HELPS YOU GET RICH

When Napoleon Hill wrote his book *Think and Grow Rich* he became famous for saying "Whatever the mind can conceive and believe, the body can achieve".

Now that was a bold and ground-breaking concept back then almost a century ago, and to be honest when I first heard this many, many years ago I thought it was all a little bit of metaphysical Hoo-Ha, but science has proven Hill to be correct as we now understand more about how the brain works and how the Reticular Activating System (RAS), which is a network of neurons in the brainstem, works.

The RAS is responsible for regulating wakefulness and sleep-wake transitions, but it also plays a part in many other important human biology functions including pulse, digestion, awareness and cardiovascular functions.

What is particularly important in the context of this discussion is the RAS's ability to bring certain things to your attention since it is the portal by which almost all information gets into your brain.

You see… your RAS filters the incoming information to your brain and decides what you are going to notice and which information is not going to come to your attention. This includes all the input from your various senses (other than smell) that your brain receives from the external world. Whatever you see, feel, hear or taste passes through the RAS.

The RAS then acts as a filter. Science suggests that our brain processes around 11 million pieces of information every second, but since only

40 bits of information can be processed consciously, this means that 99.99% of the information that comes to you is unnoticed.

Obviously this is the only way our brain can cope with the continuous flow of information floating in and demanding its attention. If you had to deal with all this information your brain just couldn't cope.

For example, you're probably sitting down while reading this chapter, but you hadn't noticed (up until now) the sensation of the seat on your body, or the ground where your feet are resting, or your breathing or heartbeat. Imagine continuously being consciously bombarded with all this information.

I guess that's why evolution has given us the RAS, a filter to extract and bring to our attention only what's important to us at that moment in time. It's a sophisticated filter between your conscious or subconscious mind prioritising what you need to know.

Your RAS responds to your name, to anything that threatens your survival and to information you need to know immediately.

The RAS takes instructions from your conscious mind and passes it onto the subconscious part of the brain which then instructs your body to take a physical action to comply with instructions from the RAS.

But what I find really interesting is that the RAS sorts through all this information from your environment and seeks data that validates your beliefs and when it finds a match your conscious mind is alerted.

Medical science has found that in some people the RAS can't sufficiently excite the brain cortex as it should, and these people have difficulty learning, poor memory and little self-control.

At the other extremes some people have illnesses such as ADD and ADHD where the RAS is overstimulated and these people have sensory hypersensitivity, are hyper vigilant, suffer from constant talking, restlessness and hyperactivity. Apparently these conditions occur because of the lack of a chemical norepinephrine (noradrenaline) in the brain.

## But what does all this have to do with developing Rich Habits?

As I said, the RAS is a sophisticated filter system that allows certain information into your brain and filters out other information.

Guess who programmed that filter? You did and so did your past experiences. The RAS screens the world through the parameters you give it, and your beliefs form those parameters.

The RAS helps you see what you would like to see and in doing this, influences your actions.

What this means is everything in your life is a reflection of your inner state. You are what you believe yourself to be. If you think people at work don't like you, your RAS is going to point out every single piece of evidence that confirms that negative belief.

As I've often said – your thoughts lead to your feelings, your feelings lead to actions and your actions lead to your results which really means your outside world is a reflection of your inner world.

This is the reason why you have to learn how to take control and reprogram your RAS to create what you want – but the good news is you can reprogram your brains Reticular Activating System to create success. This is very exciting because it means if you get your thinking correctly aligned you will be able to achieve amazing things.

In reality, your RAS acts as both a search engine and a GPS and it's easy to see why evolution encouraged this.

## How the RAS acts as a search engine

Your RAS works like a search engine looking for what you've programmed it to look for.

That's why it's important to tell your RAS what you want, not what you don't want, because when you program a specific idea or goal into your Reticular Activating System it will keep searching for it. It doesn't matter whether you're thinking about it or not, your RAS will work in the background until it finds precisely what you asked for.

Just like the search engine on your computer, it will sift through all the data presented to it (those millions of bits of information), edit out the irrelevant material and only select the relevant data to bring to your attention.

This is why it is important to create a clear picture of what you want, and then allow your RAS to start working until it finds the information for you.

*But there's a catch...*

Scientists have found that your RAS also controls your belief systems and will only recognise and select information that supports your preconceived beliefs. This means that your RAS will pay more attention to what you already believe or think (no matter whether your thoughts are right or wrong) and filter out all other information to help reinforce what you have chosen to believe.

That's why, despite being exposed to the same circumstances...

- Some see money making opportunities all around, while others only see problems, debt and difficulties.

- Some people see all the good that rich people do, while others see wealthy people as evil and greedy.

- If you believe that people are generally bad, every time you read the news you'll see tragedy, crime and death. The same time other people are optimistic and see all the good that is happening around us.

- If you believe property investing is a great way to make money, your RAS will filter for opportunities, however if you believe real estate investing is risky, your RAS will filter for all the reasons why the same properties others see as moneymaking opportunities you see as potential problems, risks and debt bombs.

So as you can see... your RAS can either work for you or against you.

Let me give you another example. Have you ever noticed when you decide to buy something you'll see it everywhere?

If you've decided to buy a white Toyota you'll find white Toyotas everywhere. If you've decided to buy a new widescreen TV you'll see advertisements for them everywhere.

This is because your RAS is filtering out the important information and bringing the car or other item of your thoughts to the forefront.

Obviously there are no more white Toyotas on the road than there were a few weeks ago, it's just there now been brought to your attention.

And this doesn't only happen while you're awake. Have you noticed how new mothers tend to be very tired yet when they eventually do get a nap, they instantly wake as soon as their baby stirs or cries?

## How the RAS acts as a GPS

If you think about it, when using a GPS you don't need to know where all the roads are located. You just decide where you want to go, but not necessarily how you want to get there, and you let the software do the rest.

You just need to know where you are now and where you want to end up and then the GPS takes into account all the data and directs you. If you take a wrong turn it puts you back on track.

That's exactly how your RAS works. Once you have decided on your goal your RAS begins to filter for everything connected with your goal and filters out all the irrelevant information, and if you veer off course it reroutes you.

A simple example is that your RAS continually filters for your name. You could be in a busy airport with lots of background noise, but if somebody calls out your name or your flight number your RAS allows you to pick that up amongst all the other extraneous noise.

Now the RAS isn't very clever… it doesn't know whether your destination is good or bad. It just knows what your dominant thoughts and beliefs are. This means if you're continuously thinking about what you don't want or like, your RAS is being programmed to lead you to what you don't want. The problem is you will see so much of what you don't like that you may end up feeling despondent as it could look like you have no hope of reaching your goals.

According to the Institute for Neuroimaging and Informatics at the University of Southern California, the average person thinks 70,000 thoughts a day. Most experts estimate that up to 95% of those thoughts are reruns of past events, or recurring thoughts.

That's why it is important to program your RAS with Rich thoughts not Poor thoughts, so you get what you really want out of life.

Of course, mental habits such as poor thinking are not easy to break. However, incremental changes, over time, will create big shifts in how you view the world and yourself.

This means you'll need to program your RAS with your self talk, affirmations, expectations, visualisations and goals.

Your mind believes what you tell it, so take charge of it. The RAS supports you when you set goals. Your mind needs goals. The RAS helps you see what you would like to see and in doing this, influences your actions.

If your expectations are positive, you automatically program your RAS to seek positive information and screen out negative information.

However, without clear goals, your Reticular Activating System is similar to a confused professional assistant with no clear instructions from you, the Boss.

But be warned… it's not as simple as *Think and Grow Rich*, the title of the book I mentioned at the beginning of this chapter. You have to do more than think, visualise or say affirmations. You have to take action.

The key is to realise that the opportunities RAS will present to you will be relative to your efforts. It won't show you the big opportunity right away. You have to follow its trail. Adopt the Rich Habits we discuss throughout this book and as a you do you will be reprograming your brain and slowly but surely you will see more and more opportunities in front of you.

When I first heard the concept of Think and Grow Rich, or what you think about you become, and was taught the concepts of visualisation and affirmations, I thought it was all "woo woo" stuff for those metaphysical people, but not for me. But then I learned these concepts are backed by science.

I know how reprogramming my way of thinking and developing Rich Habits have changed my life, so my suggestion to you is to be open to the concepts and the ideas we are sharing with you in this book. Work on developing Rich Habits and then, one by one, the small opportunities and eventually the bigger opportunities will "magically" appear, because the search engine of your mind will find them, and the GPS in your RAS will lead you there.

# CHAPTER 8
# WHY MOST PEOPLE WILL NEVER BECOME RICH

Here's a simple truth: if you want to become rich just look at what most people are doing and do the opposite!

As has already been explained in this book, the sad reality is that the most people will never achieve financial freedom. They will continue running on that mouse wheel for most of their lives, only to retire with less money than they gave the tax man during the many years they struggled with the nine to five grind.

The main reason most people will never become rich is because of their money habits — what the average person does about money — and this is because:

1. **They are not financially fluent. They don't understand how money works.**
2. **The "programming" they received about money, wealth and rich people when they were children, at the age when their brains soaked up all the information around them like a sponge.**

The fact is your brain is hardwired to think, feel and respond in a certain way to different ideas, events and objects — including money and wealth. ***We weren't born knowing how to "do" money*** and unfortunately most of us are programmed in an "un-wealthy" way.

The good news is you can be reprogrammed.

You wake up each day and for the most part you rethink 90 per cent of what you thought yesterday. Isn't that amazing? You use the same words, you go through the same motions and you often do the same things over and over again.

But I bet you're hoping for a new result. Now that's called insanity!

## What we've been programmed to think

The problem is that we learn more from our mistakes than from our successes — but in the wrong way — not in a positive way. It probably has something to do with our primitive caveman days, when we were surrounded by physical dangers. If you didn't run when the saber-toothed tiger roared, you were dead.

How is this relevant today?

We tend to remember bad experiences and often allow the negatives to steer what we do, far more than the positives.

Because of that, most people raise their children in a very risk-averse kind of way. They teach them nice, safe strategies.

Your own parents may have raised you this way: Go to school, get good grades, don't cause trouble, go to university, get a secure job, get married, stay married, have children, pay off your house and pay your taxes. In other words, toe the line and do what is expected of you.

It's safer that way isn't it?

Your parents taught you this because they loved you and wanted the best for you.

They truly believed that keeping you away from potentially risky behaviour was the best way to keep you safe. They probably learned these same old-fashioned and outdated rules from their parents, who raised them the same way. And their parents may well have learned these rules when money was scarce, in the time of the Great Depression. Back then most people didn't take risks with their money because they had so little, if any, of it.

The good news is that if you follow that advice, you will achieve the same average result as most people do, and if you're lucky you'll make it into the "middle class".

The bad news is that you'll stay in the middle class.

You may have what many people believe is a nice, safe and secure life. You'll work hard for your money all your life, pay most of what you earn in taxes and then retire; but maybe not as soon as you'd hoped. Your superannuation will give you a modest income; you'll live in a little house that's getting old and if you're really lucky, you may (after paying to simply live) have enough money left over to enjoy a few of the little pleasures of life.

What's the problem with this scenario?

Many things! But one that is glaringly obvious is that you will be stuck working hard for your money for more than 40 years and then retire, only to live an unexceptional lifestyle.

## The only thing to fear is fear itself

A big part of being human is being human. And being human means having emotions. We all feel fear, sadness, anger, love, hate, disappointment and joy. What makes us each unique is how we respond to those emotions.

I've found that one of the biggest obstacles that gets in the way of most people's financial independence is fear.

***Truth is, when it comes to risking money, we all experience fear,*** even the most successful of us. The difference is how we handle that fear. For many people, that emotion of fear generates the thought: "Don't take risks — play it safe." For others the fear of losing money makes them think: "Learn to manage risk — play it smart."

Interestingly the same emotion, but a different thought process, leads to a different result.

The thing is that you are not born being scared of money. You are taught this fear by your parents, by our society.

They teach you to be careful; they teach you not to take risks. They teach you to be "safe" — just get a nice steady job, earn a nice steady income and seek security.

They teach you not to climb mountains, but to stay in the secure valley. You see that word "security" everywhere. Have a think about it; does the name "Department of Social Security" really make you feel secure?

For most of us security is just an illusion, it's a myth. There is no security in this life, only varying degrees of risk.

When we talk about security, what are people really afraid of?

Many are afraid of failure. But have you ever really stopped to consider — what's so bad about failure?

Some people feel guilty when they've failed, others feel humiliated.

This often comes back to your childhood, when teachers made you feel bad every time you made a mistake. Some of us were good students and others not so good. Many of us had experiences at school where either children or teachers humiliated us when we made a mistake, so we've learned not to ask questions, not to step up, not to try and climb the mountains so as to not be embarrassed.

## We hide in what we think is security

To climb the mountain of financial independence you're going to have to overcome some of your fears. But the good news is, once you overcome the fear, success is just around the corner.

Sure there will be little setbacks — the climb to the top of the mountain will have some hazards along the way, but don't see them as failures — just retracements on the path to success.

## Fear can cost you money

One of the big differences between rich people and poor people is how they handle the fear of losing money. In fact, fear of losing money is one of the biggest reasons most people don't invest or why they chose poorly-performing investments.

It's no coincidence that one of the reasons so many people think investing is risky is because they are led to believe it is by people with ulterior motives for engendering fear into the masses. In fact, there is a whole financial planning industry built around fear when it comes to investing money.

I know I'm going to ruffle few feathers by saying this, but most people who go to financial planners end up with a plan to make them poor.

Most financial planners suggest you put money aside regularly, invest in mutual (managed) funds and over time build a nest egg and then at the age of 65 retire on less than your pre-retirement income.

Can you see why I say that most people plan to be poor?

They accept, without question, that when they retire their income will decrease. In other words, they plan on working hard all of their lives and then plan to become poorer once they stop working.

They say things like, "I won't need much money after I retire because I'll have paid off my house and my living expenses will go down."

But who wants to retire only to end up living a lifestyle that's worse than how you live today?

While your mortgage expenses may diminish, you'll probably find that your health and medical expenses will rise and your travel and leisure expenses are likely to increase, too. Why would you settle for less than what you have worked hard to achieve all of your life once you retire?

While most financial planners tell their clients to get out of debt, those people who become financially independent use debt to their advantage and to create a far better lifestyle than the one they had when they were working nine to five.

In fact, they use your money to get deeper in debt, while you're trying to get out of it. They use your money (borrowed from the banks) to buy investments and make more money.

## What they don't tell you about financial planners

Because we are not taught how to handle our financial affairs at school, I understand why many people consult a "licensed" financial planner to advise them on retirement planning or wealth creation. They believe that because these financial advisors are licensed, they must be trained money experts who can be trusted to some degree.

However, the financial services industry, in many cases, profits from people's ignorance about money.

Let me ask you a question: do you think to become a licensed financial advisor you need to first be a successful investor? The answer is no.

To become a financial advisor and work in the financial planning industry, you have to learn about financial products and be aware of the bureaucratic paperwork involved.

When you realise that many financial planning companies in this country are owned or controlled by banks or insurance companies, you'll understand why most financial planners are biased towards selling managed funds. This is because they get paid their commissions for advising you to buy managed funds or insurance products, and as they don't usually get paid for advising you on individual stock or property transactions, planners rarely suggest direct property or share ownership.

Please don't get me wrong, most financial planners are well-intended and point their clients to conventional savings and investment strategies that are good if you want to be average.

Of course, there are some great financial planners around — we have some at our company Metropole and of course Tom Corley is an investment-savvy financial planner. The thing is you have to dig deep to find a proficient financial planner.

And here's another risk to your financial success...

## Beware the expert

***It seems we have become a nation of "experts".*** Just check your inbox or turn on the television and there they are:

- **Experts on politics who have never run a business let alone a country.**
- **Experts on football even though they couldn't run from one side of the field to the other.**
- **Experts on celebrity who can't sing or dance themselves and...**
- **Whenever the real estate market booms we get a whole new generation of "property experts".**

Yes, we are surrounded by so-called experts — people with opinions, but very little expertise.

And you know what they say about opinions? They are like belly buttons, everyone has one, and mostly they are useless.

Also beware; you're likely to have well-meaning friends and family with varying opinions that you are going to have to watch out for. These "armchair experts" may not be any further along in their quest for financial freedom than you are, but they'll expect you to heed their words of wisdom nonetheless. Sound familiar?

These well-meaning friends have probably never really done anything more in terms of their money management than open a savings account. Yet it never ceases to amaze me how many people will willingly take investment advice from these non-investors. They'll swear black and blue that the latest fad described with enthusiasm by their friend, family member or co-worker is a sure thing and jump right in without so much as a second glance.

On the other hand, the information we're sharing with you is about the habits of the rich — what they know, think and do — you'll find that is very different to what the average person thinks and does.

And just to round things off, let's look at nine reasons most people don't get rich:

### 1. They never decide and really define, very specifically, what wealth means for them

The problem is that the average person has grown up in a family that is not wealthy. They go to school and socialise with people who are not wealthy. They work with people who are not wealthy. Their friends are not wealthy.

So, most people never decide to become wealthy. It never occurs to them, because they have no role models who are wealthy.

Of course, this is why people who grow up in homes where their parents are rich are much more likely to become rich as adults than people who grew up in homes where their parents are poor.

Unless you decide what being rich really means to you, ***unless you make a plan to become rich, there is no way you will become rich***.

### 2. Most people are too lazy to get rich

Ask someone if they'd like to become rich and they'll almost certainly say yes. But when you dig deeper you'll find they're not prepared to do what is necessary to become rich.

Sure, they're ready to buy a lottery ticket, but they're not prepared to put in the hard work, the sacrifices, the study and the effort to become rich.

I will discuss this in more detail in a future chapter, including their Success Habits, but I thought I should warn you early in the piece that becoming rich won't come easily or quickly.

Choose any role model you want to emulate in becoming rich and you'll find, no matter which industry they are in, that they've worked hard to get there. Whether it's the computer geniuses who invented Google or Facebook or pop stars that you see on TV, while life may look easy for them today, they all started their journey working very hard.

If you want to get rich, then you must do as they did. They were dedicated, focused and ambitious — they didn't sit on the couch waiting for wealth to come to them. And neither should you.

Put simply: ***you have to work hard to get rich enough not to have to work hard***.

**3. They are not prepared to pay the price**

The great majority of people have an inability to delay gratification (I'll tell you more about this in chapter 10). They feel they must spend every single dollar they make and whatever else they can borrow or buy on credit.

If you cannot delay gratification, and spend less than you earn, save the difference and then invest it, you cannot become wealthy.

Warren Buffett once said: "Wealth is the transfer of money from the impatient to the patient."

**4. Most people wait too long to start**

Most people can't wait to succeed yet they are willing to wait to get started on the road to financial success.

While they know they should invest to secure their financial future, they wait for everything to be "perfect" before they get going. They wait for the right time in the cycle, the right property, the right stocks, the right economic environment or the right interest rates. All this means they never get going.

The longer you wait to get started, the longer it will be before you get the money, success and freedom you want. It takes time to grow real wealth. ***It takes time for the power of compounding to work its magic.***

You need to understand that the timing will never be perfect nor will you ever have all the information you want. You need to develop the confidence to make an investment decision based on knowing enough and realising that you will learn the rest along the way.

**5. Fear stops them**

Fear keeps many of us from getting what we want, especially in matters of money. Be honest with yourself and count the number of times fear has prevented you from taking action and in the process cost you a lost financial opportunity.

The rich have learned to harness their fears and rather than focus on the negatives, they use fear to force them into positive action. For example, they use the fear of being stuck in their job for the rest of their lives, without the financial independence that they are craving, to motivate them to take on the commitment of investing.

Just like a river, fear can be bridged. The river of fear is only as deep and as wide as you allow it to be. And once you've crossed that river of fear and experienced the success on the other side, you usually look back and wonder why you were ever afraid.

But here's the catch: The only people who actually realise this are those that have crossed the river and stand on the other side. ***Money and success live on the other side of fear.***

**6. Waiting until they know enough**

The fear of not knowing enough prevents others from getting started investing.

However, the irony here is that the more you learn, the more you learn that you don't know! Once you start learning some basic investment concepts you suddenly realise there are a whole lot more things about investing or property that you don't understand.

That's the paradox of knowledge: the more you learn, the more you learn you don't know.

The trap is that many investors think that the way to escape this paradox is to learn even more, so they read more books, go to more seminars, listen to podcasts and watch YouTube videos.

As they learn more they find a whole heap more things they don't yet know.

The way out is to recognise that while you don't know it all, and you never will, you do know enough to get started with your investing and you will learn more along the way as you apply your knowledge in the real world, surviving any mistakes and challenges along the way.

**7. Focusing on linear income instead of passive income**

It is important to realise that not all income is created equal: some streams are linear and some are passive (as I've previously explained).

Linear income is what you get from a job. You work for an hour and get paid once for that hour's work, and that's it. If you don't turn up to work you don't get paid.

Passive income is when you work once but you continue to get paid over and over again from work you're no longer doing. The way to become wealthy is having passive income coming in whether you go to work or not.

Wouldn't it be nice to be paid hundreds of times for every hour you work?

That's what happens to investors. Initially they work long hours and save up to buy some stocks or to invest in real estate. Now their money starts working for them and keeps giving them sound investment returns "passively" in the form of capital growth and returns. Rather than getting another job, wealthy people know they need to send their money out to work for them.

To put it simply: "If you're not making money while you sleep, you'll never become rich."

**8. They give responsibility to others ("experts") instead of to themselves.**

Handing over responsibility for your financial affairs is really another form of laziness. It's not good enough to say, "I'll hand that over to someone else and they'll look after it for me."

You have to have some understanding of what you're about to embark on before you make any type of investment. It's OK to outsource the process as long as you don't outsource the understanding. You still need to understand what actually is going on. You need to understand the risk that you're about to embark on. You need to understand the rewards that you're about to enjoy.

**9. They give up when they face challenges**

There will always be challenges, so get used to that, but going through the challenges is what has made people rich, not giving up. You will only get where you wish to get to if you are willing to face the challenges along the path. Challenges are just opportunities dressed in work clothes.

So, it's really quite simple…

Decide to do these nine things that the rich do and you are much more likely to become successful and wealthy. If you don't do them, then like most people, you may never get rich.

Now in the next chapter I'll expand on this theme by outlining 39 ways that the rich think differently so you can start thinking, and achieving, the same results as they do.

# CHAPTER 9
# 39 WAYS THE RICH THINK DIFFERENTLY

There is a classic book by Napoleon Hill called *Think and Grow Rich*. While it was written almost 100 years ago, you will find it on the bookshelf of almost every successful investor. It's so important that you read it, that we'll gift you a free digital copy as a bonus when you register your copy of this book at www.RichHabitsPoorHabits.com.

Now there is good reason why the book is called *Think and Grow Rich* and not *Get a Job, Work Hard and Grow Rich*. It's because ***the rich think differently to most people*** and those who work hard at a job don't end up rich.

In my mind, your level of wealth — how rich you are — is the greatest measurement of your mindset. Aside from temporary setbacks and extraordinary fortunes of inheritance or luck, if you want to know how people think about money, look at their bank accounts.

This is probably why there is so much emotion and neurosis tied to people's relationship with money. I guess that's why I've heard it said that if you want to fix your money problems, get your head examined.

One of the big lessons I've learned in mentoring over 2,500 people in the past decade is that one of the greatest limitations to becoming rich is a deep-seated belief that somehow money is wrong and people who have a lot of it are inherently bad, crooked or selfish.

Of course, these beliefs are untrue and go back to the early childhood conditioning because of other people's (your parents) desire to rationalise away their own financial failures.

***The fact is: money is good.***

It takes money to build hospitals, churches and shelters. You need money to buy homes, cars, clothes, food, vacations and all those wonderful experiences in life.

To acquire money is not to take it away from someone else. Money tends to flow toward those people who can use it in the most productive ways to produce valuable goods and services, and who can invest it to create employment and opportunities that benefit others.

At the same time, money flows away from those who use it poorly, or who spend it in non-productive ways.

You have heard the phrase, "water seeks its own level," right? Fortunately, or unfortunately (depending on your level on the Wealth Pyramid), the same is true about money. Money will meet you where you are.

I've mentioned this before, but because it's one of the most important messages in this book, please let me remind you that:

***Your thoughts lead to your feelings, your feelings lead to your actions, and your action lead to your results.***

In other words, your inside world (your thoughts and feelings) directly affects your outside world (your actions and your habits which lead to the results you achieve).

Now don't underestimate the power of this principle. I know I did when I first read it in a book written almost a century ago (*The Science of Getting Rich* by Wallace Wattles), but once I understood the power of this principle, it was pivotal in fast tracking my success.

Of course, this concept has since been written about in many books and recently popularised by T. Harv Eker's in *Secrets of the Millionaire Mind* and Steve Siebold in *100 Ways the Rich Think Differently* (both on my recommended reading list).

So in this chapter I'm going to outline 39 ways the rich think differently to the average person because this is what determines their Rich Habits — this is what makes them act differently to most people. Remember

— if you want to become rich you'll have to study how most people (the poor) behave and then do the opposite.

Please remember that when I use the words "rich" and "poor", I don't intend any offense and I am not making value judgments — just using expressions that help contrast two very different ways of thinking. So let's look at the difference between wealth generating thoughts and impoverished ones:

First, here's a summary of some of the many ways the rich think differently:

| | The Average Person | The Rich |
|---|---|---|
| 1 | Thinks about spending their money. | Think about how to invest their money. |
| 2 | Worries about running out of money. | Think about how to use their money to make more money. |
| 3 | Believes hard work makes you rich. | Believe leverage creates wealth. |
| 4 | Believes having a job gives them security. | Know there's no such thing as "job security". |
| 5 | Believes in working for money. | Believe in working for fulfilment. |
| 6 | Want to be rich. | Are committed to being rich. |
| 7 | Sets their financial expectation low, so they're never disappointed. | Set their financial expectations high so they're always excited. |
| 8 | Focuses on obstacles in their way. | Focus on the opportunities all around them. |
| 9 | Believes life happens to them — they are a passenger. | Believe that they create their own destiny — they are the pilot of their lives. |
| 10 | Believes money will make them happier. | Know that money has little to do with happiness, but it does make your life easier and more enjoyable. |
| 11 | Believes they aren't worthy of wealth. | Believe they deserve to be rich. |
| 12 | Believes rich people are lucky. | Know luck has nothing to do with it. |
| 13 | Resents successful and rich people. | Admire other rich and successful people. |
| 14 | Thinks about money emotionally. | Think about money logically. |
| 15 | Believes it's wrong for a small group of people (the 1%) to possess most of the money. | Welcome the masses (the 99%) to join them. |
| 16 | Believes rich people are dishonest. | Believe rich people are ambitious. |
| 17 | Believes money is the root of all evil. | Believe poverty is the root of all evil. |
| 18 | Believes money changes people. | Believe money reveals people. |

| | The Average Person | The Rich |
|---|---|---|
| 19 | Believes if they become wealthy they will lose their friends. | Believe being wealthy will expand their network. |
| 20 | Believes they can't afford to give to charity. | Believe they must be generous. |
| 21 | Thinks either/or. | Know they can have both. |
| 22 | Believes they must choose between a great family life and being poor, or love and being poor. | Know they can have it all — it's not either or. |
| 23 | Sees money as a finite resource. | See money as an infinite resource. |
| 24 | Dreams of having enough money to retire. | Dream of having enough money to leave a legacy. |
| 25 | Thinks small. | Think big. |
| 26 | Believes they have to build wealth on their own. | Know that if they're the smartest person in their team, they're in trouble. |
| 27 | Believes their thinking is unrelated to their net worth. | Know their mindset is critical to their results. |
| 28 | Believes you have to be educated and smart to be rich. | Know intelligence has little to do with getting rich. |
| 29 | Believes you have to have money to make money. | Know you can use other people's money to become rich. |
| 30 | Believes the rich should support the poor. | Believe in self-reliance. |
| 31 | Teaches their children about money by example. | Interestingly the rich does the same thing. |
| 32 | Hands down their limiting beliefs about money to their children. | Hand down their empowering beliefs about money to their children. |
| 33 | Teaches their children how to survive. | Teach their children how to become wealthy. |
| 34 | Minimises the importance of money to their children. | Teach their children the importance of money. |
| 35 | Teaches their children to be happy with what they have. | Teach their children to follow their dreams and aim for the stars. |
| 36 | Don't believe in personal development. | Know that their personal wealth can't grow faster than their personal growth. |
| 37 | Thinks education finishes when you leave school and would rather be entertained than educated. | Continually learn and grow. |
| 38 | Thinks short term. | Think long-term. |
| 39 | Feels threatened by change. | Embrace change. |

What this should show you is that the poor develop narrow thinking around their current incomes and adjust their lives to fit in with their financial situation. It shows in the clothes they wear, the cars they drive and the restaurants they eat in. It all has to do with how they think.

## So where do you fit in?

How often did you find yourself on the left-hand side of this table and how can you get to be more like the people on the right? And, just importantly, how does this affect your habits and behaviours?

Whatever got you to where you are today won't get you any further, that's why you'll need to learn to think differently. That's one of the reasons ***the rich are constant readers and learners***.

At my seminars, I often ask what the attendees were taught about money when they were young, and the list usually looks something like this:

- Money doesn't grow on trees
- Filthy rich, dirty money
- We don't deserve to be rich
- You can't have money and be spiritual
- Rich people are greedy
- You have to work hard to be rich
- You shouldn't talk about money or show of your wealth

Remember we were told these things as children when we didn't have the perspective to decide whether they were right or wrong, but many of us have carried these myths into adulthood. However, today they make no sense.

Why not look at the list of the 39 ways of thinking above and see which ones strike a chord with you? Of course, you can add any I've missed that relate to you.

Then work out why you hold on to these beliefs. Do they still make sense?

Now is the time to get rid of any that you can question or that you realise are nonsense. Now is the time to discard any that simply aren't true, that are holding you back, and are stopping you from becoming rich.

More importantly now is the time to replace them with some new empowering beliefs. Why not write down a new list:

- **I deserve to be wealthy**
- **It's okay for me to be rich**
- **I'm going to be wealthy**

In fact, choose as many, if not all, of the beliefs on the right-hand side of the previous table and make them your new money beliefs.

Here's one to start with…

## Are the rich really greedy?

Many people think the rich are all greedy. That's not true. Some rich people are greedy, just as some poor people are. But most of the rich people I hang around with understand the importance of giving and society is the better for it.

In my mind when you create wealth it's your responsibility to return it to society — giving back is a necessary step in getting rich.

Even before you become rich you should adopt the practice of giving.

Why? Because Newton's law states, "For every action there is a reaction." If you're greedy, people will respond to you in kind. You have to give money to get it back. Remember, ***give and you shall receive***.

Here's another one…

***Money doesn't buy happiness***

Well that's also wrong!

My co-author Tom spent five years studying the daily habits of the rich and poor and he found that:

- **82% of the wealthy were happy, while 98% of the poor were unhappy.**
- **87% of the wealthy were happy in their marriage, while 53% of the poor were unhappy.**
- **93% of the wealthy were happy because they liked or loved what they did for a living, while 85% of the poor were unhappy.**
- **0% of the wealthy were unhappy due to finances, while 98% of the poor were unhappy.**

Tom also found that ***money problems have a ripple effect on your life***. They can result in an overall sense of unhappiness, and they can create marital stress, making both spouses unhappy in the marriage. Even worse, that stress can cause health issues and, worse still, it can negatively impact the lives of your children.

On the other hand, Tom found being rich creates an overall sense of happiness, improves your marital relationships, eliminates stress associated with money problems — which improves your overall health — and enables parents to give their kids a superior education, which lays the foundation for success in life.

If you're a parent then I'm sure you would agree that when your children are doing well in life, it makes you happy, and when they're struggling, it makes you unhappy.

So when the poor say "money doesn't buy happiness," they're wrong. Just like many of those other non-empowering beliefs that they think and say as well.

Being rich can increase happiness in many areas of your life. Tom's research found that wealth and poverty have a domino effect on all aspects of your life, so if you improve your financial condition in life, you will increase happiness in other aspects of your life.

If you want to increase your overall happiness in life, you have to end your poverty.

However...

### To have more, you must become more

These are not just clever words; they are wise truths — and stark realities for some.

I remember one of my early mentors Jim Rohn saying: "If you don't like how things are, change it. You're not a tree."

He also said that ***becoming wealthy begins with an attitude of gratitude.*** That's why I want you to take inventory of all the great wealth you already have.

Go ahead and ask yourself, "What do I feel grateful for in my life?" Take a couple of minutes to write it down.

Now, if you were to show that list to most people around the world they would call you wealthy.

You see, wealth is a matter of context and perspective that ultimately creates a feeling. Feel grateful for all you have, and you will feel instantly wealthy.

Here's the trick, once you feel wealthy you will act wealthy, and this will charge a magnet that will attract more wealth to you.

Those who believe they can become rich and are worthy of wealth are the ones who will be, because they act accordingly. People become rich because they decide to become rich — because they think like the rich think. They consistently take the necessary actions that turn their beliefs into realities.

That's why I now want you to decide that you are worthy of becoming rich. It will be your first step toward greater prosperity.

After all, people with more difficulties and far greater obstacles and limitations than you have gone on to become incredibly wealthy — so why NOT you?

People who started poorer or are less intelligent or had more difficult childhoods or no support have gone on to make great fortunes. So can you!

If you think you can, you will. ***Your attitude will determine your destiny.***

As well as being more grateful for being alive, there are a number of other success habits that rich people adopt that you can learn from. Let's discover what they are in the next chapter, shall we?

# CHAPTER 10
# THE SUCCESS HABITS OF THE RICH

Unfortunately, we live in a society that teaches us that money equals success. Like many other things, money is a tool. It's certainly not a bad thing but, ultimately, it's just another resource. Regrettably too many people worship it.

Now I didn't understand this when I began my study of rich and successful people almost 50 years ago.

Of course, I eventually learned that not all rich people are successful, and not all successful people are rich; but remember I was much younger and more naïve then and wanted it all.

So I tried to understand why some people were rich while others kept struggling financially. Over the years I attended many seminars, paid mentors and read as many books as I could on the topic of success. I modelled successful people and eventually grew successful myself.

It wasn't easy, I've had my challenges in life (mostly self-inflicted) and I've hit rock-bottom, but I got up again, learned from my mistakes and moved forward.

Over the years I have learned that…

## Being rich has little to do with the money itself

Instead, it has a lot to do with how you think about money.

This means that if you want to become rich, one of your first steps is to ***know how the wealthy think about money differently than you do,*** and to start thinking like them.

The next step is to take action and to let the action become natural by thinking the way wealthy people do and developing what we call Rich Habits, which Tom outlines in upcoming chapters.

Anyway… just like Tom did in his study, I also found rich people share similar habits just the way poor people share similar habits.

## Now before you get too offended…

As I've already explained, I'm not making a judgment when I say rich people or poor people — they are terms I use to help clarify the different ways of thinking that 1% of people exhibit from the majority of the population.

While Tom will explain many of these in detail later in this book based on his five-year study of the rich and the poor, initially I'd like to give you a brief overview by sharing…

## 66 Rich Habits of Successful People

1. The average person thinks about spending their money, while the rich think about how to invest their money.

2. The poor worry about running out of money while the rich think about how to use their money to make more money. They're not scared to take on debt, recognising leveraging other people's money is one of the fastest ways to grow their wealth. You can learn more about leveraging other people's money in my other books on investing, which you can find at www.MichaelYardneyBooks.com.au.

3. Most people believe hard work makes you rich, while the rich know that leverage creates wealth.

4. Successful people don't procrastinate. They don't spend their life waiting for the "right time" or waiting until they know it all or have figured everything out.

5. The average person believes having a job gives them security. The rich know there's no such thing as "job security".

6. Most people want to be rich. The rich are committed to being rich, which are very different things.

7. When things go wrong, the rich find a lesson, while others only see a problem.

8. The poor set their financial expectations low so they're never disappointed.On the other hand, ***the rich set their financial expectations high so they're always excited.***

9. Successful people take calculated risks — financial, emotional, professional and psychological. But once they've built their wealth they take fewer risks.

10. The rich consciously and methodically create their own success, while others hope success will find them.

11. The rich look for and find opportunities where others see obstacles.

12. The poor and middle class believe life happens to them. They are a passenger in the journey of life, while the rich believe they create their own destiny. They are the pilot of their lives.

13. Rich and successful people align themselves with like-minded people. They understand the importance of being part of a team. They create win-win relationships.

14. The poor believe money will make them happier, while the rich know that money has little to do with happiness, but it does make your life easier and more enjoyable.

15. The rich don't blame (what's the point?). They take responsibility for their actions and outcomes (or lack thereof). They know there is no such thing as a rich victim.

16. The poor believe it's wrong for a small group of people (the 1%) to possess most of the money. The rich welcomes the masses (the 99%) to join them.

17. Successful people are not necessarily more talented than the majority, yet they always find a way to maximise their potential. They get more out of themselves. They use what they have more effectively.

18. The poor believe that in order to gain something, you must sacrifice something else. You must choose between a great family life and being poor, or love and being poor, but you can't have both. The rich know they can have it all if you have an abundant mindset.

19. Successful people are solution-focused, rather than looking for problems or obstacles.

20. Successful people are fearful like everyone else, but they are not controlled or limited by fear. They use it to empower themselves.

21. The rich get up early. They know there's no shortcut so they work hard until they've accumulated a big enough asset base so they don't have to work hard any more.

22. The rich ask the right questions — ones that put them in a productive, creative mindset and a positive emotional state. They understand that the better the questions they ask, the better the answers they get and the better the results they will achieve.

23. The rich have clarity and certainty about what they want (and don't want) for their life. They actually visualise and plan their future while others are merely spectators of life.

24. While the poor believe rich people are lucky, the rich know luck has nothing to do with their success. While the poor wait for their lotto numbers to come up, the rich don't expect Lady Luck to pay them a visit; instead they aggressively pursue their dreams.

25. While the middle class believe the road to riches is through a formal education like a college degree or a masters, you'll find many of the

rich never completed high school. They favour specific knowledge in their industry over a formal education. They've learned to become more valuable by becoming an expert in their job.

26. ***The rich are voracious life-long learners.*** They constantly work at educating themselves, sometimes formally and academically; but more often informally by asking, watching, reading or listening and also experimentally by doing, trying, failing and trying again. By the way... I'm not talking about a formal education.

27. Rich people are generally rich because they have made money selling a specific knowledge they have acquired.

28. Rich and successful people are glass-half-full people — while still being practical and down-to-earth. They have an ability to find the good in everything around them rather than look for faults, problems or stumbling blocks.

29. Putting it another way... the poor focus on obstacles in their way while the rich focus on all the opportunities all around them.

30. While many people are pleasure junkies and avoid pain and discomfort at all costs, the rich understand the value and benefits of working through the tough stuff that most others avoid.

31. The poor think the rich are selfish. The rich see it as their obligation to earn more so they can contribute more — partly by setting a good example but more importantly by giving to charity and helping their community. They know that if they're not taking care of themselves, they won't be in a position to help others.

32. The poor believe they aren't worthy of wealth, while the rich believe they deserve to be rich.

33. Rich and successful people are adaptable and embrace change. They are comfortable with and embrace the new and the unfamiliar, while the majority of us are creatures of comfort and habit.

34. The poor often resent successful and rich people (you know what I mean... they're waiting for the real estate or stock market to

collapse on those who've worked hard to invest in their future). On the other hand, the rich admire other rich and successful people.

35. Successful people don't believe in, or wait, for fate, destiny, chance or luck to determine or shape their future. They believe in and are committed to actively and consciously creating their own best life.

36. The poor think about money emotionally, while the rich think about money logically.

37. Successful people have a plan for their lives and work methodically at turning that plan into a reality. They plan to become the person they plan to become, while in general, for the poor, their lives are a blundering series of unplanned events and outcomes.

38. The poor often think that rich people are dishonest, while successful people know that rich people are ambitious.

39. Most of us are conditioned to think that money is the cause of all that's unjust in the world. But money is simply a commodity, it's only as good or bad as the perception we have of it. So while the poor believe money is the root of all evil, wealthy people know that poverty is the root of all evil.

40. The poor believe money changes people. The rich understand that money reveals people.

41. The poor are worried that if they become rich they will lose their friends. The rich believe being wealthy will expand their network.

42. Successful people are resilient. They're just warming up when most would throw in the towel.

43. The poor believe their thinking is unrelated to their net worth. Successful people know their mindset is critical to their results.

44. Many people believe you have to be educated and smart to be rich. Successful people know intelligence has little to do with getting rich, but know they have to be financially fluent.

45. The poor teach their children about money by example. Interestingly, the rich do the same thing.

46. ***Successful people innovate rather than imitate.***

47. The poor believe the rich should support the poor. The rich believe in self-reliance.

48. Successful people consistently do what they need to do, irrespective of how they are feeling on a given day. They don't spend their life stopping and starting.

49. The poor believe you have to have money to make money. The rich know you can use other people's money to become rich.

50. Successful people deal with problems and challenges quickly and effectively; they don't put their head in the sand. They face their challenges and use them to improve themselves.

51. The poor hand down their limiting beliefs about money to their children. Conversely, the rich hand down their empowering beliefs about money to their children.

52. The poor teach their children how to survive. The rich teach their children how to become wealthy.

53. The poor teach their children to be happy with what they have. The rich teach their children to follow their dreams and aim for the stars. Average people set low expectations to avoid disappointment, whereas rich people set huge expectations.

54. Successful people are more effective than most at managing their emotions. They feel like we all do but they are not slaves to their emotions.

55. The poor minimise the importance of money with their children. The rich teach their children the importance of money.

56. Successful people are good communicators and they consciously work at it.

57. Successful people are secure. They do not derive their sense of self worth from what they own, who they know, where they live or what they look like.

58. Most people think their education finishes when they leave school and would rather be entertained than educated. The rich continually learn and grow.

59. Successful people are generous. They take pleasure in helping others achieve.

60. Successful people tend to be humble and they are happy to admit mistakes and to apologise. They are confident in their ability, but not arrogant. They are happy to learn from others. They are happy to make others look good rather than seek their own personal glory.

61. The poor don't believe in personal development. The rich know that their personal wealth can't grow faster than their personal growth.

62. ***Successful people are happy to swim against the tide***, to do what most won't. They are not people pleasers and they don't need constant approval.

63. Their desire to be exceptional means that successful people do things that most won't. They become exceptional by choice. We're all faced with life-shaping decisions on a regular basis. Successful people make the decisions that most won't and don't.

64. While the average person feels threatened by change, successful people embrace change.

65. While many people are reactive, successful people are proactive. They take action before they have to.

66. Successful people have balance in their lives. While they may be financially successful, they know that the terms "money" and "success" are not interchangeable. They understand that people who are successful on a financial level only are not successful at all.

## Of course it's worth realising that...

We all have some of these Rich Habits and we all exhibit some disempowering Poor Habits. The big differentiator in the see-saw of life is: do you have more of the Rich Habits or more of the Poor Habits?

The good news is that as you're learning about these concepts in our book the choice is yours. You can choose whether you will be a have or a have not.

Our aim in this book is to take you through four stages:

1. **Develop awareness of these concepts**
2. **Recognise your disempowering Poor Habits**
3. **Remove your Poor Habits and**
4. **Replace them with Rich Habits**

So that you can join the ranks of the rich.

I recently read an interesting quote: "Whoever said money can't buy happiness isn't spending it right." So in the next chapter I'm going to share some thoughts on how much money is enough.

# CHAPTER 11
# HOW TO BE HAPPIER WITH YOUR MONEY

I guess you bought this book because you want to become rich. But how much money do you need?

A lot of research has gone into whether money truly makes you happy and it has been found that, in general, humans are never satisfied. We always think that if we had a little bit more money would be happier. But when we get there, we are not.

For some people, the more money they have the more they want, but the more they have, the paradox is that it becomes less effective at bringing them joy.

I recently heard a story about a wealthy couple who were at a party hosted by a multi-millionaire.

The wife said to her husband, "Do you realise that our host makes more money in one day than you do in a year?"

Interestingly her spouse's response was: "Yes, but I have something he will never have: *enough*."

Now that's a great lesson to learn, isn't it?

## How much money is really enough?

I grew up in a poor household where money was scarce and while I can't really remember when it was, but I know I was quite young, I decided I wanted to become wealthy through property investing after seeing the lifestyle some of my friends' parents enjoyed.

What I didn't realise at the time was that it would take me at least 30 years to develop a big enough asset base to give me the sizeable passive income I desired.

And it hadn't dawned on me that along the way I would need a *real* job, I'd have to practice delayed gratification and money discipline, and I would have to work long hours and save, invest and reinvest my money.

Back then I didn't realise that you need to do the hard work early in your life so you can have an easy life later on.

What I do remember was that I wanted to be a millionaire by the age of 30 – back then (and that was more than 50 years ago) $1 million was worth a lot more than it is today.

So how much money is enough?

One million dollars might have been sufficient 50 years ago but how much is enough today? And how do you even work it out?

In his book *30 Lessons for Living: Tried and True Advice from the Wisest Americans*, gerontologist Karl Pillemer interviewed well over 1,000 elderly people (mainly aged from 80 to 100+), looking for a source of unique guidance from those who had lived "rich and fulfilling lives".

One thing I found interesting was that:

- Not one person of the thousand interviewed said that to be happy you should try to work as hard as you can to make money to buy the things you want.
- Not a single person said it's important to be at least as wealthy as the people around you, and if you have more than they do it's real success.
- No one – not a single person – said you should choose your work based on your desired future earning power.

Now to be clear…

- The elderly didn't say that money isn't important – because it is.

- They didn't rule out that more money might have made them happier because it most likely would. Remember… any problem that money can solve isn't really a problem – is it?

But it seems like the elderly people understood the important concept of enough.

Studies show that money does increase happiness.

Research Tom and I undertook before writing this book shows there's not even a known satiation point – a higher income makes virtually everyone happier, although each additional dollar delivers less happiness than the one before it.

Interestingly, psychologist Daniel Kahneman writes in the book *This Will Make You Smarter*:

> "On average, individuals with high incomes are in a better mood than people with lower income, but the difference is about a third as large as most people expect.
>
> "When you think of rich and poor people, your thoughts are inevitably focused on circumstances in which income is important.
>
> "But happiness depends on other factors more than it depends on income."

In other words, when I was young and saw all those rich landlords and wanted to become one myself, I imagined a big income would make me happier (I was pretty miserable growing up) because I thought about the luxury imported cars they drove and the nice houses they lived in, rather than the years of hard work they had to put in and family life they sacrificed.

Just look what happens to all those actors and sporting heroes who earn staggering incomes yet ruin their family lives.

## So, what does make you happier?

Not surprisingly psychological studies have looked into what makes people happy and researchers broadly agree that four major points have a big impact on making people happy:

- Control over what you're doing.
- Progress in what you're pursuing.
- Connections to other people.
- Having purpose and meaning.

That's it.

You'll notice "more money" isn't on the list.

But you can easily see how money ties into these points.

- Money can grant you freedom from being locked into a job that you don't enjoy.
- Money can provide the tools necessary to achieve progress in pursuing your goals.
- Money can afford you time off to spend time with people that matter to you.
- Money can give you the ability to provide charity and community contribution, bringing meaning and purpose to your life.

Yes, money is important in those areas where it is important, and not at all important in those areas where it is not important.

So I believe striving to be Rich, striving for financial independence is worthwhile, but it's a marathon rather than a sprint. Yet it's a race worth running because it will allow you to live your life by design. You will be more in control of your life.

But think about it… how much money is enough? How will you know when you have enough?

Will you ever know when enough is enough?

The final chapter in this section is about a concept which is central to becoming rich and successful. It's called delayed gratification. While not many people practice it, you must learn how if you want to change your financial future.

# CHAPTER 12
# THE SECRET TO DELAYED GRATIFICATION

We live in a world of consumption, where people seek immediate gratification with the latest and greatest gadgets and products as soon as they hit the shelves.

Think about Apple and the ridiculously long line of people who queue for their updated iPhones!

When it comes to money management and becoming rich, though, patience and delayed gratification makes all the difference.

Patient people are more likely to save their pennies than seek "easy" (and expensive) credit, because they are happy to wait for a new car or big screen TV.

They don't have to have it all yesterday!

## The power of delaying

One of the common Rich Habits that I've found amongst successful people is their ability to delay gratification.

***Successful people possess higher patience*** and an aptitude to postpone the enjoyment of their work.

They have an ability to work hard to accomplish a goal which isn't achieved for a long time.

Learning to delay gratification rather than seeking immediate satisfaction is essential for success, particularly when it comes to things like investing, business and making money.

One key difference between people with consumer debt and those without, everything else being equal, is that ***the person with no consumer debt has mastered delayed gratification,*** while the person with consumer debt has not.

***In its simplest form,*** the ability to wait 15 minutes to get two marshmallows instead of one marshmallow is delayed gratification — more on this fact a little later!

The ability to wait to buy something after you've saved for the item, rather than impulsively purchasing something as soon as you realise you want it, is delayed gratification.

The ability to invest money today to have money when you retire is delayed gratification. ***The real question is: how do you learn delayed gratification?***

Like I said, learning delayed gratification isn't easy but it can become a skill in your Rich Habit tool-kit if you follow a few simple tips.

1. Write down a list of money goals and put them somewhere that you can see them every day. Another idea is to tell someone else what your money goals are, perhaps a mentor, who can then help keep you accountable to them.

2. Every time you're tempted to purchase something consider whether it's a want or a need. If it's a want, such as a new suit or handbag, then delay for at least 24 hours before deciding whether to buy it. Most of the time, that 24-hour period will be enough time for you to see that you don't need it at all. For more expensive purchases, then you should delay for even longer. If you're buying that gadget online, how about putting it in your shopping cart but don't click the checkout button? Instead come back in 24 hours and if you still "need" that item then buy it. You'll be surprised how often the desire has disappeared.

3. Another strategy is to get advice from someone much older than you are to discover what they wish they'd done differently with money when they were your age. It's likely that they'll share ideas

with you that you've never thought about. And in my experience, they're probably going to disclose that they wish they'd started saving and investing earlier in life rather than spending their money on things they thought they needed at the time.

## The science behind delayed gratification

Let me explain further: Many people think that ***delayed gratification is the secret to success***. I certainly believe it's one of them.

There have been numerous studies about delayed gratification over the years, so I thought I'd share two of them with you now to illustrate how it works.

In 1972, there was an experiment that tested children's ability to delay gratification. Now, in this experiment, a researcher offered a small child a choice. They could have one marshmallow now or two marshmallows if they could wait a mere 15 minutes. The researcher left the child alone in the room with one marshmallow on a tray.

The child was filmed with a secret video camera. Of course, most of the children couldn't wait and soon ate the marshmallow straight away. However, about 30 per cent were able to delay gratification and get the second marshmallow.

Interestingly, the same children were tested for the next 30 years and guess what happened?

The ones who could wait for the second marshmallow were *more successful* later in life! They got higher test scores in school. They had fewer problems with drugs. They were much more likely to go to college. They had lower body fat. And they made more money as adults.

According to the researchers, the children in the experiment used a number of techniques to delay gratification and control themselves. Some of the children turned around so they didn't see the tray or the marshmallow. Some covered their eyes so they couldn't physically see the marshmallow. Some even kicked the desk or pulled their hair to distract themselves. Others stroked the marshmallow as if it were a doll.

Of course, these were all techniques to control their focus. Sure, they were childish techniques, but they worked. What was clear from this experiment was that 30 per cent of the children were lucky to have developed self-control from a young age. But, many people think that adults can also develop self-control through practice. With that self-control they become more successful and reach their goals.

In other words, this series of experiments proved that ***the ability to delay gratification was critical for success in life***.

If you think about it, you can see the impact on success that having the ability to delay gratification can have everywhere you look.

- If you can delay the gratification of watching television and get your homework done now, then you'll learn more and get better grades.
- If you delay the gratification of buying sweets or crisps at the store, then you'll eat healthier when you get home and be healthier, too.
- If you delay the gratification of finishing your workout early and put in a few more reps, then you'll be stronger and fitter.

So, the question we need to ask ourselves is this: Why did some children naturally have more self-control and thus were destined for success?

More research was conducted into delayed gratification to find out the answer. Researchers at the University of Rochester decided to replicate the marshmallow experiment, but with an important twist. This time, they split the children into two groups.

According to the study results, the first group of children were also exposed to unreliable experiences, such as the promise to bring bigger crayons or more stickers compared to the small selection that the children were originally given. These promises never materialised.

Conversely, the second group of children had reliable experiences where the promised better crayons and stickers were provided to them. It doesn't take Einstein to work out what consequently happened to the marshmallow experiment!

The first group, having experienced those broken promises, had no reason to trust that the researchers would ever bring a second marshmallow so they quickly ate the first one in front of them.

The second group, however, had experienced delayed gratification training because their promises were kept. So they had learned that waiting was worth it because they'd previously received better crayons and stickers. They also had the capability of waiting longer. On average, according to the results, they waited four times longer than the first group.

In other words, the researchers found that the child's ability to delay gratification and display self control was not a predetermined trait, but rather was impacted by the experiences and environment that surrounded them.

In fact, the effects of the environment were almost instantaneous. Just a few minutes of reliable or unreliable experiences was enough to push the actions of each child in one direction or another.

## Delayed gratification basics

Over the decades these marshmallow experiences have become very popular but they're only one piece of the delayed gratification puzzle.

Human behaviour (and life in general) is a lot more complex than that, so let's not pretend that one choice a four-year-old makes will determine the rest of his or her life or how rich or successful they will be.

However, my observation is that the studies do highlight a very important Rich Habit. Waiting for the second marshmallow, or better crayons or stickers, isn't easy. In fact, for children it's particularly hard.

What we can learn from this is that ***you need to find the ability to be disciplined and take action*** instead of becoming distracted and doing what's easy. Success in nearly every field requires you to ignore

Yet it's not easy to change ingrained habits and the approaches to life that you've been practicing since childhood, but once you're aware of the importance of the concept of delayed gratification, it's entirely do-able.

Start with small alterations to your thought patterns by acknowledging your habits intended to provide immediate gratification.

Remember, if it comes too quickly, chances are you will lose it again just as easily. All good things take time!

As Warren Buffet wisely said: "*Wealth is the transfer of money from the impatient to the patient.*"

## What does delayed gratification mean?

If you're wondering what I'm on about let me explain…

The definition of delayed or deferred gratification is the ability to resist the temptation for an immediate reward and therefore wait for a later reward. The later reward is generally much larger than the immediate one, and that's why it's worth the wait.

Research into the ability to delay gratification shows that there are a number of other positive outcomes from this skill, including academic success, physical and psychological health and social competence.

Similarly, a person's ability to delay gratification relates to other skills such as patience, impulse and self-control, and will power, which are all involved in self-regulatory behaviour.

So, if we think about the rich and successful, one of their key Rich Habits is the ability to delay a smaller instant reward for a later more generous one. But we need to remember that this skill isn't natural for most people.

***Humans are wired for instant gratification.*** We love it! While evolution made us that way long before our modern monetary system came about, unfortunately the desire for instant gratification doesn't help us when we're trying to become wealthy. In fact, it hurts us.

That's one of the reasons many high income earners are not "rich". You'll often find the more they earn, the more they spend and they end up on a treadmill where they tend to spend more than they earn because they need to support a lifestyle that has little or no enduring value, but has high fixed costs to maintain. Typically they spend on things like big houses, fancy cars and impressive vacations.

They live a life of instant gratification, where they live in a peer group of other big spenders and where they have to work harder and harder to maintain the lifestyle they no longer feel they have the time or energy to enjoy. This is what we typically call the rat race!

## Delayed gratification and money

When it comes to the latest gadget or fad, most people have no self-control. This is made even worse in the technological world we now live in where we all have access to instant money — real or otherwise.

Too many people use their credit cards for impulse purchases that in reality they have no way of repaying any time soon. Unfortunately, this type of mindset can quickly lead to financial ruin.

It's time to be honest with yourself — ***are you a slave to instant gratification?*** If so, there are a number of strategies to break the cycle, but first you must recognise this Poor Habit.

Let me be clear: Consumer debt is never OK. Using your credit card for impulse purchases or taking on unnecessary debt for such non-appreciating assets as cars or, worse still, a personal loan to go on holiday is never a good idea.

Too many people see the limit on their credit card as their money — it's not. When you take on consumer debt it involves using dollars you'll hopefully earn in the future for current expenses (or splurges) and paying the bank interest for the privilege of doing so!

This means that "bargain" price you paid today is likely to cost you much more over the long run because you're using credit to pay for it.

doing something easier (delaying gratification) in favour of doing something harder.

The lesson from all of this is that we all can develop the Rich Habit of delaying gratification and accepting what good things are worth waiting for.

Now, in the next section, Tom will explain his Rich Habits Program as well as the 30 Rich Habits that he identified during his five-year study of the rich and the poor. We truly believe that his research will help you understand how to profit from adopting Rich Habits, while equally importantly teaching you how to avoid the Poor Habits at all costs.

## SECTION THREE

# UNDERSTANDING RICH AND POOR HABITS

*Tom Corley*

# CHAPTER 13
# THE RICH HABITS PROGRAM

Before beginning my review of the Rich Habits Program I want to dispel a few common myths about financial success. Certain members of the media have perpetuated these myths over the years and, unfortunately, these myths have succeeded in brainwashing many people who would otherwise have pursued success.

## Myth #1 — The Rich Have Good Luck and the Poor Have Bad Luck

Many unsuccessful people rationalise that they don't have "good luck" or just aren't "lucky". They argue that in order to be financially successful you need good luck. Is good luck important to becoming successful? The answer is a resounding "Yes!" All successful people have experienced good luck. In fact, no one will ever become successful if they do not have some good luck. But let's elaborate on this truth.

There are four types of luck. The first type of luck is "random good luck". This is a type of good luck we have no control over, like winning the lottery or receiving an unexpected inheritance.

The second type of luck is "random bad luck". Like random good luck, we have no control over this, either. Events creating this type of luck are outside of our influence for the most part. Examples include coming down with a disease, getting hit by lightning, random accidents, a tree falling on your house, etc.

The third type of luck is "opportunity luck". This is good luck that is a by-product of good daily habits. Think of opportunity luck as an apple orchard. You prepare the land, plant the apple seeds and diligently nurture the trees as they grow. After some time the apple trees blossom and bear fruit. This fruit is the by-product of doing the things you needed to do over a long period of time. These apples represent opportunity luck.

Successful people do the things that are necessary over the long-term in order for opportunity luck to occur in their lives. They live the Rich Habits every single day. ***Rich Habits are like a magnet for opportunity luck.*** Many of the opportunities are completely unexpected. Some people refer to this as "the law of attraction". Opportunity luck follows the law of attraction for those who live the Rich Habits.

The fourth type of luck is "detrimental luck". Detrimental luck is the evil twin of opportunity luck. Unsuccessful people have bad habits. Like the Rich Habits, bad habits are also seeds. They will take root and grow until they too bear fruit. Unfortunately, the bad fruit birthed by bad habits brings detrimental luck into the lives of the unsuccessful. This detrimental luck might be a job loss, investment losses, foreclosure, divorce, illness or something similar.

To bring success into your life you need to attract the right kind of luck. Living the Rich Habits guarantees you will attract the right kind of luck, and opportunities will appear, seemingly out of thin air. As with low-hanging fruit, all you have to do is reach out and pick it.

## Myth #2 — Rich People Inherit Most of their Money

Depending on the study or survey, and there are many[1], between 67-80 per cent of the wealthy are self-made millionaires. These self-made millionaires either came from poverty or the middle-class. Most wealthy individuals do not inherit their wealth. They create it.

[1] 2013 study by BMO Private Bank — 67% of high-net-worth Americans were self-made millionaires and only 8 percent inherited their wealth.

## Myth #3 — Rich People Don't Work Hard

***Rich people***, particularly self-made millionaires, ***work far more hours than everyone else***. According to the Census Bureau, the average wealthy household (which the IRS defines as the top 20 per cent of income earners in the U.S.) worked five times as many hours as the average poor household. So, the rich are just harder working than everyone else? Yes. But not necessarily because they have a better work ethic. The rich work harder because they like, love or are very passionate about what they do for a living. As a result, they devote more hours to their work. Unfortunately, most people do work that they don't like. As a result, they do the bare minimum in order to keep their jobs.

When it comes to the uber-rich, those with $5 million or more in net worth, to them work has a very different meaning. Richard Branson is a famous self-made multimillionaire. He owns Virgin Atlantic, Virgin Airlines and about 20 other companies. He is known to work 12 to 14 hours a day. When he was asked if he considered what he did work he said the following: "No. I love what I do and I love the people I work with. If I told you I played 12 to 14 hours a day would you still think I was a hard worker?"

The very rich do not work, at least, not as society defines it. Sure, they devote enormous amounts of time to their jobs, but they do so because they love what they are doing. When you love what you do for a living, it no longer is work. It becomes play. Who wouldn't want to play for 14 hours every day?

## Myth #4 — Rich People Are Smarter and Better Educated

If you were to look at a "Who's Who" of wealthy individuals, you would find that nearly 50 per cent of them never completed college. And some, such as Andrew Carnegie, didn't even complete grammar (primary) school, let alone high school. The reality is that most rich people start out in life no smarter or better educated than everyone else.

What they do have that eventually makes them smarter and more knowledgeable is a desire to continuously learn as well as a desire to improve their skills. They are life-long learners who, through relentless daily self-improvement, grow every day. They invest whatever available time they have in themselves. They become the person they need to be in order for success to visit them.

## The Rich Habits

Habits represent unconscious behaviour, thinking, choices and emotions. A habit is formed when neurons (brain cells) talk to one another repetitively. Habits have a purpose. Unlike the rest of the body, the brain cannot store fuel. It has to request it from other parts of the body. As a result the brain creates habits over millions of years of evolution in order to help it function more efficiently and on less fuel. Habits save the brain from work and conserve brain fuel. So the brain naturally prefers habits.

Habits are governed by an almost fractional area of the brain called the basal ganglia. The basal ganglia resides deep within the brain, in an area called the limbic system, and is the unconscious command and control centre for habits. When the basal ganglia decides that a habit needs to go to work, it directs the brain to fire up a series of brain cells and once fired, we unconsciously find ourselves engaging in some activity, thinking, behaviour or emotion.

***Habits improve brain function.*** The brain is always looking to create habits for this reason. Habits put you on autopilot. If you have good daily success habits, this puts you on autopilot for success. If you have bad habits, this puts you on autopilot for failure. Habits are, quite simply, an amazing invention.

Unless we force ourselves to become aware of our habits, we will never be able to change our habitual behaviour, thinking, decision-making or emotions. Without habit awareness, habits tend to slip right below the radar of our consciousness.

Studies show that many of our habits are formed by the age of nine by mimicking our parents[2]. Parents have the most influence over the habits we develop in our early lives. Most of these habits we will carry with us into our adult lives. Some of this parental habit mimicking is neurological. Our brains have something called mirror neurons. The purpose of mirror neurons is to enable babies and children to mimic the behaviours and emotions of their parents. They are an ancient relic of prehistoric human evolution, whose primary purpose for existing is to aid in survival.

Only when kids become adults are they able to break free from the habits forged during their early lives. Their new habits develop from new environments, career mentors, lifelong self-education or from the school of hard knocks.

About 40 per cent of all of our daily activities are habits[3]. This means 40 per cent of the time we are all on autopilot every day. If we have more good habits than bad habits, life will be good and we will be happy. If we have more Poor Habits than Rich Habits, life will be a struggle and we will be unhappy. It's like a seesaw. For most, their seesaw has more bad habits than good habits. It's tipping in the wrong direction. Adding just a few good habits can get that seesaw tipping in the right direction and change our lives forever. Conversely, eliminating just a few bad habits can get that seesaw tipping in the right direction and also positively affect our lives.

There are two types of habits:

1. Ordinary Habits and
2. Keystone Habits

Ordinary Habits are simple, basic, standalone habits — the time we wake up in the morning, the route we take to work, how we hold a fork, etc. Keystone Habits are more complicated habits. They are unique in the habit world because they affect ordinary habits. Keystone Habits are like predators; they move around searching for and devouring ordinary daily habits that pose a threat and interfere with the Keystone Habit.

[2] Brown University Study published in The American Journal of Family Therapy in 2014 – Most habits are forged by the age of nine.

[3] Duke University Study published in Psychological Science Journal 2006 (Habits – A Repeat Performance) – 40% of daily activities are habits.

Let me give you an example:

It's New Year's Day and one of your resolutions is to lose weight. You're about 50 pounds overweight. A close friend, who is a runner, says the fastest way to lose weight is to run. So you decide to start running (Rich Habit). You hate running but after doing it a little while, you're down 15 pounds. One night you attend some social event or get together and someone you know compliments you on your weight loss and how amazing your look. You go home that night feeling happy, like you're floating on air. That compliment really got you pumped up.

The next morning you decide to cut back on junk food (Poor Habit) and stop overeating (Poor Habit). You also want to run more in order to lose more weight, so you decide to quit smoking (Poor Habit). Adopting just one Keystone Habit — running — causes the elimination of three Ordinary Habits: junk food, overeating and smoking cigarettes.

That's why Keystone Habits are so important. They automatically eliminate one or more bad Ordinary Habits. For this reason, many of the Rich Habits were designed to be Keystone Habits. This makes habit change much easier and also much faster.

## What I learned about success

I spent 5 years studying rich and poor people as you already know and here's the most important things I learned about succeeding.

When I began my study of the rich and the poor I wanted to know the answer to one question: why are some people rich and other people poor?

Five years later and over 350 interviews later, I finished my research. It wasn't an easy thing to do. I had grouped 144 questions into 20 categories, and asked over 350 millionaires and poor people these questions.

It took me five years because this wasn't just a survey I mailed out. Surveys have very limited value. I either met with these people or spoke with them over the phone.

As a result, I was able to gather far more data. If you do the math, ***I asked 51,984 questions of the rich and the poor***. That's a lot of questions!

But it was worth it. I learned an enormous amount about dealing with mistakes and disappointment.

I gained insight into what it takes to overcome the hurdles, obstacles, rejections and the emotional downs everyone who pursues success experiences.

More importantly, I learned a lot about success and failure. I learned, in particular, why some never quit on their dream and why some do.

I learned that those who never quit:

*1. Have passion energy*

Those who never quit are the ones who have found their main purpose in life.

When you find your main purpose in life you are infused with something I like to call passion energy.

This energy is a hundred times more potent than willpower energy. It allows you to work 14 hour days, day after day.

It enables you to work long stretches during those days, with intense focus and without getting tired.

You don't get tired because you love what you are doing and want to keep doing it. When you have passion energy you just don't feel like you are working at all.

*2. Have unforced focus*

Those who never quit have stumbled upon something I call unforced focus.

You probably never heard about unforced focus before. This is a type of focus that relies on the passion energy I mentioned previously. Some call this being in the flow.

In any event, it is a type of focus that allows you to put your full attention and concentration to a task for five, six and even seven hours without a break.

Its sister, forced focus, relies on willpower energy, which is usually limited to two or three hours. You use forced focus while working at a job you do not like or have no passion for.

If you find yourself struggling with focus while pursuing your dream, you have not found your main purpose in life and you will not succeed in realising your dream.

*3. Are able to compartmentalise*

Many of the self-made millionaires in my study were holding down full-time jobs or running businesses full-time while they were pursuing their dream.

***The trick is to compartmentalise.*** You need to isolate time for your bread and butter and make sure you are still doing average-to-good work on your bread and butter stuff.

Average-to-good keeps you employed or keeps your business afloat until your dream begins to pay dividends.

It will take many years before your dream begins paying off financially. You're in it for the long haul, so you need to keep your bread and butter going.

If you want to better understand this concept read the book *The Wright Brothers* by David McCullough.

*4. Are patient*

Eighty per cent of the rich in my study did not become rich until age 50. Fifty-two per cent did not become rich until age 56.

***It takes a long time to create wealth.*** Those who never quit are patient.

*5. Take calculated risks*

Those who never quit are masters at managing risk. They take risks that are well thought out.

They don't wing it or rely on chance. Because they fully understand the risks they are taking and have thought everything through, they are able to weather the ups and downs associated with pursuing success.

*6. Control their thoughts and emotions*

Eighty-one per cent of the rich made a habit of controlling their thoughts and emotions.

Not every thought needs to come out of your mouth and not every emotion needs to be expressed.

Doing so damages relationships; relationships that could otherwise open important doors for you and members of your family.

Those who never quit are able to build strong, powerful relationships with other success-minded individuals because they are careful about what they say and they are in control of their emotions.

*7. Do their homework*

Those who never quit do their homework.

They read and learn every day. They perfect their knowledge and skills every day. They just keep improving and growing through daily learning.

*8. Form a team*

Those who never quit usually have a team around them that keeps everyone motivated. They find apostles for their cause — individuals devoted to them and who share their vision and purpose.

You need the cooperation of others to help you succeed in life. Those who never quit are good at forming teams of people who cooperate together, focused on pursuing a singular dream or purpose.

No one does it on their own.

*9. Learn from their mistakes*

Mistakes are the by-product of taking calculated risks.

Those who never quit view mistakes as nothing other than learning experiences. ***Mistakes teach you what not to do.***

*10. Are open-minded*

You can't learn anything if you are closed minded.

Being open to new ideas, new ways of doing things and the opinions of others is critical to growth.

Success requires growth. You must grow into the person you need to be in order for success to visit you.

You must be open and tolerant to the opinions of others. Those who never quit are open to all opinions and all ideas.

*11. Never quit on their dream*

Those who never quit will stick to something until they succeed, go bankrupt or die.

No matter how down in the dumps you are, you must do at least five things every day to move you forward on your goals.

There will be days when everything goes wrong, when you receive nothing but rejection, when everyone ignores you and days when it feels like your back is up against the wall and your dream feels like it's collapsing under the weight of all of your failures and mistakes.

*12. Stay healthy*

"You can't make money from a hospital bed."

That's what one of the non-quitters told me during my research. Those who never quit exercise every day, they moderate their consumption of junk food, they drink alcohol in moderation, they avoid fast food restaurants, they floss every day and most don't smoke cigarettes.

*13. Don't give into fear*

Those who never quit have made a habit of overcoming their fears. They are not superstitious and believe they can overcome any obstacle that is put in their way.

*14. Are persistent*

Julie Crone was the first woman inducted into the Thoroughbred Hall of Fame with 3,704 victories under her reins.

Her motto was to keep showing up; to keep trying her best every day. Those who never quit on their dream go at it every day.

When things go wrong, and they do all the time when you pursue a dream, they manage to brush it off, learn from what went wrong, and try again.

***They persist because they are passionate about what they are doing.*** They are passionate about what they are doing because they know they found their main purpose in life.

When you find your main purpose in life it infuses you with passion energy and passion energy enables you to persist.

Conversely, those who quit:

*1. Run out of money*

They quit because they run out of money. This should never be a reason for quitting. There is always money to be found. Especially with the growth of crowd sourcing.

The real reason for not being able to find money is a failure to build relationships with individuals who have money or an inability to promote your dream adequately to those who have money.

*2. Have family issues*

The time you must devote to your dream deprives family members of your presence.

The word divorce starts to rear its ugly head. Or your kids, absent one mentor, begin behaving badly or making poor choices. Think failing out of school or drugs here.

*3. Lose their team*

Some quit because critical members of their team quit.

When you are pursuing a dream, your resources are usually very limited. Everyone on your team counts. Some more than others.

To combat this, you must develop relationships with individuals who possess skills that you need. If you don't, when you lose a key team player, it could mean the end of your dream.

*4. Don't have passion*

Some quit because they lose their passion.

In this case their WHY was not big enough or they were not pursuing their main purpose in life.

***If your WHY is big enough you will never quit.*** When you find your main purpose in life will never quit.

*5. Have health issues*

Some quit because of health reasons.

This is why I mentioned above the importance in maintaining your health. Pursuing success is a long process. It will take many years.

If you neglect your health during those years it could derail you.

*6. Are afraid*

Many who quit give into their fears: fear of losing money, fear of bankruptcy, fear of taking on debt, fear of their marriage unravelling, fear of embarrassment, fear of inadequacy, etc.

So these are some of things that I learned during my five-year study of the rich and the poor.

Let's now look at the 30 Rich Habits I have developed through my research so you can start on your journey to success and to a wealthy life.

# CHAPTER 14
# RICH HABIT NUMBER ONE

**I will adopt good daily habits and follow these good daily habits every day.**

Good daily habits are the foundation of success. Successful people differ from unsuccessful people in their daily habits. Successful people have many good daily habits and few bad daily habits.

Unsuccessful people have many bad daily habits and few good daily habits.

The secret to success is a secret because even wealthy individuals are unaware that the habits they possess are responsible for their success in life. This is why unearthing the causes for success has always been difficult. Until now.

No person will ever be truly successful until they become aware of their strengths and their weaknesses. ***Self-assessment requires self-awareness.*** In order to be able to determine which habits are helping or hurting you, you must first become aware of the habits that you have. Once you identify all of your habits, only then can you determine if they are good habits or bad habits.

For three workdays I want you to carry around a small pad of paper and write down every activity, thought or decision that is a daily habit.

You know an activity, thought or decision is a daily habit because you will, through this exercise, find yourself repeating it every day. You won't need to add it to your pad because it will already be there from the previous day. Once you have a complete list of all of your habits, the next step is to put a plus (+) or minus (-) next to each habit.

The plus represents good habits and the minus, bad habits. With your habits graded, now we move on to the next step, which is converting your bad habits into good habits.

On a piece of paper form two columns. List your bad daily habits under column one. Then I want you to invert each one of your bad daily habits and list their opposites under column two, which we'll refer to as your new good daily habits.

| **Bad Daily Habits** | **Good Daily Habits** |
|---|---|
| I watch too much television. | I limit myself to one hour of TV per day. |
| I don't exercise regularly. | I exercise 30 minutes each day. |
| I don't watch what I eat. | I eat no more than XXXX calories per day. |
| I don't do my work-related reading. | I read 30 minutes each day for learning. |
| I procrastinate. | I complete my to-do list every day. |
| I waste too much time. | I did not waste time today. |
| I smoke. | I will not smoke today. |
| I don't return phone calls right away. | I will return every phone call today. |
| I don't remember names. | I write down names & remember them. |
| I forget important dates. | I acknowledge important dates of others. |

For 30 days follow your new good daily habits. Review them once in the morning, once at noon and once at bedtime. This forces accountability. The objective is to follow as many of your new good daily habits as you can each day. My experience has been that if I am able to follow 20 to 30 per cent of my new good daily habits it's a good day.

## Good Daily Habits Work Week Checklist (sample items):

1. I read and learned something new today for my job, my business or some dream or goal I am pursuing.
2. I exercised for 30 minutes today.
3. I completed 80 per cent of my to-do list today.
4. I called at least one prospect today.
5. I did not waste time today.
6. I did one thing today that I did not want to do.
7. I stopped myself from saying something sarcastic today.
8. I stopped myself from saying something inappropriate today.
9. I stopped myself from talking today when I realised I was talking too much.
10. I ate no more than 2,000 calories today.
11. I limited myself to two beers today.
12. I worked for 30 minutes more than I am required today.
13. I called one person today, just to say hello.
14. I called everyone I know who had a birthday today to wish them a happy birthday.

## Summary

Successful people automate success by adopting good habits. They also eliminate bad habits that prevent success. This is the first Rich Habit and the most important one because it lays the foundation for the rest of the Rich Habits I will be sharing with you.

## Michael Yardney's Insight

The first step to becoming rich and successful is to evaluate your current position. How are you going? Become aware of what's working — the thoughts, actions and habits you want to keep. Then clearly identify your Poor Habits — your unproductive and disempowering habits.

The problem is, as you look at your poor habits one day at a time, they may not seem so bad, but compounding these poor habits into the future the consequences can be devastating.

# CHAPTER 15
# RICH HABIT NUMBER TWO

**I will define my dreams and then create goals around each dream. I will focus on my dream-goals every day.**

You may never have heard of dream-setting before. ***Dream-setting is the springboard for the realisation of your dreams.*** If you don't dream-set, you can never realise your dreams and, thus, live your dream life. Your life is very much a construction project. It's really a simple two-step process:

1. Draw up the blueprints for your ideal life
2. Construct your life

Seems pretty simple, doesn't it?

The components of your life's blueprint are all of the things that make a perfect life: the job you want to have, what you would love to do for a living, the place you want to live, the life partner you'd like to share your life with, the places you'd like to travel to, the wealth you'd like to accumulate, etc.

These are known as dreams. You start building your ideal life by defining all of your dreams which, when taken together, become the blueprint of your life.

Your goals are your construction team. You need to define all of the goals that will make all of your dreams become a reality. You design your goals around each dream. One dream could require the achievement of one, five or 10 goals.

The realisation of each dream happens when you accomplish the series of goals that are required in order for each specific dream to be realised.

Dream-setting lays the foundation for the goal-setting process. Let me explain this dream-setting process in a little more detail:

1. Step One — Ask yourself what you want your ideal life to be in 10, 15 or 20 years' time. Then write down every detail of your ideal future life. Be very specific in the details: the income you earn, the house you live in, the boat you own, the car you drive, the money you've accumulated, etc.

2. Step Two — Using this detailed description of your ideal future life, make a bullet point list of each one of the details that represent your ideal life. These would be the income you earn, the house you live in, the boat your own, etc. These details represent each one of your dreams. It takes the realisation of many dreams in order to produce the life of your dreams. Each dream is like a rung on the ladder. As you realise each dream it takes you up another rung on your ladder. When you reach the top of your ladder you'll know it, for that is the moment you realise you're living the life of your dreams.

Only after you've defined each dream does the goal-setting process begin. This goal-setting process requires you to build goals around each one of your dreams. In order to build goals around each dream you need to ask yourself two questions:

1. What would I need to do and what activities would I need to engage in, in order for each dream to come true?

2. Can I perform those activities?

If the answer to question two is yes, then those activities represent your goals. A goal is not some mystical thing. It is not some broad objective. This is one of the reasons so many fail in achieving their goals. They pursue things they were taught to be goals that are actually dreams.

Dreams are broad objectives and very different from a goal. A goal is only a goal when it involves physical action ***and*** you have the knowledge and skills to engage in that activity. If you don't have the knowledge and skills to engage in that activity, you cannot and will not achieve the goal.

This is then number one reason why so many fail to achieve their goals in life. They lack the knowledge or skills to take the action that is required in order to complete the goal.

Goals = action. Dreams = broad objectives, like making $100,000 a year, or buying a home or accumulating $50,000.

These are all dreams. ***Goals are the action steps*** you must take in order to realise each dream.

As an example, let's say your dream is to accumulate $50,000. Now what's the goal or goals behind your dream? Your goal might be to save $1,000 a month for 50 months. This $50,000 dream may also require another goal: I will reduce my spending by $1,000 a month, so that I can save that $1,000 a month.

Once you understand what a goal is, you can achieve 100 per cent of all of your goals. Most people, unfortunately, mistake a dream for a goal and that is why most fail at achieving their goals.

Let's summarise this process:

1. Paint a picture with words of your ideal life.
2. Define each dream that must be realised in order to have your ideal future life.
3. Establish specific goals around each one of your dreams.
4. Take action. Pursue and achieve each of the specific goals that will make each dream come true.

You then repeat this process for each dream. When you realise each one of your dreams, your ideal future life will then become your actual real life.

## Daily Goals

Before beginning each day, compile a daily to-do list. On this list, automatically populate it with daily action steps that will help move you towards achieving each one of the goals that, when achieved, will move you closer to realising each one of your dreams.

Some dreams might have five or more goals that need to be accomplished. Some goals might have five or more action items that must be accomplished. Define those action items and automatically process them into your to-do list. Set a specific time in which you will tackle each goal-related action item.

Successful people like to focus on these dream goals by blocking off time during their day. Often that time is in the early morning, when they are least distracted. During the day, mark off each completed goal-related action item and congratulate yourself on its accomplishment. At the end of the day evaluate your to-do list. This forces accountability. Your to-do list becomes your accountability partner.

## Monthly Goals

Monthly goals are really nothing more than a scorecard. It tells you whether or not your daily goals are working. For example, if you're trying to save $50,000 over the next 50 months, your monthly goal would be saving $1,000 by the end of the month.

Did it happen?

No? Well, why not? Time to pivot. Maybe you need to cut back more on my expenses? Maybe you need to work more hours to earn more income? Your monthly goals are directly related to the achievement of your daily goals.

## Current Year Goals

The same principle and logic that applied to the monthly goals process applies to the current year goals process. Your current year goal is nothing more than a scorecard. Did you save $12,000 this year towards your $50,000 dream? If not, the problem was not with your current year goal. The problem was in not achieving your monthly goals. Failing to meet your monthly goals is the red flag that says something went wrong with the daily goal process. It is the monthly goal stage that sends up a red flag that you need to pivot — to change something you are doing at the daily goal level. Your current year goals are nothing more than a mirror, reflecting the fact that the daily action you are taking is working.

## Example of Dream-Setting/ Goal-Setting process

*Dream:* I will pass the CPA exam this year.

*Daily Goal:* I will study for 90 minutes every work day for the next six months.

Monthly Goals: I have two monthly goals — Monthly Goal #1: To study 150 hours and Monthly Goal #2: To get a grade of 80 on the practice tests I take during the month.

Now let's say that at the end of the month you fail every one of the practice tests. What does that mean? That's a red flag that says, time to pivot. You may have to increase the number of minutes you devote each work day or increase the number of minutes you study over the weekends. Monthly goals = red flags. They tell you that you are either on track or not on track.

## Long-term Goals

Long-term goals are dreams in disguise. You cannot achieve a dream. You can only realise a dream by achieving your daily goals, monthly goals and current year goals. Goals are the gateway to the realisation of dreams. They are the construction team for dreams. For some, this might be upsetting, but I suspect for most, you are breathing a sigh of relief. The relief is that you are not a loser who repetitively fails to achieve your long-term goals! You've been failing because ***you've been given the wrong definition of a goal***.

So let me clarify the definition of a goal:

***A goal is only a goal when it has two things: #1 Physical Activity and #2 100 per cent Achievevability means you have the knowledge and skills to perform the physical activity required.***

If you can perform the activity, the only thing holding you back is taking action.

A useful technique to assist you in keeping your dreams in sight is the use of a vision board. A vision board is an actual picture of each one of your dreams.

This may be a picture of the house you desire to buy, a picture of the business you hope to own one day, or a picture of the type of place you hope to retire to one day.

Before he rose to great fame, comedian Jim Carey wrote out a cheque to himself for $10 million and kept that cheque in a place where he would see it every day. It represented a vision-board of a dream he had — to be paid $10 million for a movie. When the opportunity arose for a leading role in a movie, guess what Jim Carey's demand for compensation was? $10 million — and he got it!

***Successful people build goals around their dreams.***

They are long-term thinkers, constantly looking to the future, their ideal future life, in an effort to determine where they are in terms of accomplishing their goals. They continuously pivot and make course corrections when the actions they are taking are not getting them closer to realising their goals.

Unsuccessful people have either not defined their dreams or they give up on their dreams when success does not happen overnight.

Those without any dreams are not goal-oriented. Like leaves on an autumn day, they float in the air aimlessly, without direction. They allow the distractions of daily living to affect their ability to perform their duties at work. They allow themselves to become easily distracted by things that have nothing to do with their work. Since they are not pursuing any dreams or any major purpose in life, they have no goals to focus on.

The few unsuccessful people who actually do pursue a dream, quit when the going gets tough. They then shift their attention to the next thing that catches their eye. They jump from one venture to the next when success is not immediate and the money comes hard. You've seen these types of unsuccessful people all around you. Each year they are obsessed about something new that will make them a lot of money, such as becoming a published author, developing phone apps, creating YouTube videos, becoming a real estate investor, business coach, trainer, financial planner, inventor, etc.

I like to call this Bright Shiny Object Syndrome, which prevents individuals from succeeding in life because they lack focus, patience and persistence — three success habits that are a prerequisite for success. This malady prevents them from developing the necessary skills and knowledge that would otherwise enable them to grow into the person they need to be in order for success to visit them.

## Summary

Successful people dream-set and then build goals around each one of their dreams.

### Michael Yardney's Insight

While it's good to have an end to journey towards, in the end it's really the journey that matters.

# CHAPTER 16
# RICH HABIT NUMBER THREE

**I will devote at least 30 minutes each day to increasing my knowledge and improving my skills. I will invest in myself every day.**

Successful people engage in self-improvement every day. For the most part this involves reading.

They read anything and everything related to their job, their business, a dream they are pursuing or the goals behind their dreams. They become students of their industry, profession, trade or niche and keep up-to-date with changes that occur. They do not waste their time on things like TV, watching movies or scouring the internet.

Each day successful individuals devote blocks of time to better themselves by studying subject matter that will improve them in some way or by practicing some skill. This daily habit eventually transforms them into experts or professionals in their field.

***Successful people see time as the most valuable asset they possess.***

They coordinate their dreams and goals with daily self-improvement. This may involve obtaining an additional license, a degree or developing a new niche. They are continuously engaged in some constructive project to increase their skill-sets, promote their business or careers, keep their minds sharp or expand their knowledge.

Knowledge and learning are the foundation and springboard for success. It's impossible to know everything, to be a know-it-all. Therefore, you must focus your study on specific areas that will create the greatest return for the time you invest in your learning.

Let's touch on these key areas:

1. Learn everything about your job and the industry you are in.
2. Learn everything about the things you are passionate about in life.
3. Learn everything about the people who are important in your life.
4. Learn everything about significant current events.
5. Learn at least one new fact every day.
6. Learn at least one new word every day.
7. Learn about one novel thing every month, something outside your comfort zone that will challenge your thinking.

Unsuccessful people are not students of their industry, profession or trade. They do not engage in daily practice to perfect a skill. They do not routinely follow their industry. They do not regularly read industry periodicals. They would rather spend hours each day watching television, reading for entertainment or surfing the net. They use rationalisation to justify their negligence in improving themselves.

Self-improvement involves engaging in some activity every day that will improve your mind, expand your knowledge or hone your skills. Expanding knowledge within your industry is a self-improvement activity that you must engage in. This can be done by regularly reading your industry periodicals and advancing your career by obtaining additional licenses, skill-sets or new niches for your business. Career-specific self-improvement activities are necessary to increase skills and take advantage of opportunities. You will notice that, as your knowledge base grows, or as your skills improve, opportunities begin to present themselves.

Choose a time when there are fewer distractions and you can set aside a block of time. Sometimes this is possible in the early morning hours prior to beginning your normal workday. At a minimum, set aside 30 minutes each day for these activities. Thirty minutes per day may not seem like much, but over time it adds up to a significant amount of self-improvement. No matter what time of the day works best for you, engage in daily self-improvement activities without interruptions.

## Summary

Successful people devote a minimum of 30 minutes each day to learning and improving their skills.

### Michael Yardney's Insight

I've found you can often learn more about getting rich from a person who went bankrupt than you can from Bill Gates. That's because it's more common to be stupid than it is to be brilliant, so you should spend more effort trying to avoid bad money decisions than making good ones.

I've read that in professional tennis, 80% of the points are won, while in amateur tennis, 80% are lost. The same is true with getting rich: Beginners should focus on avoiding mistakes and become experts on making great moves.

# CHAPTER 17
# RICH HABIT NUMBER FOUR

**I will devote 30 minutes to exercise every day. I will eat healthy food every day.**

***Successful people*** make a concerted effort to eat right and exercise every day. They consider not only what they eat, but also how much they eat. They ***manage their consumption of food.***

Successful people do not binge or overindulge in food or drink. If they do slip, it is managed overindulgence, relegated to that of an infrequent occurrence rather than a regular occurrence, such as a holiday meal or a party.

For successful people, exercise is a daily routine like brushing their teeth. They understand that daily exercise improves their bodies and minds. Daily exercise has so many benefits.

Let's run through them:

- *Exercise Improves Mental Function:* Exercise, particularly aerobic exercise, floods the bloodstream with oxygen. This oxygen eventually makes its way to the brain. One of the purposes of oxygen is to act like a sponge, soaking up the waste within each cell. Since the brain uses 20 per cent of our oxygen reserves, increased oxygen flow into the brain soaks up more waste inside brain cells, making them cleaner and healthier.

  Twenty to 30 minutes of aerobic exercise every day has been proven to stimulate the growth of axon branches on each brain cell. The number of axon branches you have is directly related to how intelligent you are. So aerobic exercise makes you more intelligent, increases neurogenesis (growth of new brain cells) and creates new synapses (brain cells that talk to one another).

Exercise does this by increasing blood flow into the Dentate Gyrus. The Dentate Gyrus is part of our brain's Hippocampus, a region involved in memory formation and neurogenesis. Exercise, therefore, increases the growth of new and existing brain cells as well as the number of synapses you have inside your brain. Exercise also stimulates the production of Brain Derived Neurotrophic Factor (BDFN). BDFN is miracle grow for the neurons inside our brain, making them bigger and healthier.

- *Exercise Improves Health and Increases Your Productivity:* Aerobic exercise increases blood flow, feeds the body with oxygen and strengthens the heart. Weight-bearing aerobic exercises, such as walking, jogging or running, reduces the risk of osteoporosis. Aerobic exercise helps lower blood pressure and control blood sugar. If you've had a heart attack, aerobic exercise helps prevent subsequent attacks.

  Aerobic exercise boosts your high-density lipoprotein (HDL or "good") cholesterol and lowers your low-density lipoprotein (LDL or "bad") cholesterol. The result? Less build-up of plaques in your arteries. Studies show that people who engage in regular aerobic exercise live longer than those who don't exercise regularly.

  Oxygen, as I mentioned above, acts like a sponge. It soaks up waste products inside every cell and converts this waste product into carbon dioxide. The blood carries this carbon dioxide to the lungs, which then removes the carbon dioxide from our bodies by exhaling it into the environment. Aerobic exercise reduces the risk of many conditions, including obesity, heart disease, high blood pressure, Type 2 diabetes, stroke and certain types of cancer. Healthier people have fewer sick days, more energy, fewer diseases and this translates into more productivity at work. More productivity makes you more valuable to your organisation, customers or clients, which translates into more value and ultimately more money.

- *Exercise Reduces the Effects of Stress:* When we feel stress, there is a domino effect of physiology that takes place inside our bodies. Thinking negative thoughts creates stress. When the body detects stress, the hypothalamus increases the release of epinephrine and norepinephrine. These hormones make the heart beat faster and prepare the body for fight or flight. If the stress lingers, a gene on chromosome 10, called CYP17, is activated. This gene goes to work to convert cholesterol to cortisol. Cortisol is used in virtually every part of the body and its purpose is to integrate the body and the mind. The body and mind then work in harmony to escape the outside world danger responsible for the stress.

  One of cortisol's side effects, unfortunately, is that it depresses the immune system by reducing the production of lymphocytes — white blood cells. The gene CYP17 also turns on another gene called TCF, which suppresses the creation of a protein called interleukin 2. Interleukin 2's purpose is to put white blood cells on high alert. White blood cells are our main defence against viruses, diseases, germs and any parasites that infect the body. Long-term stress, therefore, impairs our immune system's ability to fight off these viruses, diseases, germs and parasites.

  Aerobic exercise floods the body with oxygen, as mentioned above, and this increased oxygen reduces the effects of stress on the body. Because aerobic exercise contributes to an overall feeling of well-being through the release of certain hormones, it acts as a stress reducer. Aerobic exercise is like a double in baseball; it reduces the effects of stress while at the same time reducing stress itself.

- *Exercise Makes Us Feel Happier*: Happiness is, for the most part, activity-driven. Forty per cent of all happiness is the result of engaging in frequent happiness activities. ***Aerobic exercise is a happiness activity*** because it contributes to an overall feeling of well-being by releasing endorphins, natural painkillers that promote an increased sense of well-being and make us feel "happier".

- *Exercise Stimulates the Production of Erythropoietin (EPO):* EPO is responsible for the creation of new red blood cells in bone marrow. New red blood cells have more haemoglobin, which enables them to carry more oxygen to the body. Oxygen = fuel for the brain, tissues and muscles. Exercise increases the ability of red blood cells to fuel the body.
- *Exercise Activates an Enzyme called Telomerase:* Telomerase protects telomeres. Telomeres are like caps at the end of every chromosome. Telomeres control the number of times a cell can divide. Cells that lose their telomere die. When cells die it's called aging. Exercise, therefore, increases the life span of cells, allowing you to live longer.
- *Exercise Increases the Volume of Nerve Tissue in the Hippocampus:* The Hippocampus is a part of the brain responsible for memory and learning. Exercise, therefore, increases your ability to remember and learn.
- *Exercise Can Reduce the Risk of Cancer:* Regular exercise of 30 minutes a day, five days a week has been proven to reduce the incidence of cancer from 25 per cent to 50 per cent.
- *Exercise Increases Your Confidence:* Exercise elevates your testosterone level; testosterone is a hormone that not only accelerates muscle recovery, it also elevates your confidence, making you feel more in control of your life. When you feel more confident, you are more inclined to pursue opportunities that challenge you, enabling you to grow as an individual. Confidence boosts your desire to take on those new challenges and learn new things, important qualities inherent in great leaders and self-made millionaires.
- *Exercise Increases Willpower:* Daily exercise not only benefits your muscles and health, it also boosts your willpower and self-control. Why is willpower so important? Depletion of willpower results in bad decision-making and causes you to lapse into old bad habits.

> The latest science on willpower indicates that willpower depletion, also known as decision fatigue, is behind drug addiction, alcoholism, overeating, infidelity, gambling and many other vices. When your willpower is depleted, watch out. The wake you leave behind can be devastating: damaged family relationships, friendships and work relationships, poor health, and bad finances (spontaneous purchases occur when willpower is low) will send your life spiralling downward. So, you need to rid yourself of your demons by exercising every day. You and everyone around you will be better off for it.

Successful people have a system or routine for weight management that works best for them. Some have sophisticated systems, some less sophisticated, but they "manage" their weight. Managing weight means monitoring the amount of food consumed every day and engaging in a daily exercise regimen.

Unsuccessful people have no consistent, day-to-day control over their health. They are always in search of the latest and greatest quick-fix diet idea.

Unsuccessful people deal with health matters sporadically and usually require outside influences to motivate them to eat less or eat differently. This is the reason why there are so many diet books out there. With little control over their eating habits, they go through phases of gaining and losing weight again and again. This behaviour takes a toll on the body, which eventually manifests as medical disorders, such as high blood pressure, diabetes, heart disease and the like.

Unsuccessful people approach exercise the same way they approach their consumption of food, requiring some outside force to momentarily motivate them. When that motivation wears off, they fall back into bad habits, stop exercising and gain weight as part of a cycle that recurs throughout their lives.

An easy way to monitor food consumption is to count the calories after every meal or snack and document daily consumption. In beginning a weight management program, first gain an understanding of the specific foods you eat on a daily basis.

During the first 30 days of your weight management program you will need to track what you normally eat and figure out the number of calories for each food item.

During this 30-day period you will be able to identify certain foods that are high in calories and you can thereafter choose to avoid those high-calorie foods, at least on a regular basis. Use the Tracking Schedule at the end of this section to help you track your calories for the next 30 days.

Do not confuse monitoring and managing food consumption with dieting. They are not the same.

Diets don't work in managing weight in the long-term. The reason is that they are too restrictive, unsustainable and, quite frankly, take the fun out of life. Managing the consumption of food does not mean starving or never again eating special treats. You are going to eat treats from time to time and you should not feel guilty about this.

You simply need to understand that you can't eat those high-calorie foods every day, as this will likely push you over your daily caloric threshold, which is the level you need to stay within in order to lose or maintain your weight. You should be free to eat and drink the things you like when the spirit moves you.

But you need to understand that eating some of the foods you love might mean occasionally exceeding your caloric threshold for that day, which is fine as long as this is the exception rather than the rule.

Monitoring food consumption only gets you halfway toward managing weight. You must engage in a daily aerobic exercise regimen for at least 20 to 30 minutes a day, five days per week. Jogging outdoors provides the most effective results. The number of calories burned with running is greater by about one-third than an indoor treadmill, Stairmaster or stationary bike. Lifting weights, sit-ups, push-ups and the like are good supplements to any basic aerobic activity, but they are not substitutes for aerobic activity.

By themselves, these exercises will not help you lose weight as much as they will help you shape and tone your body. Aerobic activity is the most reliable activity to help you lose weight and should be the foundation for your exercise regimen.

Morning may be the best time to engage in an exercise activity. By preceding the work day with exercise you are less likely to be pulled away by scheduling issues or conflicts that often occur during the day.

A great tool to monitor your weight is the Rich Habits Weight Management Tracking Schedule. Tracking takes only five minutes each day.

You will begin to see patterns in your weight management that enable you to better understand your body and allow you to gain control over your weight. Within two months of completing the Rich Habits Weight Management Tracking Schedule you will be able to determine your individual daily caloric threshold and you can then manage your calorie intake to lose or maintain your weight. For example, assume your daily threshold is 2,100 calories per day given the level of exercise you do. If you consume less than 2,100 calories each day, you will lose weight every day.

## Summary

My Study found successful people manage their consumption of food and engage in regular daily exercise.

# RICH HABITS WEIGHT MANAGEMENT TRACKING SCHEDULE

| Beginning weight | | Goal weight | | End weight | |
|---|---|---|---|---|---|

| Average daily calorie goal for the month | | Weight goal for the month | |
|---|---|---|---|

| Day | Date | Weight | Cardio time (run, jog, etc.) | Weight training time | Other exercise time | Breakfast calories | Lunch calories | Dinner calories | Total calories for today | Cumulative calories for the month | Average daily calories |
|---|---|---|---|---|---|---|---|---|---|---|---|
| | | | | | | | | | | | |
| | | | | | | | | | | | |
| | | | | | | | | | | | |
| | | | | | | | | | | | |
| | | | | | | | | | | | |
| | | | | | | | | | | | |
| | | | | | | | | | | | |
| | | | | | | | | | | | |
| | | | | | | | | | | | |
| | | | | | | | | | | | |
| | | | | | | | | | | | |
| | | | | | | | | | | | |
| | | | | | | | | | | | |
| | | | | | | | | | | | |
| | | | | | | | | | | | |

# RICH HABITS WEIGHT MANAGEMENT TRACKING SCHEDULE (CONT)

| Day | Date | Weight | Cardio time (run, jog, etc.) | Weight training time | Other exercise time | Breakfast calories | Lunch calories | Dinner calories | Total calories for today | Cumulative calories for the month | Average daily calories |
|---|---|---|---|---|---|---|---|---|---|---|---|
| | | | | | | | | | | | |
| | | | | | | | | | | | |
| | | | | | | | | | | | |
| | | | | | | | | | | | |
| | | | | | | | | | | | |
| | | | | | | | | | | | |
| | | | | | | | | | | | |
| | | | | | | | | | | | |
| | | | | | | | | | | | |
| | | | | | | | | | | | |
| | | | | | | | | | | | |
| | | | | | | | | | | | |
| | | | | | | | | | | | |
| | | | | | | | | | | | |
| | | | | | | | | | | | |
| | | | | | | | | | | | |

# CHAPTER 18
# RICH HABIT NUMBER FIVE

**I will seek to build strong relationships with other success-minded people.**

There are two extreme types of people out there with whom we form relationships: Rich Relationships and Toxic Relationships.

***Rich Relationships help lift you up in life.*** They are always happy, optimistic, grateful, enthusiastic, open-minded and life-long learner-types who help elevate your chances for success.

Toxic Relationships drag you down in life, sabotaging any chance for any success you might have.

Unfortunately — we seek out others who share our habits. Habits spread like a virus throughout our social networks. As a result, we pick up most of our habits from those in our environment: parents, teachers, family, friends, work colleagues, neighbours, mentors, celebrities, coaches, etc.

If you're overweight, there's a good chance that your friends or family members are overweight. If you're a smoker there's a good chance that your friends or family are smokers. It is also one of the reasons why individuals who join a weight loss group, such as Weight Watchers, have a greater chance of losing weight — you are spending time with others who share your desire to lose weight.

One of the short-cuts to habit change is to change your environment, or those you associate with on a consistent basis.

Those you associate with on a frequent basis are part of your environment.

If you want to adopt a good habit, such as daily exercise, you increase your chances by associating with other individuals who already have the daily exercise habit or who are trying to adopt that habit. This forces accountability, one of the keys to habit change.

Association accountability is also commonly known as peer pressure. If you want to adopt a good habit, one sure-fire way is to create a new, specific peer group around that habit. These new peers will put pressure on you to stick to your new habit.

One of the hallmarks of successful people is the conscious effort they make to associate with other success-minded individuals.

If a close relationship is a spendthrift, they limit how much time they spend with those individuals. If a close relationship is conscientious with their money, they increase the amount of time they spent with those individuals. If an individual has an optimistic mindset, they flock to them like bugs to a light.

Who we associate with on a regular basis affects the level of success we experience in life.

We can choose to be Rich by Association or Poor by Association.

Rich by Association means we surround ourselves with other success-minded people. Poor by Association means we surround ourselves with individuals who have a poverty mindset.

Successful individuals put a high value on the individuals they want to associate with. To successful people, relationships are like gold. They tend to relationships like a farmer tends crops, nurturing them every day, remembering names, birthdays, gifts for newborns and interacting frequently. Successful people seek to help their relationships and their business associates, even when there is nothing in it for them. They are focused on others, rather than on themselves.

## The Power of Networking

For successful people, networking is a prerequisite to their success. They develop systems and processes as tools to assist them in networking efforts. They search for reasons to reach out to their contacts, such as birthdays or congratulatory calls, cards or gifts. They attend important celebrations and milestones such as graduations, funerals and weddings. They network with individuals who are like-minded. They do not waste their time developing or nurturing relationships with toxic individuals. They reduce all ties to relationships that are harmful or destructive. They stay clear of individuals who are perpetually in a state of turmoil. Many times this turmoil is financial in nature. These toxic individuals have bad habits and can drag you down along with them.

***Successful people are students of relationship building.*** They faithfully return phone calls right away. They continuously seek out ways to improve their relationships.

Unsuccessful people typically associate with other unsuccessful people or Toxic Relationship types. They are Poor by Association. They have a "What have you done for me lately?" attitude about relationships.

Some, oddly enough, even consider it a virtue when they intentionally short-change others. If an individual cannot provide them with some immediate value, they are ignored until needed. No calls, emails or cards on birthdays. No gifts congratulating their "friends" or associates on the important events in their lives.

Unsuccessful people are not good networkers. They don't seek to improve their relationships with others on a continuous and regular basis. They do not return phone calls right away, and sometimes not at all.

Unsuccessful people adopt a "put out the fire" mindset in managing relationships. When a crisis arises, and unsuccessful people often have sudden crises in their lives, they reach out for help. Oftentimes, they seek assistance from an individual they have neglected. When it comes to relationships, unsuccessful people simply do not care enough to invest time in developing relationships.

## Avoid Toxic Relationships

If you want to be successful, you need to forge Rich Relationships and avoid Toxic Relationships.

Toxic Relationships have certain unique characteristics:

1. **Negative Types** — They always seem depressed, down, pessimistic, angry, unhappy and ungrateful. They envy those who are doing well in life. They ridicule anyone trying to better their lives. They seem to always have a negative opinion. To them, the world is a mean, unfair and painful existence. They drown their misery in drugs or alcohol. They have very powerful biases. They see life as unfair and embrace any ideology that advocates for the punishment of those who are rich and successful.

2. **Deceptive Types** — They are perpetual liars. They cannot be trusted. They seek, by whatever means necessary, to take what is not theirs. They are adept at spinning the truth. They are experts in rationalising their bad behaviour. Nothing is ever their fault. They are never to blame. They see others as marks, targets, not people.

3. **Critical Types** — They are very critical of others. They seem to always have an opinion that is critical of something. They condemn and blame society, the government, their parents, the schools, their boss, their spouse, etc. Everything is a problem. Nothing is ever straight forward or simple to them. They complain about everything in their lives and every person in their life. They are very rarely happy and never grateful for what they have.

4. **Backstabber Types** — These are people you cannot trust. They are not only looking out for their own interest, they have a maniacal habit of hurting their relationships either intentionally or unintentionally. They have very low self-esteem, confidence and do not like anyone who is trying to better their life. They love to gossip about others. They have no long-term relationships and move from one new relationship to the next, causing havoc wherever they go. The danger with backstabbers is that you never see it coming. They wear a mask when they are in your presence

that belies their true selves. You only find out who they really are after the damage is done.

5. **Financial Train Wreck Types** — They are always deep in debt, borrowing money from their friends and family and never repaying that debt. They are perpetually unemployed, in between jobs, jumping from one career to the next. There is always one emergency after another and they have a nasty habit of calling upon you at the last minute to bail them out. As a result, they consume a great deal of your time and money.

6. **Lazy Types** — These types are always looking for the home run, quick fix, the easy money. They do not want to put in the time and effort to achieve success. They believe success is about random good luck. They approach others with business opportunities that can't miss. They do not invest time in their relationships, in their careers or in their businesses. They gamble. They get others to invest their money in their latest schemes. They take irrational risk, rather than calculated risk.

7. **Victim Types** — Victim types have an entitlement mindset. They believe those who are doing better in life have an obligation to help those who are struggling financially in life. They see the wealthy as beneficiaries of mere good luck. Conversely, they see themselves as the victims of mere bad luck. They do not take individual responsibility for their lives. They do not blame themselves for their financial circumstances. They feel they just got a raw deal in life.

8. **Addicted Types** — They are addicted to drugs, food, alcohol, gambling, sex, risk, you name it. They have no control over their behaviour. They have no willpower. They always let you down. Their lives are a mess. Their relationships are a mess. Their finances are a mess. They are leeches who will suck the life out of you.

Successful people employ a system in managing their relationships.

Some have systems that can be quite sophisticated and utilise the latest in technology and software.

Whatever system you create for yourself, find a way to track various types of information about each of your contacts.

Besides names, addresses, phone numbers and email information, you should capture other important data such as: professions, birthdays, spouse names, spouse birthdays, names of children, colleges attended, graduate school attended, law school attended, etc. Also track their hobbies, interests, books they like to read, along with any other important data. "Important" means important to your contact.

The most common contact management system is Outlook. Almost anyone with a computer has Outlook. Some cell phones even link up with Outlook, giving you the ability to carry contact information with you.

Having the greatest contact management system in the world does you no good unless you put your system to good use. The most basic system provides a process that reminds you of a contact's birthday so you can reach out to them to wish them a happy birthday.

Even if you do not regularly communicate with a specific person, this minimum amount of contact keeps your relationship alive. Birthday calls allow you to maintain a relationship by being in touch at least once a year. Your contact may reciprocate, thus increasing the frequency of your contacts with this individual to two times per year.

I have never met a successful person who has not shared with me the same nasty little secret... they have difficulty remembering names just like everyone else. To overcome this failing, however, successful people create systems to help them remember names of people they want to remember.

A good way to remember names is to group your contacts by category. For example you can group contacts into the following categories:

- Tennis contacts
- Golf contacts
- Bowling contacts
- Club contacts
- Neighbour contacts

- College friends
- Business partner's friends
- Work associates and their families, church/synagogue/mosque, or community contacts, etc.

Before any event in which you are likely to run into one or more of your contacts you can pull out that category's group of contacts and review their names just before you go to the event. Names are important to each one of us and we all appreciate when someone feels we're important enough to be remembered by name.

## Summary

Successful people foster, grow and improve their relationships with other success-minded individuals and limit their exposure to toxic people.

### Michael Yardney's Insight

One of my early mentors, Jim Rohn, taught me that we are the average of the five people we spend the most time with. When it comes to relationships, we are greatly influenced, whether we like it or not, by those closest to us. It affects our way of thinking, our self-esteem and our decisions.

# CHAPTER 19
# RICH HABIT NUMBER SIX

**I will live every day in a state of moderation.**

To live in moderation means to live a balanced life — no extremes.

***Successful people*** avoid excesses, wild emotional swings, addictions, obsessions, binging, starvation, extravagances and fanatical behaviour. They ***keep their thoughts and emotions on a short leash***. They understand the need to be on an even keel and in control of their lives.

Successful people understand that life is a marathon and not a sprint. They moderate their work hours, eating habits, exercise, alcohol intake, watching television, reading, internet use, phone conversations, emails, text messages, conversations, entertainment, sexual relations, and so on. Their personalities reflect this moderate mindset.

They do not become overly excited or excessively melancholy. They are even-tempered and slow to anger or excitement. Their moderate mindset puts family, friends, colleagues, and business partners at ease, which helps improve relationships. As a consequence, people enjoy being around them. There is a comfort level in dealing with them in all matters.

Successful people eat, drink, entertain and live moderate lifestyles. Contrary to what many believe, their homes, cars, personal effects, vacations, etc., are not extravagant. Warren Buffet, one of the wealthiest individuals in the world, lives in the same home that he was married in more than 55 years ago.

His home is modest with no fence or surrounding wall. While he owns a private jet business, he prefers to fly commercial airlines. He drives back and forth to work in his car every day. Warren Buffet lives this Rich Habit on a daily basis.

Unsuccessful people live in extremes. They eat too much and drink too much. They overreact to events. They permit their emotions to swing in extreme manners, which create great conflict and pain in their relationships. Emotions such as anger, happiness, love, hate, jealousy and envy are placed on a very long leash, perhaps reeled in momentarily when their most important relationships are placed in jeopardy. They obsess over food, drink, sex, drugs, gossip, personal possessions, their opinions, their thoughts and their actions.

Unsuccessful people have little control over their lives.

They have wild swings in their moods, which result in strained health, relationships and finances. They have a "keeping up with the Joneses" mindset. Their spending patterns are continuously influenced by others. If they fall into money somehow, they spend this money on big homes and expensive cars to impress others. Mortgages and loans stretch them financially. Many refinance their homes in an effort to maintain their lifestyles.

An unexpected event, such as a job loss, temporary disability or sudden decline in earnings, results in immediate financial catastrophe because unsuccessful people live pay day to pay day. They have no savings or financial safety net. Their priorities are misplaced. They are incapable of living moderate lifestyles, prioritising their needs correctly or living within their means.

## Summary

Successful people do everything in moderation. They avoid excess.

**Michael Yardney's Insight**

Living a life of moderation allows you to find and enjoy balance in your life. The opposite of moderation is living in extremes and, interestingly, too much of a good thing usually become something unenjoyable.

You see… spending money to show people how much money you have is the surest way to have less money.

Money buys "things" like cars, clothes or jewellery. But wealth is the stuff you don't see — the assets the rich build up to give them financial freedom, such as cash, stocks, bonds, real estate. These buys freedom and security. Pick which one you want wisely.

# CHAPTER 20
# RICH HABIT NUMBER SEVEN

**I will take action on my goals every day.**

Whether or not we're aware of it, there are two wars raging inside each one of us: Taking Action or Procrastinating.

Procrastination prevents even the most talented individuals from realising success in life. Most people have this Poor Habit and it is not an accident that most people struggle financially in life.

Success has many moving parts and procrastination is a big moving part.

One of the main contributors to procrastination is not being passionate about what you do for a living. We simply like to do the things we like to do and we put off the things we do not like to do. There is a feeling of dread and fear associated with doing things we don't want to do but have to do.

So we procrastinate until the pain of the consequences of not doing the thing we dread and fear outweighs the dread and fear of doing it.

***Procrastination is a big reason why most are struggling financially in life.***

It damages our credibility with employers and fellow colleagues at work. It also affects the quality of our work and this affects the business we or our employer receives from customers, clients and business relationships.

Procrastination brands us as someone who cannot be trusted or whose work product is poor. Worse, procrastination can lead to litigation, which causes stress and financial costs that can run into the tens of thousands of dollars.

Successful people take action on their dreams and goals. When we take action on our dreams and goals it moves us forward in life. Action creates ripples, which produces feedback and is critical in understanding if we are on the right track or the wrong track.

That feedback enables us to pivot, to make course corrections. Action fosters happiness. It reduces stress that is the by-product of not doing the things we know we should be doing in life.

Unsuccessful people procrastinate, which creates problems that require immediate attention. They are constantly putting out the fires in their lives. Procrastination increases the risk of forgetting something important or dealing with a critical matter in an emergency setting, which risks mistakes, errors and legal liabilities that can result in lawsuits.

Procrastination prevents us from moving forward. It is the reason most are stuck in life.

Procrastination leads to poor quality in whatever service or product we are selling. The lives of unsuccessful people are haphazard, confused and complicated.

They cannot accomplish much as they are constantly putting out one fire after another. They react instead to outside forces, which command their immediate attention. They have no control over their lives or their daily schedules. They feel powerless and directionless.

***Procrastination is driven by dread and fear.***

We dread taking action because of the fear of pain. The pain is the imagined physical or mental effort it will take to complete the task or goal. It is also the consequences of taking action, since all action creates ripples of feedback. Sometimes that feedback is good, sometimes bad. We fear negative feedback. But negative feedback is critical to success in life. It lets us know if we are on the right or wrong path.

For those who procrastinate habitually, the pain of taking action outweighs the pain of not taking action. Procrastinators distract themselves by doing other things that are not so demanding or painful. But our subconscious, our old brain, never allows us to forget that we have an uncompleted task. It constantly nags us and reminds us that we have an uncompleted task. It does this through stress, an unconscious advanced warning system built into our physiology.

The subconscious intuitively knows that completing that task is important in helping to improve our lives and that procrastinating on the task will only have negative consequences, damaging our life. The brain nudges us, via stress, to take action — a stress that never goes away until we take action. Stress creates a state of unhappiness.

So procrastination creates unhappiness.

Believe it or not, the voice of procrastination screams just as loud and clear in the minds of those who excel in life, as it does in the minds of those who do not. The difference is how successful people stop that voice of procrastination in its tracks.

Here are five tools that can help anyone silence the voice of procrastination forever:

## Tool #1 — To-do Lists

In my study, successful people often relied on "to-do" lists to help them get things done.

There are two types of daily to-dos:

1. Goal To-Dos — These are daily tasks tied to monthly, yearly and long-term goals. These are almost always fixed in nature, meaning the same to-dos show up every day on the to-do list. For example: "Make 10 Telemarketing Phone Calls".

2. Non-Goal To-Dos — These are to-dos that are unrelated to any goals. They may be administrative tasks (i.e. Respond to Emails), client tasks (i.e. Meeting with Client) or daily obligations (i.e. Go to Bank). They may be fixed, daily tasks or they may vary daily.

## Tool #2 — The Daily Five

Every day, successful people incorporate into their daily to-do list five things to accomplish before the day ends. The Daily Five can represent five things that are unrelated to your nine to five job. They can be five things that you do every day that move you toward accomplishing some goal or realising some dream or purpose in life.

## Tool #3 — Setting and Communicating Artificial Deadlines

When we set deadlines and communicate those deadlines to third parties directly affected by the completion of a task, we increase the urgency for completing the task. It elevates it from a mere "to-do" to a personal promise we make to another individual. It puts pressure on us to fulfil our promise and meet the deadline.

## Tool #4 — Accountability Partners

An Accountability Partner is someone we meet with regularly (weekly, for example) who holds our feet to the fire in accomplishing our tasks. This can be one or more individuals. Knowing that there are others who will hold us accountable to perform certain tasks also elevates those tasks from mere "to-dos". We all perform better when we know others are watching.

## Tool #5 — "Do It Now" Affirmations

No one likes to be nagged. Whether we realise it or not, nagging alters our behaviour. We tend to get something done that we don't want to do when we are repeatedly nagged about it. The "Do It Now" affirmation is a self-nagging technique that really works. By repeating the words "Do It Now" over and over again, we are effectively nagging ourselves. When I uncovered this tool during my research, I began using it to nag myself into doing things I regularly procrastinated on, like time and billing. Now all I have to do is think about the affirmation in order for the nagging to alter my behaviour and force me to get a task done.

You are the commander in chief of this war raging inside you.

Take command of your forces. Take action. You can only win the war by taking action on your goals and dreams. ***Overcome your fear and dread of taking action.***

Do not procrastinate or delay in activities that should be performed on any given day.

When the thought of putting off something enters your mind, immediately cast this thought out by saying, "Do It Now" or using any of the other strategies provided. Find what works for you and use it. Do not allow thoughts of procrastination even a second of life.

Once you are fully engaged in an activity, you will soon find yourself absorbed in the activity and all thoughts of deferring the task will be gone. You will feel exhilarated in accomplishing the task and feel in control of your life.

## Summary

Successful people do not procrastinate. They use tools and strategies to silence the voice of procrastination. They have a "Do It Now" mindset. As a result, they are responsive to clients, patients, business partners, family and friends.

### Michael Yardney's Insight

When you learn to treat procrastination as a Poor Habit rather than a choice, you'll be on your way to success.

# CHAPTER 21
# RICH HABIT NUMBER EIGHT

**I will engage in Rich Thinking every day.**

Have you ever been to a horse track?

If you have, you know that right before the race begins the horses are chaotically ushered into their starting gates. The gates remain closed, until the gun goes off, at which point the gates open and the horses stream out like bullets from a gun, headed towards the finish-line.

But until the gates open, nothing happens. The race does not begin until the gates are opened.

For most people, their metaphorical gates are closed their entire lives. Their thinking holds them back from starting their race to achieve and win.

Any mental thought, often repeated, becomes a habitual thought. ***Habitual thoughts direct you to take certain actions that can be good or bad.***

As long as your thinking is mired in negativity, pessimism, closed off to new ideas and suffocated by limiting beliefs, you will never begin your race or reach your finish line.

That race represents the pursuit and achievement of the goals behind your dreams. That finish line represents the realisation of those dreams. Ninety-nine per cent of the population never gets out of the gate because their thinking holds them back.

According to the latest science on the ability to solve complex problems through creative thought, better known as insight, negativity inhibits your ability to think clearly.

Unhappy people tend to have unhappy, pessimistic thoughts.

Conversely, happy people tend to have happy, optimistic thoughts.

Cognitive psychologists call this tendency to see the world through either a negative or positive lens, mood congruency. When the lens through which you view the world is negative, your focus is narrowed and you see nothing but your problems.

You become blind to solutions and opportunities. A negative mental outlook causes tunnel vision, limiting creativity.

If you're one of those struggling in life financially, a negative mental outlook acts like gasoline, fuelling the flames of negativity and perpetuating a life of unemployment, poverty or near poverty.

Conversely, a positive mental outlook, according to that same science, enhances creative problem-solving. A positive mental outlook expands your thinking and consciousness. It opens your mind to solutions and opportunities. If you are poor, a positive mental outlook is your only means of escaping a life of unemployment, poverty or near poverty.

Successful people are positive, enthusiastic, energetic, mostly happy and well-balanced individuals. They feel powerful, in control, confident and energised. This is not by accident. They are disciples of Rich Thinking. When they talk to themselves, their words are uplifting, not critical.

They engage in habitual positive self-talk. They use positive affirmations to reinforce their attitude and create a positive mindset. They do not get down on themselves when problems occur. They have adopted the Rich Thinking that problems and obstacles are opportunities and learning experiences.

Successful people control their thoughts. Bad thoughts are displaced immediately by good thoughts.

They understand that allowing a bad thought even a second of life will permit them to take root and eventually change their behaviour in a negative way. They feed their minds with positive, good thoughts and let them take root, eventually blossoming and one day bearing fruit.

Successful people also use visualisation techniques to alter or reinforce their mindset. Contrary to what you may believe, successful people also have dire thoughts that enter their minds.

How could they not, with all of the negative news that we are constantly bombarded with from the various media outlets?

Every day the media feeds us negative thoughts. The negative information causes fear, anxiety and angst. It is easy to fall victim to this barrage of negativity. Successful people realise this and try to minimise their consumption of television, radio or internet sites that are negative.

Rather, they watch or listen to programs that are constructive or uplifting. They read positive newspaper or magazine articles and stay away from the negative ones.

***Successful people control what they see and hear every day.***

Lastly, successful people are grateful for all that life has given them. They express thanks every day, oftentimes before sleep or upon waking in the morning.

Some even maintain a list, which they read every day, setting forth all they are grateful for.

## Why is gratitude so important?

Gratitude is the gateway to optimism and a positive mental outlook. Gratitude forces you to become aware of the good things about your life. My car started today, I was able to feed my family, I have a roof over my head, I'm healthy, I'm alive, I have a loving family, etc.

When you shift your thinking to the good things about your life, you cause your brain to begin to shift from negative to positive.

If you practice gratitude every day, eventually your positive mental outlook will overpower your negative mental outlook. Gratitude changes the lens through which you view your world, from negative to positive.

And when that does happen you'll begin to see solutions instead of problems. Ideas will pop into your head that will help you climb your way out of your unemployment, poverty or near poverty.

Expressing gratitude every day is not some pseudo, new age mumbo jumbo. Gratitude is the gateway to optimism and a positive mental outlook. It's the means to transforming your life from one filled with limitations to one filled with unlimited opportunities.

***Unsuccessful people have a negative mental outlook.*** They are critical of themselves and everyone they come into contact with.

They are often their own, and everyone else's, worst critics. They engage in negative, destructive thinking. They allow bad thoughts to enter their minds and take root, which eventually causes bad behaviour. They lack motivation, enthusiasm and often fall into states of mental depression that can last for days or weeks at a time. They watch too many negative programs on television or on the internet. They buy newspapers with headlines designed to stir negative emotions. They frequent negative internet sites. They feel hopeless and powerless.

## How can you tell if someone has a negative mental outlook?

The symptoms are as follows:

- *Victim Mindset:* These types of unsuccessful people believe that their financial circumstances are dictated by forces outside their control such as Wall Street, rich people intent on keeping them poor, government policies, the economy, bad schools, growing up in a bad neighbourhood, bad luck, etc.

- *Closed-Minded:* Unsuccessful people are closed-minded and unwilling to embrace new ideas, new thinking or opinions that differ from their own. One of the hallmarks of self-made millionaires is the ability to be open-minded to new ideas, new knowledge and new ways of thinking.

- *Ideological Constraints:* Unsuccessful people hold on to ideologies that keep them from growing out of their poverty. They carry with them beliefs that rich people are bad, money is the root of all evil, those born into poverty can't escape poverty, that you need a college education to escape poverty, etc. The ability to cast aside our ideological constraints allows us to expand our thinking, to grow and to evolve.

- *Intellectual Constraints:* Unsuccessful people believe they are not smart and that is one of the reasons they are poor. Everyone has the potential for genius. We are all born with the genius gene. What keeps the switch to that gene in the off position is our belief that we don't have the intelligence to rise above our financial circumstances in life.

- *Immediate Gratification:* Unsuccessful people look for short-term solutions to their long-term problem. They play the lottery, they gamble on sports or they go to casinos with the hope of funding their retirement. Escaping poverty and creating wealth takes time but the only way our ship will come in is if we build a dock big enough to anchor it.

One of the most successful techniques to help alter our mindset is to employ positive affirmations.

Positive affirmations reprogram our old brain, also known as the subconscious. Our old brain has been around millions of years longer than our new brain (our neocortex also known as our conscious brain).

It is far more powerful than our new brain. One of its powers is the ability to direct our behaviour without us knowing it. When we use positive affirmations to reprogram our old brain it will go to work behind the scenes to alter our behaviour. It sends messages to us in the form of intuition and insight. Intuition and insight causes us to pivot and change course.

## Positive affirmations

- "I complete my 'to-do' list every day."
- "I accomplish my goals."
- "I am lucky."
- "I am successful."
- "I make $300,000 a year."
- "I own a vacation home in Long Beach Island."
- "I am a senior executive in my company."
- "I pay for my child's college tuition out of my earnings or savings."
- "I love my job."
- "I love working with others."
- "I am confident."
- "I have a large network of relationships."
- "I call my parents every week."
- "I am a certified public accountant."
- "I live my life in moderation."

Positive affirmations represent the picture of the individual you hope to be, the things you hope to achieve, assets you hope to own or the income you hope to have one day.

They must be specific and in the present tense to be effective. ***Make a list of positive affirmations and keep them by your side.*** Review them once in the morning, once in the afternoon and right before you go to sleep.

Let these positive affirmations seep into your mind every day. They represent your most positive, good thoughts and they will eventually take root.

Events and circumstances will begin to manifest themselves around your positive thinking and opportunities will appear seemingly out of thin air.

## Summary

Successful people avoid negative thinking. They engage in Rich Thinking every single day.

### Michael Yardney's Insight

Having negative thoughts is normal and when something's bothering you, you know that getting your mind off it is easier said than done. But rehashing negative thoughts over and over in your head is unpleasant and counterproductive, so heed Tom's great advice in this chapter and develop the habit of Rich Thinking.

# CHAPTER 22
# RICH HABIT NUMBER NINE

**I will save 10 per cent of my income and live off of the remaining 90 per cent.**

***Successful people pay themselves first.***

Before any bills get paid, successful people set aside at least 10 per cent of their income into some savings, investment or retirement vehicle. They invest their money wisely, watch over their investments regularly and set realistic goals for their investment returns.

They have high credit scores, know their net worth and monitor their personal balance sheet. They use only the most qualified financial professionals to maximise their returns and minimise their taxes. They employ the services of experts like certified public accountants, certified financial planners or attorneys. They use these professionals to help them manage their money and their taxes.

## Successful people have a retirement plan

They participate to the fullest extent permitted by law in retirement plans. Many of these retirement plans allow individuals to put away, in a tax-deferred manner, a large portion of their income each year. If their company does not have a retirement plan, they create their own retirement plan by funding individual retirement accounts.

They add to these accounts with every pay cheque. They have retirement goals. They monitor their retirement plan regularly and make course corrections in an effort to reach their retirement goal.

## Unsuccessful people pay themselves last

They live pay day to pay day, spending every penny to support their lifestyle. They are poor savers and carry excessive amounts of debt. They have home equity loans, which are tapped out. Their credit cards are maxed out, and they can barely make the monthly minimum payments. They have poor credit scores.

Unsuccessful people do not contribute to retirement plans. Some gamble excessively and view the lottery as their retirement plan. They take risks, which are either unnecessary or not well thought out. They don't set aside at least 10 per cent of their income and, consequently, when they reach retirement age, they do not have enough retirement savings to allow them to retire with financial security.

They rationalise that they cannot afford to set aside 10 per cent of their earnings. They are unwilling to alter their lifestyle in order to save adequately. More often than not, unsuccessful people have no choice but to continue working well into their retirement years or rely on family or the government.

## Summary

Successful people pay themselves first by putting a minimum of 10 per cent of their income into savings or retirement plans.

### Michael Yardney's Insight

The formula for becoming rich is to spend less than you earn, save the difference and when you have enough saved up, to invest your money for the future.

An important Rich Habit is to pay yourself first and spend what's left. On the other hand, a common Poor Habit is to spend your money living and save what's left. The problem is there's rarely anything left over.

# CHAPTER 23
# RICH HABIT NUMBER 10

## I will control my words and emotions every day.

Not every thought needs to come out of your mouth and not every emotion needs to be expressed.

***Successful people are the masters of their words and emotions.*** They understand that saying whatever is on your mind could damage relationships with individuals who could help move them forward in achieving their dreams and goals.

They do not fall prey to anger, jealousy, excitability, sadness or other petty emotions. They cast out all bad emotions. They do not allow them even a second of life.

They understand that negative emotions cause them to make bad decisions that result in bad consequences. They replace these bad emotions with positive emotions.

They use the following technique when faced with a difficult situation that presents itself: "Think, Evaluate and React." Thinking gives them time to understand the situation. Evaluating the situation buys more time to determine the correct course of action.

Reacting is the last thing they do and most likely will be the appropriate reaction, as they took the time to choose their reaction.

## The words we use every day create perceptions

They are like magnets, drawing to us all sorts of people.

Rich people figured that out long before they ever became rich. The more words you know, the better your ability to communicate what you know. If you want to create the perception that you are smart, you must increase your knowledge of words and use them in conversation. Learning new words helps you grow as an individual. They increase your confidence. They transform you.

Successful people are very much aware of the words they use when they communicate to others. They choose words that will not offend others. They use words to reinforce the perception they have of themselves and use their words to also reinforce the perception others have about them.

Successful people are too busy to allow themselves to sink into a negative emotional state. They engage in productive activities, which take their minds off their troubles. They are constantly engaged in projects or self-improvement activities that promote positive feelings about themselves. Successful people feel as if they have total control over their emotions.

Unsuccessful people are unaware of the words they are using every day. They unknowingly use words that offend others, damaging relationships. They use words that create a perception in the eyes of others that is not favourable.

Unsuccessful people fall prey to petty emotions.

They let their emotions rule their behaviour. They become easily depressed and feel as if they have no control over their lives. They react before thinking. They have adopted the bad habit of "Ready, Fire, Aim." As a consequence of this, there are many unsuccessful people sitting in prisons throughout the world.

## Summary

Successful people control their words and emotions.

# CHAPTER 24
# RICH HABIT NUMBER 11

**I will do work that I love.**

Most of us are very good followers. We do as we are told. We become accustomed doing as we are told; this habit forms early in our lives.

For our own good our parents make us do things we don't want to do: wake up early for school, eat broccoli, do homework, house chores, etc. Doing what we are told is conditioned into us from a very early age.

But then we become adults.

Physiologically, this metamorphosis begins at about the age of 14 and continues until about age 21. Some parents who recognise this transformation slowly begin handing over decision-making for our lives to us. They encourage us to take individual responsibility. They let us make mistakes and experience some of life's harsh realities, standing by to offer advice and direction when things go wrong.

Unfortunately, parents like this are in the minority.

Most continue to exert control over the lives of their children well into their 20s, preventing them from becoming independent thinkers and doers. They are sometimes referred to as helicopter parents. We then pursue the goals and dreams of our parents rather than our own goals and dreams. We put our ladder on our parents' wall and climb that ladder most of our lives.

At some point, we realise we are unhappy doing what we are doing and become despondent or depressed about the work we do. This unhappiness usually begins to manifest in our mid- to late- 30s, when we have children of our own. We get stuck between a rock and a hard place because we believe we have no choice but to continue to climb our parents' ladder in order to provide for our family.

## How do you break free?

How do you take your ladder off someone else's wall and move it to your own wall?

***Successful people pursue work that they love.***

Because they are doing work that they love, they devote more time to it. They get labelled as "workaholics", which is ironic because they never actually feel like they are working hard at all. To them work is play. It's fun and it's enjoyable. They look forward to it. Because they are devoting more time to their work, they become expert in what they do.

Successful people find that niche in life that they can monetise and which energises them with passion. Passion provides them with the desire to engage in an activity until they become expert in it. With passion they are able to power through their mistakes and learn what works and what doesn't work.

## Unsuccessful people have their ladder on someone else's wall

They do not like what they do for a living. The poorest of the poor typically hate what they do for a living. As a result, they do the bare minimum to keep their job or earn a living. Because they devote the bare minimum to their jobs, they never become true experts in what they do.

You need to take action on your goals and dreams. Devote small blocks of time in the pursuit of your own individual goals and dreams, either early in the morning, late at night or on the weekends. It is possible to scale your own wall if you devote some time — any time — each and every day. In the beginning it will take some discipline.

But once you get going, passion energy will replace willpower energy. This passion will only continue to grow and energise you. Eventually, your daily investment will get you higher up your ladder and closer to the top of your wall. You will begin to feel happy and enthusiastic as you climb your own wall.

Experts are paid the most for their knowledge and skills. Expertise expands our means (income), which enables us to accumulate enormous wealth over time. The more we practice, the more money we make and the more wealth we accumulate. In time, what we practice becomes a habit.

The beauty of habits is that they endow us with instantaneous recall as well as effortless performance of our perfected skills. ***Passionate practice prevents poor performance*** by perfecting our knowledge and skills.

Passion is the number one and, by far, most important attribute of successful people. It is the catalyst that transforms ordinary individuals into exceptional individuals.

When you pursue something you are truly passionate about, your life will change for the better. You know you have found that thing you are truly passionate about when it occupies your thinking 24/7. It consumes your waking moments and your dreams. Why is passion so important?

- Passion creates persistence.
- Passion transforms even the laziest person into a workaholic.
- Passion infuses you with creativity.
- Passion allows you to overcome mistakes and failures.
- Passion turns obstacles the size of mountains into paved roads.
- Passion produces unforced focus, the most powerful type of focus.
- Passion gives you unlimited energy.
- Passion produces extreme willpower, the most powerful type of willpower.

While it is still possible to "do well" in life without passion, you will never reach your full potential without it. Your success will be stunted; a fraction of what it could be.

Finding your passion in life should be your main focus because with passion all of your wishes and dreams will eventually become your reality. Passion forces you to grow into the person you need to become in order for success to visit you. It is the first domino of success.

- Passion sets in motion all of the other success dominos.
- Passion trumps education.
- Passion trumps work ethic.
- Passion trumps intelligence.
- Passion trumps working capital.
- Passion trumps skills and years of technical proficiency.
- Passion trumps any advantage those who lack passion might have in life.

Those few who find passion in something simply blow the doors off those who lack passion. It is not even a competition. Passion is like a light switch. When it is turned on, it triggers a domino effect of other success characteristics. It is the catalyst for all success. Passion allows you to overcome every obstacle, every mistake and every failure. Nothing can stand in the way of a person with passion. Those imbued with passion never quit and so they never fail.

## Summary

Successful people find ways to make money doing something they love.

### Michael Yardney's Insight

We've all heard the expression: "Do what you love, and you'll never work another day in your life."

I know I absolutely love what I do and I'm lucky to make a good living at it. But beware: this doesn't mean your entire career will be a walk in the park. It doesn't mean you won't have to work hard — you will. The rich have worked hard and invested their money so that their money eventually works hard for them so they don't have to work hard any more. But interestingly, once they reach that point, the rich usually keep working because it's their passion.

# CHAPTER 25
# RICH HABIT NUMBER 12

## I will never quit on my dreams.

Those with the most persistence are the most successful in life and accumulate the most wealth.

***Persistence means never quitting on your dreams.*** Successful people pursue their dreams until they succeed, die or become incapacitated. Not even bankruptcy or divorce stops them from pursuing their dreams.

Persistence means taking action every day on the goals behind our dreams, whether we feel like it or not. It means never giving in to our doubts. Some days go our way, but most of the days in pursuit of a dream will not go our way. That's just the way it is.

## Realising a dream takes time and persistence

When things don't go our way, those are the days our minds can get filled with doubts. What sets successful people apart from everyone else is that they persist even when life does not cooperate and fills their mind with doubts.

Persistence means we stay on task despite all of the mistakes. Successful people view their mistakes as nothing more than learning experiences. Persistence means we pick ourselves up after suffering devastating failure after failure. We only fail when we quit.

Persistence means not letting rejection or being ignored stop us from moving forward. When we are pursuing a dream we will be faced with rejection and we will be ignored. It's part of the process. We cannot take it personally. We need to take emotion out of it. When we get rejected or ignored just say "next" and move on.

Persistence means not allowing distractions to shift our focus. It's easy to let distractions get in the way. Successful people push aside distractions and focus on what's important. They have a big picture view that acts like a force field, deflecting all distractions from their path.

Persistence means not letting fear stop us in our tracks. Fear is the main reason most quit on a dream. Successful people make a habit of taking action, despite their fears.

Most unsuccessful people do not pursue their dreams. They are held back by fear and doubt. They do not believe in themselves enough to pursue a dream. They have limiting beliefs that tell them they are not smart enough, educated enough, hard-working enough or capable of pursuing their dreams.

Those few unsuccessful people who do pursue their dreams, eventually quit on their dreams.

They fall victim to Bright Shiny Object Syndrome, which I mentioned in a previous section. When something does not immediately pay off, they move on to the thing that attracts their attention. They shift their focus to something else when things get hard.

Unsuccessful people perpetually chase something new because the thing they were previously pursuing did not immediately pay off, was too hard or was just taking far longer than they expected.

## Summary

Success takes time. Those who succeed never quit. Long-term persistence is a requirement for success.

**Michael Yardney's Insight**

No one is born a failure, but in my mind if you have not failed you can't succeed — there is nobody who is successful today who has not previously failed.

Successful people know better than to quit whenever they fail. They get up one more time. It doesn't matter how much you fail, if you persist you will succeed.

Remember Winston Churchill's famous quote: "Never give in — never, never, never, never, in nothing great or small, large or petty, never give in except to convictions of honour and good sense. Never yield to force; never yield to the apparently overwhelming might of the enemy."

# CHAPTER 26
# RICH HABIT NUMBER 13

**I will embrace only positive beliefs and eliminate all negative beliefs.**

Why do the rich get richer and the poor get poorer? Why does poverty perpetuate itself from one generation to the next?

The answer is our beliefs.

Our beliefs can either create wealth or create poverty. If we believe we are smart, we are right. If we believe we are dumb, we are right. If we believe life is our oyster, we are right. If we believe life is a struggle, we are right.

***What we believe determines who we become in life.***

Our beliefs are stored deep in our old brain, also known as the subconscious mind.

Our old brain differs dramatically from our new brain (also known as our conscious mind). Our old brain has been around for millions of years, whereas our new brain has only been around for a few hundred thousand years. Our old brain is immeasurably more powerful than our new brain. It is the only part of the brain that can actually multitask.

Simultaneously, it controls our autonomic system, directs our behaviour, stores our habits, it is where our emotions reside and warehouses our beliefs.

Beliefs represent emotionalised thought programming our old brain has accepted. If we want to change our circumstances in life we need to start by changing our beliefs. In order to do that we need to create positive emotionalised thoughts and avoid negative emotionalised thoughts.

Each one of us has inherited from our parents, environment and our upbringing certain beliefs that direct our behaviour, thinking, emotions and the choices we make in life.

When these beliefs close our mind to new ideas, new knowledge and new ways of thinking, they hold us back in life. They inhibit our ability to grow as individuals. One way to tell if our beliefs are preventing us from growing as individuals is our reaction to new information or new discoveries. If our knee-jerk reaction is to immediately dismiss any new information as bogus then we have a closed-minded, limiting, negative belief.

One of the hallmarks of successful people is their ability to be open-minded to new ideas, new knowledge and new ways of thinking. They are able to cast aside their limiting, negative beliefs and expand their thinking, to grow and to evolve.

Unsuccessful people have limiting, negative beliefs that hold them back in life. These beliefs are like stop signs, preventing them from pursuing anything that their beliefs tell them are not possible.

***Our daily habits mirror our beliefs.*** "I'm not smart" forges the habits of not studying, not listening and not focusing. "I can't lose weight" forges the habits of eating too much, eating poorly and not exercising.

A belief is formed in two ways:

1. Through repetitive programming that may be internal — our thoughts — or external — repetitive statements made by influence relationships such as our parents, teachers, friends, family, etc.

2. Through life events that were anchored to strong negative emotions (disappointment caused by a failure event) or strong positive emotions (happiness caused by a success event).

The early part of everyone's life is fraught with mistakes and failure events: we engage in new activities and make mistakes or fail at an activity. These mistakes and failures are life's way of telling us we are doing something wrong. They are not intended to negatively affect the rest of our lives. They are intended to positively affect the rest of our lives by teaching us what not to do.

Unfortunately, the people around us, our parents, friends, teachers, etc., unintentionally resort to destructive criticism that affects most of us for the rest of our lives. This criticism sticks because it is tied to negative emotions. Once a negative emotion is coupled with a destructive criticism, it becomes a limiting belief.

Parents, teachers, company managers and anyone in the position of authority have the capacity to eliminate the limiting beliefs and bad habits of their children, students and employees. We all need to positively inspire everyone we are in a position to influence in our lives.

One person can change the entire life of another person by simply giving them a new belief to believe in, which will, in turn, rid them of their corresponding bad daily habits forever.

Here are some limiting beliefs that could be holding you back in life:

- Poor people can't become rich.
- Rich people have good luck and poor people have bad luck.
- I am not smart.
- Everyone thinks I'm ugly.
- I never have enough money.
- I can't do anything right — everything I try I fail at.
- People don't like me.
- I'm disorganised and have no discipline.
- I'm not good at (fill in the blank): school, cooking, work, reading, relationships, etc.
- I can't lose weight.

Each one of these limiting beliefs is an individual mini-computer program which alters our behaviour in a negative way. These limiting beliefs are responsible for the life we have. If we are unhappy and want to change our circumstances in life, we need to replace these limiting beliefs with positive, uplifting beliefs. It can be done.

Here are some powerful strategies that will reprogram your subconscious and completely transform your life.

If you follow these strategies for 30 days the reprogramming will stick and you will shift your mindset from negative to positive.

## The Five Year Letter

The Five Year Letter is a lot of fun. It gets the imagination going and when you're done you will feel immediately better about yourself. Kids particularly enjoy this activity. Here's how it works:

Imagine it is five years from now and you are writing a letter to yourself explaining what your life is like five years from now. In a perfect world what would you like your life to look like in five years' time? You want to paint a picture of your life five years from now that is the perfect, ideal life. It is the life you would want to have if you could snap your fingers today. Describe in your letter where you live, what kind of house you live in, what car you drive, what you do for a living, how much money you make, etc. Describe what you've done during the past five years — the goals you've accomplished and the dreams that have come true. ***The Five Year Letter will become a blueprint for your future life.***

## Write Your Obituary

This exercise forces you to evaluate your current life and gives you an opportunity to rewrite your script for the future. What would you like your perfect obituary to say? How would you like the world to remember you? Include all of the things you would like to accomplish in your life. Don't skimp. List all of the dreams you realised in your life. Your obituary should make you in awe of yourself. Really lay it on. Let it pour forth your greatness and success. Let it paint a picture of the ideal person you would like to be. Like the Five Year Letter, let this Obituary become the blueprint of your ideal future life and your future you.

## Make a List of Your Wishes and Dreams

List every wish or dream you would like to come true. Then reduce it to the top five wishes or dreams you would like to come true over the next five years.

## Create Goals around Your Wishes and Dreams

Goals help us to focus on accomplishing our dreams. Goals help bring clarity to what we are trying to accomplish in life. Goals work like a magnifying glass works in focusing the sunlight. Goals help focus our activities.

Once you identify the actions required, you have your goals. The only remaining issue is whether or not you have the ability to perform the actions required.

## Create a Success Log

This is a listing of all of your successes in life. Its purpose is to put a stop to the negative self-criticism we all seem to engage in. It's a tool that helps shift our thinking from negative to positive.

***Positive thinking attracts good things into our life*** by reprogramming our old brain positively. Negative thinking attracts bad things into our life by negatively programming our old brain. The Success Log helps shift our thinking from negative to positive. As we read through all of the successes in our life we become positive.

This programs our old brain to be success-focused and not failure-focused. It's a psychological pat on the back and it works. Every time you screw up, pull out your Success Log and begin reading. It will stop you from beating yourself up the rest of the day and prevent you from going negative.

Mistakes and failures are nothing more than lessons to be learned. They are not a reflection of our incompetence, lack of education or some character flaw. They are just things to learn from. The Success Log helps put mistakes and failures in their proper context and keeps us on the path of Prosperity Thinking.

## Create Daily Affirmations around your Goals

Affirmations need to be in the present tense and represent a future state of being. For example: "I am my company's #1 salesperson."

Affirmations only work when they are tied to our goals, dreams or main purpose in life.

## Create a Vision Board

A Vision Board is a visual representation of all of the things we desire in life. Cut out and paste pictures to your Vision Board that represent the ideal house you would like to live in, the ideal car you drive, the ideal profession, the size of your bank account, places you would like to go on vacation, things you would like to do, people you would like to meet or become friends or do business with, etc.

Keep this Vision Board where you can see it and look at it in the morning just after waking up and at night, just before going to bed.

## Meditate Once in the Morning

Sit in a chair and get comfortable. Close your eyes. Feel your eyes relax; then your whole head; then your neck; then your shoulders; then your chest; then your arms; then your waist; then your legs; and then your feet.

Take 30 deep breaths and visualise each number in your head. Let all thoughts drift by, one after the other.

Visualise your big dream coming true. Visualise all of your goals being realised. Visualise your ideal life, with your ideal home, ideal job, your substantial income, and your good health. See yourself happy and successful. Ask for help in overcoming any obstacles that are currently in your way. Open your eyes and say, "I am happy".

## Summary

Successful people don't accept beliefs that stunt their growth. They understand that when beliefs prevent change and growth, they hold them back in life and prevent them from becoming the person they need to be in order for success to visit them.

# CHAPTER 27
# RICH HABIT NUMBER 14

## I will seek out success mentors.

In order to be successful, we must learn to walk in the footsteps of the wealthy.

The fastest, most effective way to do this is to find a success mentor. ***Finding a success mentor is the fast-track to becoming wealthy.*** Mentors regularly and actively participate in our success by teaching us what to do and what not to do. They share with us valuable life lessons they learned either from their own mentor or from the school of hard knocks.

Finding a success mentor is one of the best and least painful ways to become rich.

Successful people find success mentors in many different aspects of their lives. Unsuccessful people do not.

## Here are five ways to find success mentors:

1. **Parents** — Parents are often the only opportunity any of us have at having a success mentor in life. This is why parenting is so important. Parents need to be success mentors to their children. They need to teach their children good daily success habits. If they don't, it is likely their children will struggle in life financially.

2. **Teachers** — Good teachers are good mentors. Teachers can reinforce the mentoring children receive at home from their parents or step in to provide the much-needed success mentoring absent at home.

3. **Supervisors** — For those not fortunate enough to have had parents or teachers who provided success mentoring, finding someone at work who can act as a mentor will ensure success in life. Find someone at work who you admire, trust and respect and just ask them to be your mentor. This person should be at least two levels above you.

4. **Reading** — Many successful people attribute their success in life to self-help, success authors such as Dale Carnegie, Earl Nightingale, Og Mandino or Jack Canfield. Books can take the place of real-life success mentors.

5. **School of Hard Knocks** — When you learn good daily success habits through the school of hard knocks you are essentially your own mentor. You teach yourself what not to do. You learn from your mistakes and failures. This is the hard way because those mistakes and failures cost you in both time, money and emotion.

Understanding failure is more important than understanding success.

If you want to succeed in life you must learn what not to do. There are two ways to learn what not to do when pursuing a dream or something you are passionate about:

1. **The Easy Way** — Find a success mentor and learn from their mistakes and failures.

2. **The Hard Way** — Taking action and learning through the School of Hard Knocks what works and what doesn't work. This is the hard way because it often costs you time and money to learn what not to do. It is also an emotional rollercoaster ride — negative emotions, when things go wrong, and positive emotions, when things go right. The Hard Way requires an enormous amount of persistence and patience.

If you're poor or middle-class, you can find these success mentors at work, in non-profit organisations, in trade groups, business groups, charities, etc. They can be found in books or in mastermind groups. A mastermind group is typically five or six individuals who meet physically or virtually once a week to share best practices, advice and to help you troubleshoot issues and problems.

## Summary

In order to be successful, you must walk in the footsteps of the wealthy. Finding your own success mentor is the fastest path to riches!

### Michael Yardney's Insight

As Isaac Newton once said, "If I have seen further, it is by standing on the shoulders of giants."

Both Tom and I feel having mentors is so important that we've devoted another chapter to it later in the book.

# CHAPTER 28
# RICH HABIT NUMBER 15

**I will focus on my dreams and goals every day. I will not let myself get distracted from my goals.**

Most people are completely oblivious to their own behaviours, habits and thinking as well as conversations of others, actions of others and their surroundings. Study after study has been conducted regarding this and they even came up with a phrase to describe it — In-attentional Blindness.

The main cause of In-attentional Blindness is the conscious brain's inability to multi-task — to consciously do two things at once.

We are only able to consciously focus on one thing at a time. Everything else simply fades away, ignored by our conscious mind. Our brain's Reticular Activating System (RAS) and thalamus block all sensory input, other than that input needed to complete a task or that input needed to help us with something we are intensely focused on, such as a goal. This RAS and thalamus will only deviate from this filtering function when something unexpected or novel comes to its attention.

Our ability to focus intently on one thing is one of humanity's greatest assets.

While this might appear to be an inherent deficiency, it isn't. The power to focus and ignore almost everything outside our focus is why humanity has been able to send a man to the moon, build the Brooklyn Bridge, split the atom and achieve so much.

The ability to focus so intently on one thing is actually our strength.

It is the reason why famous, successful people like James Cameron (director of the Terminator movies, *Titanic* and *Avatar*) Jim Carey (famous comedian/actor) and JK Rowling (Harry Potter author) can lift themselves out of incredible poverty and magically transform themselves into self-made millionaires. All three, at one time, were so poor their home was their car.

Unfortunately, the vast majority of individuals hold on to the belief that it is virtually impossible for a poor person to break free of poverty and become rich.

This one limiting belief is the reason why we have so many stuck in a generational cycle of poverty and the reason why so many politicians are therefore able to buy the votes of the poor by simply offering them entitlements, as the only means for escaping their poverty.

Any individual who accepts this belief is unable to use the power of focus to rid themselves of their adverse financial circumstances. And that is unfortunate, because ***the power of focus is the poor person's escape hatch***. It can lift any individual out of the direst of financial circumstances.

## Successful people understand that you cannot achieve any goal without intense, uninterrupted focus

Most unsuccessful people, however, spend a vast majority of their time multi-tasking, which only distracts them from focusing on important tasks. Important tasks represent those things you should be doing every day that help move you forward in achieving some goal or some life dream.

Distractions pull you away from important tasks. Successful people understand that in order to accomplish important tasks, they need to isolate blocks of uninterrupted time during their day engaged in intense focus.

Let me expand a little on focus. There are two types of focus:

1. Forced Focus and
2. Unforced Focus.

Forced Focus relies on the new brain, our conscious brain, also known as the neocortex.

With Forced Focus we rely on willpower to focus. Willpower has a short life — usually two to three hours at a time. Using willpower to focus our attention on something rapidly drains the brain of glucose (brain fuel). So, the brain does not like to use willpower. It prefers emotion power, which is released by a much more powerful type of focus called Unforced Focus.

Unforced Focus does not rely on willpower, the energy source that comes from our new brain. Instead, it relies on emotion, the energy source that comes from our old brain. Unforced Focus occurs when we pursue something we are very passionate about and which stirs our emotions. It enables us to learn at an accelerated rate because it enables us to engage in extended periods of uninterrupted focus.
New knowledge and new skills are easier to obtain when we are in the flow of Unforced Focus.

Unforced Focus is the most intense type of focus you can have. Edison had it, Tesla had it, Einstein had it and Steve Jobs had it. People who are able to tap into Unforced Focus can work on something with laser-like attention for many hours, for many days, for many weeks and even for many years.

When you are in the presence of Unforced Focus you know it. You are unable to pull yourself away from an activity. The key to turning on Unforced Focus is the pursuit of a dream or the goals behind a dream. These things tap into the emotion centre of the old brain. ***Successful people use Unforced Focus to achieve their dreams*** and the goals behind their dreams.

Unsuccessful people do not pursue goals, a purpose or a dream. As a result, they are never able to take advantage of the incredible power of Unforced Focus. They have to rely on willpower-driven Forced Focus. They are literally using only part of their brain.

## Summary

Successful people consistently pursue their goals and their dreams. They engage in daily intense focus.

# CHAPTER 29
# RICH HABIT NUMBER 16

## I will set only good goals and avoid bad goals.

You hardly ever hear anyone talk about goals in a negative context.

Goals are almost always perceived to be good. But there are goals that add no real value to your life when achieved yet consume valuable resources. So, how do you know when a goal is good or bad?

***Good goals create long-term benefits and long-term happiness when achieved.*** They allow you to grow as an individual and alter your behaviour in a positive way.

Good goals get you from point A to point B. Point B being a better place, such as more wealth, improved health, a better job, higher income, a better school system for your kids, etc. An example of a good goal would be to lose 20 pounds. Setting a weight loss goal often involves a daily regimen of exercise, healthy eating and encourages a better lifestyle.

Good health results from exercising and eating right. It may also motivate you to moderate your consumption of alcohol or to quit smoking. When the weight eventually comes off, you enjoy the compliments, feel healthier and all of this creates a type of permanent happiness known as fulfilment.

## Here are some other examples of good goals:

- **Becoming an Expert** — Many successful people are niche experts. They devote time on the side, every day, to developing an expertise in a specific area within their industry. Niche experts have more value and, thus, make more money.

- **Starting a Side Business** — Many successful people started their successful business while working for someone else. It is possible to grow a side business while still maintaining your full-time job. This could not only add additional current income but could eventually give you the freedom to leave your job and devote yourself full-time to your business.
- **Improving the way you look** — Many successful people exercise with weights regularly. Lifting weights to build a stronger, healthier body will improve the way you look. When you look good, you feel more confident in yourself. That self-confidence is picked up by others around you, making you even more attractive.
- **Become a Speaker** — Some successful people are good speakers. Joining Toastmasters or some similar speaker organisation in order to develop your speaking skills will benefit you in the long-term. Being a good speaker sets you apart from the competition at work and within your industry. Being a good speaker gets you noticed by others in your industry. This could mean a better job with more pay and more responsibility.
- **Become a Writer** — Some successful people write for industry magazines and newsletters. Others write books or have a blog. Starting a blog is an excellent way to develop your writing skills. Becoming a good writer stamps you as an expert on the topics you write about. This opens the door of opportunity for promotions at work, new job opportunities within your industry or additional income streams.

## Bad Goals

Bad goals create short-term happiness and no long-term benefits when achieved. An example of a bad goal would be to own a Ferrari. In order to own a Ferrari you must make more money. Making more money will likely involve either more work or taking excessive financial risk (i.e. gambling). There's a cost-benefit to working more — you invest time that you will never recoup.

Don't misunderstand me here. Working more to make more money can be a good thing. But where the goal goes south is when you then use that money to buy things, like a Ferrari.

The happiness you derive from owning more or better stuff will fade over time, since happiness derived from buying most things is usually short-term. You will eventually revert back to your genetic happiness baseline — after a few weeks, the Ferrari becomes just a car you drive. The lost time with the family, however, can never be recouped.

If the goal, instead, was to judiciously invest that extra money you earned into a calculated risk, such as a side business, an investment or a vacation home that enables you to spend more time with your family, then it transforms the "work more/earn more" goal into a good goal.

### Some other examples of bad goals:

- **Winning the Lottery** — Becoming rich by gambling in any way is a bad goal. The odds of winning are remote and costs you money that could otherwise be saved or invested prudently for future wealth creation.

- **Buying an Expensive Home** — Unless this is a need (i.e. expanding family), buying a bigger house is a bad goal. Bigger houses require more upkeep, higher utilities bills and more in interest that you pay to the bank.

- **Buying an Expensive Boat** — This is another example of a bad goal. Boats are costly and the money you spend on the boat could be better used for funding your retirement plan or building an investment portfolio.

- **Taking an Exotic Vacation** — While travelling to exotic locations can have some educational benefits, saving your hard-earned money just to spend on an expensive vacation means not having that money to build wealth.

- **Destroying Your Competition** — When you focus on destroying your competition as a means to increase your market share, rather than improving upon the products or service you offer, you hurt your business and damage relationships within your industry; relationships who might be in a position to hire you or partner with you one day. Engaging in competitive warfare often accomplishes only one thing: reduced profits and burned bridges.

***The benefits of achieving a goal should create long-term benefits:*** a stronger business, more time with the family, more knowledge or expertise, financial independence, improved health, etc. When the achievement of a goal does not improve your life for the long-term, it's a bad goal. Goals pursued to own more things or to create some momentary pleasure are a wasted investment. Be careful of the goals you pursue. Not all goals are created equal.

Successful people understand the difference between a good goal and a bad goal. They don't waste their time on goals which do not create long-term success and happiness.

Unsuccessful people focus on goals that will not create long-term success. They pursue goals that will give them short-term happiness and immediate gratification.

## Summary

Focus on only those goals that will create long-term benefits and help you move closer to realising your dreams.

# CHAPTER 30
# RICH HABIT NUMBER 17

**I will not fear risk. I will take risks that help me achieve my goals and realise my dreams.**

Successful people are risk-takers.

They take risks that make most others cower in fear. ***Risk is a necessary component of success.*** You cannot possibly succeed without taking risk.

But the risk I am referring to is not the type of risk that gamblers take. The risk successful people take is known as Calculated Risk. This is a type of risk that requires thoughtful analysis. It requires that you study all of the variables of any initiative that involves some risk.

Calculated Risk means you've identified every potential scenario that could lead to failure.

When you take Calculated Risk, you prepare yourself for all possible contingencies. It requires a lot of work and thought. As a result, you are never blindsided when something goes wrong. You never panic when things go wrong. You have well thought-out contingency plans for each contingency. You're prepared for the worst. That's Calculated Risk.

## Unsuccessful people take Uncalculated Risks

Gambling is an example of Uncalculated Risk. Uncalculated Risk requires no thought, no analysis, no work and very little investment in time. Gambling is the poor person's risk.

## Results of My 5 Year Study

My study confirmed that the Rich are willing to take risks. When asked the question: *"I've taken a risk in search of wealth"*, 63% of Rich people agreed while only 6% of Poor people agreed.

A lot of the wealthy people in my study were business owners who started their own businesses. They became successes because they were master self-educators who learned from the school of hard knocks. In fact, 27% of the wealthy people in my study admitted that they failed at least once in life or in business, compared with 2% of the poor. Failure is like scar tissue on the brain — the lessons last forever.

## Summary

Successful people are not afraid to take risks. They are not afraid to invest time, money and thought into pursuing something they are passionate about.

# CHAPTER 31
# RICH HABIT NUMBER 18

**I will exercise patience every day.**

Focus, persistence and patience are three common traits of all successful people, but patience may be the hardest trait to learn.

Success takes time. It doesn't happen overnight.

And success has its ups and downs. Some days things go your way, but most of the time they don't. When things don't go your way, it's easy to become frustrated and to quit. Most people do. And most people are unsuccessful.

But ***successful people don't quit.***

They patiently pursue their goals and their dreams. They take a long view of success. They accept that it may take them years or even a lifetime to realise success. They are patient.

They don't fall victim to Bright Shiny Object Syndrome. They stick to one thing for many years. This patience enables them to gain knowledge, skills, buys them time to pivot and allows them to focus on their goals and dreams. Patience eventually provides solutions to all of our problems.

Sometimes that solution is an idea, a strategy or even that critically important person who joins our effort. Without patience none of those ideas, strategies or apostles would be possible. Patience creates Opportunity Luck, the luck that is a trademark of all successful people.

Every successful person experiences the frustration of patience. Opportunity Luck did not visit Colonel Sanders until he was in his mid-60s. Rodney Dangerfield was 46 before he got his first break on The Ed Sullivan Show. Before becoming president, Abraham Lincoln lost several runs for public office. Successful people patiently pursue their goals and dreams.

Unsuccessful people lack patience. As soon as they hit a roadblock, instead of pivoting, they quit. They lack the patience that is required in order for success to happen. As a result, Opportunity Luck never has a chance of happening. They never find solutions to problems. They never find that apostle who helps them achieve their goals or realise their dreams.

## Summary

Successful people patiently persist.

### Michael Yardney's Insight

I love Warren Buffet's quote: *"Wealth is the transfer of money from the impatient to the patient."*

# CHAPTER 32
# RICH HABIT NUMBER 19

**I will seek to exceed the expectations of others.**

Successful people seek to exceed the expectations of others in everything they do.

Doing so helps build trust and confidence others have in you. It makes others believe in you. As a result, they are more than happy to give you more responsibility. This results in increased opportunities down the road.

In order to exceed expectations, ***successful people have developed the habit of under-promising and over-delivering***.

They set themselves up for success even before they take on any challenge. Successful people make it a habit of changing the other person's perception of reality, out of the gate, reducing their expectations at the beginning of the promise stage.

By reducing expectations this way, they set themselves up for success, making it easier to exceed expectations by over delivering. This allows them to "wow" them at the end.

Unsuccessful people have a tendency to want to "wow" others at the beginning and not at the end. So, they make promises out of the gate that exceed another person's expectations. They "wow" them at the beginning. That's backwards.

Unsuccessful people set the bar too high in the beginning and then fail to meet the expectations of others. This results in distrust and a loss of confidence that others have in you. Eventually, responsibilities will be taken away from you and this results in a loss of opportunity down the road.

## Summary

Successful people exceed the expectations of others by managing the expectations process at the very beginning of any project or initiative.

### Michael Yardney's Insight

While I agree with Tom: I don't necessarily do things for other people's respect, I just want to exceed my own expectations.

# CHAPTER 33
# RICH HABIT NUMBER 20

**I will create multiple streams of income.**

Successful people do not rely on one stream of income.

They create multiple income streams during their lives. They have "several poles in many ponds" and are able to draw income from other sources when one source is temporarily impaired.

Some of the additional streams may include: a side business, real estate rentals, REITs, tenants-in-common real estate investments, triple net leases, stock market investments, annuities, private equity investments, part ownership in businesses, financing investments, ancillary product or services and royalties (patents, books, oil, timber).

***Each additional stream gives them extra money*** that they can then use to invest in order to create other streams of income.

Unsuccessful people rely on one stream of income — their job.

They put "one pole in one pond" and when that single income stream is impacted by an economic downturn or job loss, they suffer financially. Even worse, the vast majority of those just getting by do not like what they do for a living. As a result, they feel imprisoned by their jobs. They are what I call wage slaves.

If you're raising a family, it's not easy. It's already hard.

But, understand this, as your kids get older, it gets easier. As they near college age, your kid-related commitments begin to decline. You will eventually have more time to commit to growing those income streams.

Now, while your kids are young, is actually the best time to take baby steps and begin slowly building something on the side. I'm talking about no more than five to 10 hours a week, devoting yourself to something you are passionate about and that can eventually be monetised.

I'm talking about investing in yourself and your future now so that you can reap the dividends down the road. And trust me, you'll be glad you did because as your kids get older, their financial needs become larger.

Those income streams will eventually kick in enough income to allow you to quit your full-time job and allow you to hire individuals to help you manage your investments. This will free you up to enjoy the dividends: a vacation home that becomes a hub for your adult children, financial independence so that you don't become a financial burden on your children, a retirement free from financial worries and money to help your adult children buy their own homes.

## Putting all of your eggs in one basket is simply a recipe for financial disaster

If that basket breaks, what do you do? If you want to make your life easier down the road, you need to invest in yourself now. Find something you are truly passionate about and that has potential to generate an additional stream of income. Passion is the key. Passion is, by far, the most important attribute of self-made millionaires as I've mentioned previously. It is the catalyst that transforms ordinary individuals into self-made millionaires. When you pursue something you are truly passionate about, you are somehow able to find the time to devote to it.

But ***you'll never find your passion unless you try***. You must take action and invest in yourself today in order to create the future life you desire.

## How do you create multiple streams of income?

- **Save, Save, Save** — Save 10 to 20 per cent of your net income every year and then invest it.

- **Expand Your Means** — Start a side business or side career that generates additional income.
- **Create Multiple Investment Baskets** — Invest your savings and additional income into investments that generate passive income such as: residential and commercial rental properties, tenancy in common investments (TICS), triple net leases, equity investments (stocks, bonds, mutual funds), annuities, permanent life insurance, royalty-generating property (timber, oil and gas), boat rentals, etc. If you can't do it on your own, partner with others and keep building your portfolio of assets that generate passive income.

## Summary

If you want to become wealthy, you need to create multiple streams of income.

### Michael Yardney's Insight

The wealthy know that you need more than one stream or source of income to be rich today. If you think back to the 1950s when, in most families, only the husband worked, how many streams of income did a family need to survive?

Only one.

Yet today, very few families can survive on less than two streams of income, with both the husband and wife working. And the way things are going, that won't be enough in the future. It would be wise to have multiple streams of income flowing through your adult life.

Wealthy people have always known this. They generate income through wages or their businesses and also from their various investments such as real estate, shares and managed funds. If one stream dries up, they have many more to support them. If one of their businesses goes broke, they have other sources of income available.

Do you have multiple streams of income flowing into your life at this time?

Maybe it's time to add another one — but not by getting another job!

What I am talking about is recurring income that you receive whether you are working or not. Another name for this is passive income because it is money you make when you are asleep.

So, first, it is important to understand that not all incomes are created equal. Some streams are linear and some are recurring. Now here's the question that will determine whether your income streams are linear or recurring: **how many times do you get paid for every hour you work?**

If you have answered only once, then your income is linear.

But that's where the poor get it wrong — they try to obtain multiple streams of income the hard way. They either get themselves another job, or they try to make a go of network marketing or they make hard work out of real estate by attempting strategies such as managing their own properties or leasing out their properties room by room in an attempt to increase their cash flow.

They are building the wrong sort of income — they're just getting themselves another job.

What you need is *passive* and *recurring* income — income that comes into your life whether you work or not. This is the type of income that can be deposited into your bank account while you are off holidaying on the other side of the world. The secret of the wealthy is not that they have more money, but that they have more time freedom, because their income is passive, and they can spend time on anything they want.

**What percentage of your income is recurring?**

If you're smart, you will start to develop some streams of passively earned recurring income. Eventually this will give you the time freedom to do what you want when you want.

> One way you can do this is to buy stocks or income-earning real estate. Whether you're working or not, the dividends or rental income will continue to come in and over the years the value of your stocks or your property's value will increase.

# CHAPTER 34
# RICH HABIT NUMBER 21

**I will use the power of leverage to help me achieve my goals and realise my dreams.**

***Successful people use the power of leverage*** to help them with their goals and dreams.

Leverage means using all of your assets, knowledge, skills, time, money and relationships to get what you want or need in life. As an example, successful people reach out to their like-minded Rich Relationships to introduce them to individuals or groups who can help them in some way. These individuals are able to open doors that were previously shut to them.

## Another example is how successful people leverage time

There are only 24 hours in every day for every individual. With respect to time, we are all on equal footing. Successful people understand that in order to leverage time they need others to help them pull their cart to move them forward in achieving their goals and realising their dreams.

Ten people working together for one purpose equals 240 hours a day. One more example is how successful people leverage knowledge and skills. They understand that they cannot possibly know everything or be good at everything, so successful people leverage the knowledge and skills of their network of relationships. They tap into the collective knowledge and skills of everyone in their inner circle to help them with their goals and dreams.

Unsuccessful people do not use the power of leverage to help them in life.

They rely on no one but themselves. Because they do not possess many of the Rich Habits, such as relationship building, networking, giving first and many others, they do not have much to leverage.

When you understand the power leverage has, you can gain access to the assets, skills, knowledge, money and influence of others.

Leverage helps you multiply the number of hours in your day when you partner with others towards a common end.

## Summary

Successful people use the power of leverage every day to help move them forward in achieving their goals and dreams.

## Michael Yardney's Insight

Have you ever wondered why it's easier for people who have money to make more of it? I mean, why is it that the second and the third million are so much easier to earn than the first million?

They use the Rich Habit of leverage and I'm not just talking about borrowing money. As Tom explains there are at least four ways the Rich use leverage.

Let's look at them…

*1. Money*

One of the biggest differences between how wealthy people and the average person go about building wealth isn't how they invest the money that they have… it's how they leverage and use the money they don't have that makes them wealthy.

While the poor are afraid of taking on debt, the wealthy have mastered the art of using money that they don't have to build their wealth. They use borrowed money to magnify their investment activities and enjoy enhanced, accelerated returns.

*2. Relationships*

Wealthy people build a great team around themselves realising that they don't have to be an expert in every field if they develop a good network.

Having a great network around you enables you to leverage off other people's expertise. I often say "if you are the smartest person in your team you are in trouble."

In this world, it's not what you know and it's not even who you know... it's who who you know knows. That wasn't a typo. Your network of relationships is critical to growing your wealth, not just for what they themselves know, but often for the people they know who could also help you.

*3. Time*

The Rich have learned how to leverage their time putting it to its highest and best use. They do this by outsourcing these minor tasks to their property manager and to other contractors.

Instead they use their time to learn more, develop their relationships or find more deals.

*4. Their mind*

One of the greatest points of leverage is leveraging your "mind". What we're trying to teach you in this book is how wealthy people think differently to the average person.

I remember Robert Kiyosaki saying in one of his Rich Dad Poor Dad books that a cynic's reality does not let anything new in, while a fool's reality does not have the ability to keep foolish ideas out.

Stretch your mind to look for opportunities to leverage in new ways.

# CHAPTER 35
# RICH HABIT NUMBER 22

**I will not allow fear or doubt to prevent me from taking action on my goals and my dreams.**

Most of us are completely unaware of our thoughts.

If you stop to listen to your thoughts, to be aware of them, you'd find most of them are negative. But you only realise you are having these negative thoughts when you force yourself to become aware of them. Awareness is the key. The new age term for this is "mindfulness".

Physiologically, these negative thoughts, the voice inside our heads, emanates from an area of the brain called the amygdala. The amygdala resides in the limbic system portion of the old brain. It never stops talking to us.

It's there for a purpose.

Think of it as something like a radar system, warning you of danger. It broadcasts worry, fear or doubts. This voice whispers all sorts of negative things when you embark on something new or something that involves risk.

The triggers for this voice are new goals, pursuing a dream, investing our money in a new business or a new project, new job opportunities, a possible promotion with new responsibilities, etc. It says things to us like:

- You could fail.
- You could lose money.
- You might do a bad job and get fired.
- It may result in bankruptcy.

These voices are warnings to stop what we are doing and reverse course back to our comfort zone.

While unsuccessful people give in to the voices, successful people ignore those voices.

They pursue goals, dreams, new business opportunities and new challenges in life in spite of the fears and the doubts that they have. How is it that successful people are able to overcome the negative voices of doubt and fear?

## What do they do to overcome those voices?

Successful individuals play something I call The What If Game:

- What if I succeed?
- What if I love doing this?
- What if I make more money than I expect?
- What if it's not as hard as I thought?
- What if it makes me happy?
- What if it helps my family?
- What if it creates the life of my dreams?
- What if it makes me more valuable?

The What If Game stops negativity in its tracks and replaces it with positivity. It defuses all of the fears, doubts and uncertainties we all face when pursuing something worthwhile. It immediately changes the way you think. It gives you courage to move forward.

The next time you are faced with a difficult decision, play The What If Game. Don't give in to the demon voices because what if the demon voices are just wrong?

## Summary

Successful people do not give in to doubt and fear.

# CHAPTER 36
# RICH HABIT NUMBER 23

## I will seek feedback from others.

Successful people are in constant pursuit of feedback.

They make a habit of it. Feedback improves any product or service they offer in their business or careers. Successful people see feedback as a reconnaissance mission. It gives them the ability to obtain valuable information that will add value to everything they do.

***Making a habit of seeking feedback sets successful people apart*** from everyone else and enables them to learn and improve. Successful people seek feedback from their colleagues, supervisors, staff, clients, customers and business partners.

## Unsuccessful people avoid feedback

The fear of criticism holds them back.

Fear is a negative emotion that holds them back in life. They give in to their fear of criticism.

You need to learn everything about what you're doing in order to find out if you are on the right path or if you need to change what you're doing and how you're doing it. It is far less costly to seek feedback than to lose time and money learning what not to do via the School of Hard Knocks.

Learning via the School of Hard Knocks is the hard, expensive way; seeking feedback is the easier, less costly path towards success. Feedback guarantees success or, at the very least, guarantees that you will not fail. If you typically avoid feedback, you are operating out of fear.

## Summary

Continuous self-improvement is one of the hallmarks of successful people. Successful people seek feedback in order to help them learn and improve.

# CHAPTER 37
# RICH HABIT NUMBER 24

**I will ask for what I want or need.**

"Ask and it shall be given" is one of the most famous verses in the Bible.

There's a very good reason for this. When you ask for what you want or need there's the real possibility that you will get it.

Successful people understand this so they make a habit of asking for what they want or need from others.

***Unsuccessful people don't ask for what they want or need.***

Why? Fear.

Actually, they have two types of fear:

1. **Fear of Rejection** — To unsuccessful people, rejection makes them feel embarrassed, humiliated or demeaned in some way.

2. **Fear of Obligation** — Obligation means you owe someone. Someone did you a favour and now you owe them. Unsuccessful people don't ask others for help because they don't want to feel like they are obligated to them.

On the other hand, successful people use two strategies to help them overcome these two fears:

1. **They Manage Their Own Expectations** — When we expect a "yes" after asking for help but receive a "no", we immediately become unhappy or depressed. Successful people understand this. So, to prevent it from happening they manage their expectations by

conditioning themselves for a "no" when they ask for help. They actually expect to be rejected. If they are rejected, they're OK with it. They don't become unhappy or depressed because they expected a no. If someone surprises them and says "yes", they instantly become happy, optimistic and enthusiastic.

2. **They Understand That Obligation Creates Partnerships —** Successful people understand that when they are obligated to someone it actually strengthens the relationship they have with that person. Obligation forges partnerships. Successful people understand that they need partnerships to succeed in life. Obligation is a way to gain valuable partners.

## Summary

Successful people ask others for what they want or need in order to gain partners to their cause.

# CHAPTER 38
# RICH HABIT NUMBER 25

**I will make my own personalised to-don't list and follow it every day.**

We've all heard about to-do lists. The best to-do lists incorporate daily activities that help you move yourself forward in life towards accomplishing your goals and realising your dreams.

But you probably never heard of a "to-don't list".

A to-don't list is a list that includes things you should never do because they are either time-wasters, bad habits or things that hold you back from having a happy and successful life.

A typical to-don't list might include the following:

- Don't watch more than one hour of TV today.
- Don't waste time today on Facebook, Twitter, YouTube, etc.
- Don't envy anyone today.
- Don't make any impulse purchases today.
- Don't gossip today.
- Don't gamble today.
- Don't drink in excess today.
- Don't lose my temper today.
- Don't ignore my family today.
- Don't read negative news articles today.
- Don't procrastinate today.
- Don't ridicule anyone today.
- Don't hate anyone today.
- Don't smoke a cigarette today.
- Don't be negative today.

Each to-don't can be transformed into your own personalised Rich Habit.

***Successful people understand that to-don't lists are just as important as to-do lists.***

They figured out that knowing what not to do is just as important in achieving success as knowing what to do.

Unsuccessful people are not aware of the things they are doing that are holding them back in life.

To-don't lists help keep you aware of the things you should not be doing. To-do's, while a great success tool, only get you half way there. To-don'ts take you the rest of the way. To-don't lists force you to become aware of the things you are doing that might be holding you back in life.

## Summary

Successful people are as much aware of the things they should not be doing as they are of the things they should be doing.

### Michael Yardney's Insight

I've made more money in my life by saying "no" to things than by saying yes to perceived opportunities. But not only do I have a to-don't list regarding business and investment, I have a very long one for my personal life which includes the following:

1. Don't worry — most of the things you worry about will never occur and those that will are likely to seem petty in five years' time.

2. Don't always be right — I've found that often in relationships you can either be right or be happy — so be selective in your battles. There are many roads to the right destination.

3. Don't look at things from a short-term perspective — take a big picture view.

4. Don't follow the crowd — don't do what everyone else is doing, because if you do, at best you'll be average.

5. Don't wait for the perfect time — there will never really be a "right time" for anything in life.

6. Don't wait to start until you know everything — that time will never come. Get started, knowing you don't have all the information, and learn and improve along the way.

7. Don't judge other people — it's easy to jump to conclusions — but that's prejudgment or bias. Instead listen and try to understand the other person's point of view.

8. Don't try to be perfect — sure you should strive for the best, but let go of perfectionism.

9. Don't brood over your mistakes — they're part of growing and learning so don't think of what could have been.

10. Don't ignore your friends and loved ones — after all, your true wealth is what you're left with when they take all your money, property and stocks away.

11. Don't neglect your present joys — this is really the Rich Habit of being grateful.

# CHAPTER 39
# RICH HABIT NUMBER 26

**I will not be afraid to ask questions in order to learn from others.**

The common misconception is that successful people don't ask questions because they already know all the answers.

If someone is perpetually asking questions, the perception goes that they must need to because they're not that smart or knowledgeable. In reality, ***asking questions is the smartest thing you can do*** if you want to succeed in life.

Successful people figured this out long before they ever became successful.

They are obsessed with asking questions. They understand that the information they gain by asking questions is just another way to gain knowledge. To them, asking questions saves them a lot of time in learning new information.

Unsuccessful people are afraid to ask questions.

They fear that by asking questions others may think less of them. As a result, they limit how much they can learn from others.

## Summary

Successful people are not afraid to ask questions. They know that asking questions is an efficient means to gaining knowledge.

**Michael Yardney's Insight**

Successful people share a childhood attribute — they're curious, they ask questions and have a sense of wonder.

# CHAPTER 40
# RICH HABIT NUMBER 27

**I will seek to give my time without any expectation of benefiting.**

Successful people understand that in order to get, you must first give.

It is one of the universal laws of success that has never changed. You must first give value to others if you want to succeed in life.

Unsuccessful people have a me first, you last philosophy.

They want to know what's in it for them before they give their time to anyone. They have a selfish view of the world.

Just look at the board of directors on any non-profit /or charity.

Many of the individuals who run non-profits or charities happen to be successful people. Does that surprise you? It shouldn't.

Birds of a feather like to flock together.

If you want to find out where many of the rich and successful congregate, join a local charity or non-profit. This is one of the avenues the rich use to develop relationships with other success-minded people.

Those relationships often end up doing business together and helping one another thrive and succeed. You won't find many selfish individuals volunteering at charities or non-profits. It goes against their me first, you last philosophy.

## Summary

***Successful people give of their time without any expectation that they will benefit financially.*** They are more interested in improving the lives of others than they are of improving their lives.

# CHAPTER 41
# RICH HABIT NUMBER 28

**I will make an effort to be happy every day.**

One of the problems with happiness is that we have all been programmed to seek happiness, as if it were some goal.

So we go out and buy stuff to make us happy. Purchasing things creates short-term happiness. Eventually that happiness fades away. Meanwhile, the money's gone or the debt has to be paid and that creates unhappiness.

Or we pursue careers that will give us the greatest potential for high compensation because we believe that if we make a lot of money we can purchase happiness with our high earnings. So, we work long hours, slaving away, and over time we realise we are unhappy.

We don't like what we do for a living. When that happens, it really doesn't matter how big our house is, how nice a car we drive or how much stuff we're able to shove down our family's throats.

## Happiness is not a goal

It's a state of mind; a state of being.
The three-step formula for happiness is as follows:

1. **Be first:** Be the person you want to be. If that's happy, be happy for what you have. If that's a writer, become a writer. If that's a business owner, become a business owner. If that's a better father or husband, be a better father or husband.

2. **Do next:** Do the things today that make you the person you want to be. Start expressing gratitude for the things you have today, start writing today, start that business today and start doing things that make you a better father or husband today.

3. **Have:** When you Be and Do, you will eventually get what you desire. If that's happiness, you will have happiness. If that's a career as a writer, you will have that career. If it's your own business, you will have that business. If it's a family that adores you, you will have it.

***Successful people make happiness a daily habit.***

They invest in their long-term happiness by pursuing activities (goals and dreams) that produce long-term happiness down the road. They associate with others who are happy and avoid unhappy people.

They express gratitude for what they have which enables them to focus on the positive rather than focus on the negative — what they lack. They avoid activities that produce short-term happiness because they understand that those activities usually produce long-term unhappiness (i.e. drugs, drinking, etc.).

Unsuccessful people are unhappy and most of those unhappy people will do anything to pursue happiness.

Unfortunately, some of the methods they use to pursue happiness are destructive. Drugs, alcohol, infidelity, gambling and many other vices are examples of activities that unsuccessful people engage in to find temporary happiness. These vices eventually become Poor Habits.

When these Poor Habits no longer bring about their short-term happiness, they tend to move on to another vice, which soon becomes another Poor Habit. This trend often continues for an entire lifetime. It is a destructive trend that causes divorce, job loss, poor health and, ultimately, an unhappy life.

## Some background on Happiness

Various studies have been done on happiness. Sonja Lyubomirsky's research on happiness determined the following:

- 50 per cent of happiness is genetic.

- 40 per cent of happiness comes from activities.
- 10 per cent of happiness is determined by your circumstances.

***Your genetic makeup determines your "happiness baseline".*** This is the baseline you revert to before and after happiness and unhappiness events. This baseline is the reason why buying mega-mansions, expensive cars, jewellery, etc. does not create long-term happiness. It is also the reason why events in your life that make you unhappy, such as the loss of a loved one, divorce and failure do not create long-term unhappiness.

Eventually everyone reverts back to their genetic happiness baseline.

Since only 10 per cent of happiness is circumstance-based, pursuing wealth, as an end to itself, will only increase happiness incrementally. The only true way to increase long-term happiness is to engage in activities that produce happiness.

Here are some strategies and tools that will help you increase your happiness:

- **Manage Expectations** — All too often we look at life through rose coloured glasses. While optimism is critical to success, the biggest cause of unhappiness is not meeting expectations we set for ourselves. What we need, when we pursue a big goal, a dream or our main purpose in life, is a dose of reality.

  When pursuing a big goal, dream or your purpose, you need to break that journey down into manageable tasks that are 100 per cent achievable. This guarantees that you will meet expectations and avoid unhappiness. It also sets you up to surprise yourself by exceeding your expectations, thus creating happiness.

- **Practiced Optimism** — Optimism isn't something you are born with. It needs to become a routine; it needs to become a daily habit. Successful people understand this. They practice optimistic thinking every day. It's part of their daily routine.

Some of the tools they use include:
*Daily Meditation* — two to five minutes each day, morning and night. Visualise realising your dreams and goals. See yourself living your ideal future life.

*Vision Boards* — five to 10 pictures of the things you want in your life. Tape these pictures onto cardboard, a scroll on your desktop or post them where you can view them every day.

*Daily Affirmations* — these represent short statements affirming the realisation of your dreams and goals.

*Cancel Command* — any time a negative thought or emotion enters your mind immediately recognise it and cancel it from your mind before it takes root.

*Scripting Your Future Life* — successful people write out a few paragraphs of what their future, ideal life looks like. They read this script at least once a week. This script keeps them focused on the big picture and keeps them in a positive mindset.

- **Live in the Moment** — Have you ever been at a party, fun event or family gathering and your mind was elsewhere, thinking about work, projects that need to get done, issues you have with people, worrying over your finances, bills, etc.?

  What a waste of a good happiness event! Living in the moment means clearing your mind of all thoughts and enjoying the moment, enjoying the present.

  ***When you live in the moment, you create a happiness event.*** When you allow other thoughts to interfere with a happiness event, you lose that happiness event forever.

- **Overcome One Fear** — Overcoming fear alters your thinking. It will reprogram your mind from negative to positive. It will increase your level of confidence.

Doing something that scares you will take you out of your comfort zone and make you anxious and nervous. It will also exhilarate you. Human beings were not intended to be slaves to our fears. Our core fears reside in the limbic system portion of our brains.

The neocortex, the most recent evolutionary portion of our brain, has the ability to consciously overcome our fears. When you take on a fear, both parts of the brain begin to compete against each other.

The neocortex is far superior in terms of size. It has billions more neurons than the limbic system. It can easily overcome any fear. Become the master of fear and not its slave and you will experience happiness.

- **Mentor Others** — Mentorship is a two-way street. The benefits accrue on both sides. Mentors learn from those they mentor. They create devoted, cult-like followers. They benefit financially — mentors and their mentees often work together.

  But more importantly, the act of mentoring others is a happiness activity. It creates happiness for both parties.

- **Volunteer** — When you volunteer, you are giving back to your community. You also get to meet new people and grow stronger relationships. Volunteers derive an emotional satisfaction in helping others inside their community. Volunteering is a happiness activity.

- **Exercise** — Exercising is a happiness activity. While the activity itself is not a happiness event, when completed, it creates a feeling of overall happiness. We feel happy because we've done something that is good for our body. The more you exercise, the happier you will be.

- **Learn Something New** — Believe it or not, learning something new will make you happier. When we learn something new, the brain creates new neural synapses (connections), and this neural stimulation creates a physiological feeling of self-satisfaction and increased confidence. We simply feel better about ourselves.

This is not an accident.

These physiological feelings of happiness are the brain's way of rewarding us for engaging in good brain behaviour. The brain's secondary purpose (the first being to keep us alive) is to learn. When we learn new things, we actually increase the mass of our brain (new synapses = new mass). The brain is one of the very few internal organs whose mass increases by use. The more we engage in learning, the more the brain will reward us with feelings of happiness.

Each time you learn something new, therefore, you are creating a happiness event. Devote 20 to 30 minutes each day, reading something that will help you on the job or increase your knowledge in some hobby or passion you might have. Learn and be happy.

- **Meditate** — Meditation is good brain management. It's like a vacation for the brain. It reduces stress, triggers the creative forces within our subconscious and increases telomerase (an enzyme that keeps telomeres healthy. Telomeres close off each chromosome's DNA. When telomeres fray, cells die. This is why we age. Our cells stop dividing and die and this leads to aging). If you've never meditated, set a goal of meditating for 60 seconds every day in the morning, immediately after waking up, or at night, right before bedtime. It will make you feel more relaxed and induce a state of happiness. Every time you meditate it is a happiness activity.
- **Practice Gratitude** — Have you ever noticed some people are always upbeat, positive, enthusiastic and seem happy? ***Being in a positive, upbeat emotional state fosters happiness.*** You may think some are just genetically predisposed to be this way, but you'd be wrong. Wealthy, successful people have certain happiness habits that create this positive mindset. Somewhere along the line these successful people discovered one of the secrets to happiness: practicing gratitude.

There is always something to be grateful for. Practicing gratitude, every day, provides a reality check on our lives. It stops negative thinking in its tracks. It changes our thinking from negative to positive. When we force ourselves to reflect daily on all of the blessings we have in life (health, a job, a home, a family, friends, etc.), it stops us from thinking about all the things we don't have, and this changes our perspective.

A prerequisite for success and happiness in life is to function from a positive mindset. Every day express gratitude for five things you are grateful for in life. Create an attitude of daily gratitude and, in time, you will add another happiness activity to your life. The more happiness activities you engage in, the more happiness you create.

- **Associate With Other Happy People** — Birds of a feather flock together. If you want to be happier you need to associate with other happy people. You need to spend a minimum of one hour a week with other happy people. You also need to reduce the time you spend with unhappy people to less than one hour per week.

  When you make new acquaintances with other happy people, they will, in time, introduce you to their relationships, who also happen to be other happy people. The more happy people you associate with in life, the happier you will be.

- **Laugh** — The more you laugh, the happier you become. ***Laughter reduces stress and pain.*** It also fires up brain cells.

  Much like aerobic activity, laughter increases blood flow throughout the body. It boosts your immune system by creating infection-fighting antibodies and laughter triggers the release of endorphins, which promote a sense of well-being.

  Every day read, listen to or watch something that makes you laugh. Start out your day with a good laugh. It's like a form of meditation that's also fun and easy.

- **Pursue Dreams and Goals** — Pursuing a dream and the goals behind the dream creates happiness. Research shows that we are genetically engineered to be goal-oriented.

When we pursue a new goal we activate existing brain cells or create new brain cell connections (synapses). New dendrites and synapses form inside the brain when we pursue a goal. The brain likes this and releases certain neurochemicals that create a feeling of pleasure or happiness as we learn new things in pursuit of our goal.

Every time you learn something new in pursuit of your goal, you trigger a happiness event. This physiology is why those who pursue goals consider the pursuit of a goal or dream more gratifying than the actual achievement of the goal or realisation of the dream.

- **Do Something Creative** — Human beings were intended to be creative. It's hardwired into our DNA. ***Creative pursuits unleash our inner genius.*** We all have the creative gene. When we pursue anything creative, it triggers positive emotions and creates new neural pathways.

  Our brains like it when we create new neural pathways, so it rewards us with an infusion of neurochemicals that produce a feeling of euphoria. Every time we engage in a creative pursuit, we are engaging in a happiness activity.

- **Pursue a Major Purpose or Something You Love** — Most people are not following their own main purpose in life. They are following someone else's. It may be a main purpose of a mother, father, spouse or some other significant presence in their life. When you are not following your main purpose, you are not happy.

  You do not look forward to Mondays or any other work day. You see life as drudgery and anxiously await the weekends, holidays and vacation time. You pursue post-work activities that are often unhealthy, such as excessive alcohol consumption. You are often mired in negative, depressed thoughts. That's not what life intended for you.

  Life intended that each of us pursue our own individual main purpose. Doing so awakens our inner genius and stimulates the creative parts of our brain that make humans so unique. You will not be happy and successful in life pursuing someone else's agenda. You need to pursue your own agenda; you need to follow your own individual main purpose in life.

## Summary

Successful people pursue activities that create happiness.

# CHAPTER 42
# RICH HABIT NUMBER 29

**I will train others how to treat me.**

Successful people understand that if you want to be respected and be treated properly by others you must train them to respect and treat you properly.

They do not let other people walk all over them. They say no more than they say yes. They train people to treat them with respect. They train others to value their time.

Unsuccessful people allow others to walk all over them. Because they have low self-esteem and do not value their time like successful people, they allow others to abuse them.

Here are a few guidelines for training others to treat you with the respect you deserve:

- Stop saying yes to everything. Saying no sends a message that your time is valuable. The occasional no lets others know that they cannot walk all over you. It takes courage to say no.

  Don't let fear hold you back. No is like a stop sign that says "I am not your slave". Saying yes to everything is another sign that says "I am your slave". ***Saying yes all the time trains others to walk all over you.***

- Don't give into others just to get along. Surrendering all of your time to the will of others sends a powerful message that you are weak. Be obstinate every now and then.

It lets others know that you are a force to be reckoned with, that you are strong and confident. Giving in trains others that you are weak.

- Don't vacillate. Stand your ground on things you believe in. If you constantly change your mind or allow others to change your opinion, you send a message that you can be manipulated. You train others to manipulate you.

## Summary

Successful people train others how to treat them.

### Michael Yardney's Insight

Confucius taught us: "Respect yourself and others will respect you."

# CHAPTER 43
# RICH HABIT NUMBER 30

**I will seek to find apostles to help me achieve my goals and realise my dreams.**

Steve Jobs had Steve Wozniak.
Bill Gates had Paul Allen.
Warren Buffet had Charlie Munger.
Jack Canfield had Mark Victor Hansen.

***Self-made millionaires don't get there on their own.*** The greatest wealth accumulation occurs through the pursuit and realisation of a dream. And almost 100 per cent of the time it requires a team effort.

Those individuals who are able to elevate themselves from ordinary to self-made millionaire status are the ones who have found their apostles — fanatics who share their dream and their passion for that dream.

Probably the most famous individual who found the yang to their yin was Jesus Christ. He actually found 12 apostles to help him spread his important message and his cause. Jesus succeeded, not simply because of the importance of his message, but because he found 12 others who also believed in his message and his cause. If it were not for his apostles, the world would not know about Jesus or his message.

Successful people are able to put together a team of one or more individuals who buy into their dream and their goals.

They are able to find individuals who commit themselves 100 per cent to their cause.

Successful people understand that finding apostles to their cause turns dreams into reality.

Unsuccessful people are not very good at building teams to help them succeed in life. They go it alone and hope for success.

But finding apostles is not an easy thing to do.

Most people who will be drawn to your cause won't become apostles. It's hard to find people who will commit themselves 100 per cent to your dream.

Most everyone you will find are pursuing their own initiatives, projects, dreams and goals. You have to keep searching to find your apostles. But it's worth the effort. You don't need 12. Just one apostle is all you need to make the magic happen.

Anyone who's struggled in finding their yang knows it's a very difficult and frustrating journey.

The right apostles are those who commit to your dream. They become fanatics to your cause. Their commitment is 100 per cent. Finding your "apostles" means you've found a team who will all pull the same cart. Apostles will have a single-minded focus; they will all be devoted to turning your dream into a reality.

## Summary

The realisation of your dream grows exponentially for every apostle that joins your team. Ordinary people become self-made millionaires when they find their apostles.

### Michael Yardney's Insight

Tom and I practice this Rich Habit regularly and an excellent example of it is our collaboration for this book. We've learned that alone we can run faster, but together we can run further.

# CHAPTER 44
# SUMMARY OF THE RICH HABITS

So now you know the 30 Rich Habits that can change your life with a little effort and commitment to change. Here they are again in a summarised format to help you make them part of your life — right now!

1. I WILL adopt good daily habits and follow these good daily habits every day.

2. I WILL define my dreams and then create goals around each dream. I will focus on my dream-goals every day.

3. I WILL devote at least 30 minutes each day to increasing my knowledge and improving my skills. I will invest in myself every day.

4. I WILL devote 30 minutes to exercise every day. I will eat healthy food every day.

5. I WILL seek to build strong relationships with other success-minded people.

6. I WILL live every day in a state of moderation.

7. I WILL take action on my goals every day.

8. I WILL engage in Rich Thinking every day.

9. I WILL save ten per cent of my income and live off the remaining 90 per cent.

10. I WILL control my words and emotions every day.

11. I WILL do work that I love.

12. I WILL never quit on my dreams.
13. I WILL embrace only positive beliefs and eliminate all negative beliefs.
14. I WILL seek out success mentors.
15. I WILL focus on my dreams and my goals every day.
16. I WILL set only good goals and avoid bad goals.
17. I WILL not fear risk. I will take risks that help me achieve my goals and realise my dreams.
18. I WILL exercise patience every day.
19. I WILL seek to exceed the expectations of others.
20. I WILL create multiple streams of income.
21. I WILL use the power of leverage to help me achieve my goals and realise my dreams.
22. I WILL not allow fear or doubt to prevent me from taking action on my goals and dreams.
23. I WILL seek feedback from others.
24. I WILL ask for what I want or what I need.
25. I WILL make my own personalised to-don't list and follow it every day.
26. I WILL ask questions in order to learn from others.
27. I WILL seek to give to those deserving of my time without any expectation of benefiting.
28. I WILL make an effort to be happy every day.
29. I WILL train others how to treat me.
30. I WILL seek to find apostles to help me achieve my goals and realise my dreams.

# CHAPTER 45
# YOU REALLY MUST UNDERSTAND THESE 4 PATHS TO WEALTH

One of the most profound discoveries I made in my five-year Rich Habits Study was the fact that there are four paths to wealth:

1. Saver/Investor Path
2. Big Company Climber Path
3. Virtuoso Path
4. Dreamer/Entrepreneur Path

Why is this so revolutionary?

Everyone inherits certain genes from their parents, which helps shape their personality. Also, everyone is raised in different environments – we are all raised in different households, in different neighbourhoods, go to different schools, etc. Our unique genes and upbringing help to shape the individuals we become as adults.

For example, some people are outgoing, others shy. Some are risk takers, others risk averse. Some can shoulder great stress without affecting their health and relationships; others crumble under too much stress.

You see, everyone is different and because everyone is different, their path to accumulating wealth must be in alignment with their particular personality.

A shy, risk averse, anxious individual would find the life of a Dreamer/Entrepreneur or Big Company Climber ill-suited for their personality. Most likely, they would probably hate being in either of those two work environments. Such individuals would be better suited pursuing wealth by following the Saver/Investor or Virtuoso Path. Either path would work best for them, given their personality type.

Likewise, outgoing individuals who love high-risk challenges and seem immune to stress, are perfectly suited for the Big Company Climber Path or the Dreamer/Entrepreneur Path. If these individuals worked in a back-office job, they would likely hate their job.

Because there are four paths to wealth, it is critical for those who seek wealth to understand which path is right for them.

If you pick the wrong path, success will be elusive. Most people, unfortunately, choose the wrong path.

According to a 2012 survey conducted by "Big 4" accounting firm Deloitte, 80% of those surveyed did not like their jobs. In another survey conducted by Gallup in 2013, 63% of the 230,000 employees in the survey said they were unhappy with their jobs.

In my Rich habits Study, 97% of the poor in my Study said that they did not like their job and 58% said they actually hated their job. I believe many of the poor are poor because they are doing work that does not suit their particular personality-types. They hate the work they do because they are on the wrong path to wealth.

When you don't like what you do for a living, you'll do the bare minimum, just to keep your job. You certainly won't devote extracurricular time to becoming better at a job you hate.

I also learned from my Study that 86% of the wealthy liked their job and that 7% loved their job. One of the main reasons these individuals became rich was because they were doing work that fit their personality profile. When you love what you do for a living, you'll devote more time to becoming better at what you do.

So let's look at these 4 paths in more detail…

## Path #1 Saver-Investor Path

The Saver-Investor millionaires in my Rich Habits Study forged the habit of paying themselves first and learning to live off what's left. The first bill they paid was the fixed percentage of net income they saved with every pay cheque.

When you make a decision to save first, this forces you to reduce your cost of living, so that you are able to reach your goal of saving 20% or more of your net pay. This allows you to put your savings to work by prudently and consistently investing those savings, thus growing your wealth.

The typical saver-investor in my study accumulated an average of $3,260,000 over an average of 32 years.

This path does not require any unique set of skills, special knowledge, significant risks or oppressive work hours or isolating you from your family and friends. The Saver-Investor Path is not only the easiest path to building wealth, but it's also the guaranteed path to building wealth.

1. **Middle-Class Income:** It's hard to save when you are poor. Most of the poor are barely able to meet the costs of even a low standard of living. But, if you have a middle-class income and keep your standard of living low, this will give you the ability to save.

2. **Discipline:** The typical Saver-Investor saves 20% or more of their income and lives off what's left. This requires discipline in saving first and discipline in minimising how much money you spend.

3. **Consistency:** Saver-Investors consistently save and consistently invest their savings so that their wealth can grow every year.

4. **Time:** It takes an average of 32 years for a Saver-Investor to accumulate their wealth.

This path requires that you start early – almost immediately upon entering the adult work force. If you start later in life, and still desire to retire wealthy, you will have to increase your savings rate by 10% for every ten years you failed to save. And you will have to work longer.

For example, if you decide to pursue the Saver-Investor Path in your mid-thirties, you will have to increase your annual saving to 30% of your net income and work into your mid-sixties. If you start in your mid-forties, you will have to increase your annual savings to 40% of net income and work into your mid-seventies.

***Personality Traits of Savers Investors***

- Risk Averse: Saver-Investors have a low risk tolerance. They are unwilling to take risks they deem to be too great.

- Balance Work-Life: They are unwilling to work excessive work hours. They prefer a balanced approach to their lives. They desire to have and to spend their free time with family and friends. They derive their happiness from people, not things. They stick with one, two or three employers their entire lives.

- Disciplined: Saver-Investors have a financial plan that they follow and they stick to it. They are disciplined in saving and investing their money over many years. Many use budgets and financial plans to help them stick to the savings and investment plan. They begin their savings and investment plan early in life, usually in their mid to late 20s.

- Frugal: They spend their money wisely. They seek the best product of service at the lowest price. They avoid Want Spending, Emotionally-Driven Spontaneous Spending, Supersizing Their Life, Peer Pressure Spending and Lifestyle Creep.

- Modest Standard of Living: Their standard of living is modest, allowing them to save and invest 20% or more of their net income. Their homes, cars and vacation spending are modest. They are uninterested in accumulating things or buying expensive things. Things have little meaning or value to them. They place a higher value on their time than on things: they prefer to spend their non-work time with family and friends.

- Debt Averse: Saver-Investors avoid accumulating debt. They pay off their mortgages early. They avoid using credit cards or accumulating any credit card debt. They buy high-quality used cars for cash or with the small car loans, which they pay off early.

- Low Stress Tolerance: They are averse to stress. They seek out jobs that have a low degree of stress. They are happy being a cog in the wheel where they work and, therefore, are not interested in seeking positions that carry with it burdensome responsibilities or additional stress. They are happy with doing their job and receiving a pay cheque for the work they perform.

**Common Rich Habits of Savers Investors**

- I Will Save and Invest My Income: Saver-Investors, more than any class of self-made millionaires, forge the Rich Habit of consistently saving 20% or more of their net income. This enabled them to then prudently invest their savings over many years. To help them save and invest, Saver-Investors used a strategy I call the Bucket System. They use the Bucket System to help them identify specific savings priorities and then devoted a percentage of their savings to each bucket: Wedding, First Home, Emergency Fund, College Savings, Investments, Retirement, etc.

- I Will Live Each Day in a State of Moderation: Saver-Investors, more than any class of self-made millionaires, forge the Rich Habit of living their lives in moderation. They do nothing in excess, except spend time with family and friends.

- I Will Never Quit on My Dreams: No matter what happened in their lives, they never quit on their dream of saving and investing their way to becoming self-made millionaires.

- I Will Focus on my Dreams and Goals Every Day: The Dream for Saver-Investors self-made millionaires is to save and invest their way to wealth. The goals they used to manufacture that dream were:

    - Frugal Spending/Modest Standard of Living: Saver-Investors focus like a laser, every day, on frugally spending their money so that they can create a standard of living that allows them to save and invest 20% or more of their net income.

  - Invest Consistently: Saver-Investors consistently invest their savings. This consistency allows them to take advantage of Dollar Cost Averaging and helps them consistently build their wealth over many years.

- I Will Take Calculated Risks: Many of the Saver-Investors in my Rich Habits Study were what I call "Home Depot Investors" – they did their own investing. This requires that they do their homework before making any investment. They often relied upon financial advisors to help provide them with information to enable them to select suitable investments. The Non-Home Depot Investors relied upon financial planners or financial advisors in crafting and implementing an investment plan. They regularly communicated with their financial advisors – they devoted about 3-4 hours every month in discussions with their financial advisors.

- I Will Ask Questions in Order to Learn From Others: Saver-Investors ask their financial advisors many questions regarding their investments: investment-related questions, tax-planning questions, legal questions, questions regarding the fees of various investments.

- I Will Create Multiple Streams of Income: Over the course of their lives, Saver-Investors created multiple revenue streams: Interest Income, Dividend Income, Annuity Income, Rental Income and Capital Gain Income.

- I Will Seek Feedback From Others: Saver-Investors often rely on financial experts to help them select their investments.

- Law of Association: Saver-Investors surround themselves with other Saver-Investors. Because habits spread like a virus throughout your social networks, it's important for Saver-Investors to limit their exposure to individuals who do not share their Saver-Investor mindset: Risk averse, frugal spending, consistently saving money, prudently investing their savings, maintaining a modest standard of living.

- Frugal With Their Money: Saver-Investors have forged the Rich Habit of seeking the highest quality product or service and the lowest price.

## Path #2 Big Company Climber Path

Big Company Climbers are individuals who work for a big company and spend their entire careers climbing the company ladder until they reach the upper echelons – senior executive status.

Many of the Big Company Climbers in my Rich Habits Study worked for large publicly-held companies but many also worked for non-public, privately-held companies, such as large medical groups, large CPA firms, large engineering companies, large law firms and other large companies.

In my Rich Habits Study, it took Climbers about 22 years to accumulate an average Net Worth of $3.4 million. Much of that wealth came from either stock compensation or a partnership share of profits.

**Requirements**

- Long Work Hours: Like the Dreamers, Climbers have to work long hours. Most Climbers have to travel regularly. Airports, hotel rooms and taxis become a way of life. And very often, Climbers have to work during weekends and on vacations.

- Political Expertise: Besides the hard work, Climbers must possess expert political skills. Those who do are able to outmanoeuvre their internal competitors – other Climbers, biting at their heels and stabbing them in the back, as opportunities present themselves. There is always some other Climber seeking to undermine you to advance their personal agenda, which is usually the same as yours – climbing further up the company ladder.

- Power Relationships: Climbers need mad relationship-building skills. Those who succeed in reaching the upper echelons of a big company are almost certainly the best at building relationships, both within the organisation they work for and within their industry. Building these strong, powerful relationships, however, takes time, energy and money: frequent phone calls, constant entertainment, attending weddings, birthday parties or funerals and sending thoughtful cards for special occasions. Just managing all those Power Relationships can take up a big part of your workday.

- Risk: Like the Dreamer Path, the Climber Path has some unique risks. If the company struggles financially, for whatever reason, your time investment in that company may not be rewarded, to the extent you expected.

**Personality Traits of Big Company Climbers**

- Embrace Formal Education: Big Company Climbers have, at a minimum, a college degree. Some have advanced degrees, such as MBAs, specific Graduate Degrees and some even have PhDs.
- Embrace Self-Education: They devote thirty minutes or more every day to self-education. They read industry-related periodicals, blogs and books. They are students of their industry and the field they work in.
- Political: Big Company Climbers are very political within their company and industry. Their political savvy enables them to climb the ladder within their company or industry. They built strategic alliances with higher-up Influencers within their company and industry, in the hopes that those relationships will pay dividends in the form of promotions or senior executive job offers. They can withstand the political back-stabbing that is common in many large organisations. They devote part of every day to building and maintaining their relationships with their Influencers.
- Strong Work Ethic: They are willing to work oppressive work hours in an effort to climb to company ladder. They are willing to travel often on company business, which takes them away from family and friends. They prioritise work over family and friends. Work comes first for Big Company Climbers.
- High Stress Tolerance: Big Company Climbers have an innate or leaned ability to handle high degrees of stress.
- High Risk Tolerance: They are willing to take risks in an effort to climb the company ladder. They will take on high level projects and increased responsibilities in an effort to elevate their status within their company. They are willing to take the risk of the downsides

of these projects/responsibilities – failing to meet expectations of others within the organisation. They will devote their work lives to one organization, knowing that their future wealth depends on the success of that organisation. If the company struggles, or fails, they struggle or fail. They put all of their eggs in one basket – the company they work for.

- Outgoing and Sociable: They enjoy working in teams and with people. They are gregarious and outgoing individuals. They enjoy socialising with others. They draw their energy from the people they work with. They enjoy speaking and presenting to both small and large groups.

- Competitive: Big Company climbers thrive in competitive environments. They very much enjoy competing with others. They have a winner-takes-all mindset.

**Strategy – How Big-Company Climbers Make Themselves UN-FIREABLE**

I uncovered three career-related strategies that successful Big Company Climbers in my rich Habits Study used in order to make themselves indispensable to their employers:

1. **Daily Self-Education Reading.** As I mentioned above, Big Company Climbers devote a minimum of thirty minutes every day to growing and maintaining their knowledge-base with respect to their career and industry. Their daily self-education reading helped to make them among the most knowledgeable not only within their company, but also within their industry.

2. **Writing.** Thirty-eight percent of the Big Company Climbers in my rich Habits Study engaged in some form of consistent career-related writing, with 18% devoting time to writing for industry-related magazines/blogs. Writing is a form of communication. Because you are writing on a specific topic, you must gain a more comprehensive understanding of that topic than reading alone can provide. Successful individuals engage in writing in a number of ways including: company newsletters, industry newsletters, newspaper articles, industry publication articles, Internet articles

and customer/client letters and blogs. Writing helps you get noticed in your industry and fosters the perception of you as an expert. The knowledge you gain from writing increases your value to your employer, customers or clients.

3. **Speaking.** Twenty-three percent of the Big Company Climbers engaged in career-related speaking, with 12% speaking at trade group/industry functions. Speaking, like writing, is a form of communication. It requires a greater understanding of a subject matter than reading or writing alone can provide.

In a speaking engagement you may be asked questions and this forces you to a higher level of topic comprehension – when you are "the expert" on a speaking topic, you must fully comprehend that topic inside and out, in order to be prepared to accurately respond accurately to many questions.

Speaking requires a more detailed study that reading and writing, together, cannot provide. Speaking forces you to dig deeper and expand your knowledge-base. Speaking elevates your perceived expertise in the eyes of your audience, who may be fellow supervisors, customers, clients, or senior executives at competing companies.

Utilising one or more of the career-related, self-improvement strategies will make you more valuable within your industry and indispensable to your employer, customers or clients. When you are perceived as indispensable you become UN-FIREABLE.

**Common Rich Habits of Big Company Climbers**

- I Will Adopt Good Habits: Big Company Climbers make a concerted effort to self-assess their good and bad habits. This helps them to "know thyself", which is a key to growing into the person you need to become in order for success to visit you.
- I will Define My Dreams: AKA Dream-Setting. They created a vision for where they wanted to be in ten or twenty years. This vision became their blueprint, which helped them to create the life of their dreams.

- I Will Devote at Least 30 Minutes Each Day to Self-Education: Big Company Climbers devote 30 minutes or more every day to reading to learn. Typically they focused their reading on material that was directly related to their company, industry or job.

- I Will Devote 30 Minutes or More to Daily Exercise: They exercise every day. Their core exercise is aerobic exercise, but many also engage in weights and/or resistance exercises.

- I Will Seek to Build Strong Powerful Relationships with Influencers: Big Company Climbers devote a significant amount of their available time in building and maintaining strong relationships with Influencers within their company and industry.

- I Will Control My Words and Emotions: Because there is a great deal of stress during their climb up the big company ladder, Big Company Climbers are required to forge the Rich Habit of controlling their words and emotions. Losing your temper and saying something you regret can very quickly destroy a career built over many years.

- I Will Create Goals Around My Dreams: They create goals around each one of their dreams.

- I Will Engage in Positive Thinking Every Day: Big Company Climbers are upbeat and optimistic. This enables them to see solutions to problems and overcome obstacles.

- I Will Seek Out Success Mentors: Mentors are the fast-track to success. Mentors help teach Big Company Climbers what works and what doesn't work. Mentors also infect Big Company Climbers with their good habits.

- I Will Never Quit on My Dreams: They do not quit on their dreams and goals. They stick to them for many years. They understand that climbing the ladder in a big company takes a long time and they are willing to do what it takes to climb that ladder.

- I Will Seek to Meet or Exceed the Expectations of Others: Big Company Climbers seek to meet or exceeding the expectations of their supervisors or those who rely on them. This helps build trust in and faith in their abilities.
- I Will Not Allow Fear or Doubt to Stop Me from My Goals and Dreams: They take risks others are unwilling to take. They take on additional responsibilities, important projects or help lead major initiatives. As they succeed, they are recognised and promoted throughout their careers.
- I Will Seek Feedback from Others: In an effort to improve their performance, Big Company Climbers regularly seek feedback about their performance from those they work with, supervisors and customers/clients.
- I Wil Ask Questions in Order to Learn From Others: In an effort to learn from others within their organisation, Big Company Climbers are not afraid to ask questions from those they work with, experts within their company or industry or their supervisors.
- I Will Train Others How to Treat Me: Big Company Climbers understand that true leaders are respected. That respect must often be earned but it also must be demanded of others.

## Path #3 Virtuoso Path

When you are a Virtuoso, it means you are among the top experts in your industry or field. That expertise may be knowledge-based or skill-based. Virtuosos are paid a high premium for their expertise. That high premium means they can earn more money than their non-Virtuoso peers.

**Requirements**

- Significant Investment: Becoming a Virtuoso requires an enormous investment in time, and often money. Knowledge-based Virtuosos spend many years in continuous study. Oftentimes, this requires formal education, such as advanced degrees (PhD, Medical Degrees,

Law Degrees, etc.). Skill-based Virtuosos devote themselves to many years of deliberate practice and analytical practice. Deliberate practice requires thousands of hours honing your skills. Analytical practice often requires the services of a coach, mentor or expert who can provide immediate feedback. This feedback, in most cases, costs money.

- Long Hours: Like the Dreamer and Climber, the Virtuoso has to work long hours, not only in perfecting their knowledge or skills, but also in maintaining and using them. Virtuosos are rare and, therefore, in high demand. That high demand means many long hours serving the needs of others in exchange for money.

**Personality Traits of Knowledge-Based Virtuosos**

- Embrace Formal Education: Like the Big Company Climbers, Knowledge-Based Virtuosos have, at a minimum, a college degree. Most have one or more advanced degrees, such as Master's Degrees or PhDs.

- Embrace Self-Education: Virtuosos devote two hour or more, every day, to self-education. They read industry-related periodicals, blogs and books. They are students of their industry and the field they work in.

- Low Stress Tolerance: Knowledge-Based Virtuosos have a low stress tolerance. They prefer calm, peace and quiet to perform at their best.

- Introverted: Most Virtuosos are happiest at work when working alone or in isolation. They do not enjoy socialising as they see it as a time-waster. They do not enjoy speaking to small or large groups, but often must engage in this activity, as others seek out their knowledge and expertise.

- Strong Concentration and Focus: Knowledge-Based Virtuosos have innate or developed strong powers of concentration and focus. They can devote many hours at a time to concentrated study and analysis. They have very disciplined minds.

- Non-Competitive: Most Knowledge-Based Virtuosos do not enjoy competition very much.

**Personality Traits of Skill-Based Virtuosos**

- Embrace Formal Education: Certain Skill-Based Virtuosos, such as Surgeons, Engineers and Scientists have, at a minimum, a college degree. Most have one or more advanced degrees, such as Master's Degrees or PhDs.

- Embrace Daily Practice: Skill-Based Virtuosos practice their craft a minimum of three to four hours a day. They engage in two distinct types of practice:

    - Deliberate Practice – Practicing their skills or subsets of their skills repeatedly to improve or maintain such skills.

    - Analytical Practice – Practicing under the watchful eyes of a coach or mentor who provides detailed feedback regarding their performance.

- High Stress Tolerance: Because their success is dependent upon their performance, Skill-Based Virtuosos have an innate or highly developed high tolerance for stress. In fact, many Skill-Based virtuosos thrive under stress, meaning their performance improves when they are under stress.

- Innate Talent: Many Skill-Based Virtuosos were born with one or more unique innate talents, which they discovered early in life and to which they devoted their lives to perfecting, through daily practice. The most successful Skill-Based Virtuosos have complimentary talents that they use in their profession.

- Strong Concentration and Focus: Skill-Based Virtuosos can practice for long hours at a stretch due to their strong powers of concentration and focus. They have very disciplined minds.

- Highly Competitive: Skill-Based Virtuosos thrive in competitive environments. They have a winner-takes-all mindset.

- Creative: Skill-Based Virtuosos are creative. This enables them to develop new or unique skills or modify/improve existing skills.

**Common Rich Habits of Virtuosos**

- I Will Define My Dreams and Create Goals Around Each Dream (Dream-Setting): Virtuosos have a plan. They know where they want to be ten, 20 years into the future. Because they have a clear vision of where they are going, they are willing to put in the work and have forged growth habits to help them automate their continuous growth in knowledge or skills.
- I will Devote Time Each Day to Daily Self-Improvement: Knowledge-Based Virtuosos engage in a minimum of two hours a day to self-education to maintain and grow their knowledge-base. Skill-Based Virtuosos devote three to four hours a day to Deliberate and Analytical Practice.
- I Will Save and Invest Part of My Income: Like the Saver-Investors, most Knowledge-Based Virtuosos forge the Rich Habit of consistently saving 20% or more of their net income. This enables them to then prudently invest their savings over many years.
- I Will Take Action on My Goals Every Day: Virtuoso goals include daily education and/or practice. They have specific goals they are pursuing which will make them more knowledgeable or expert in what they do.
- I Will Live Each Day in a State of Moderation: Knowledge-based Virtuosos live fairly modest lifestyles, which allows them to save and invest.
- I Will Do Work That I Like or Love: Virtuoso's, second only to Dreamer-Entrepreneurs, like or love what they do for a living, especially Skill-based Virtuosos.
- I Will Never Quit on My Dreams: It takes many years for Virtuosos to become expert in what they do. This requires persistence and a Never Quit mindset.

- I Will Seek Out Success Mentors: Virtuosos typically have success mentors they have apprenticed for or expert coaches who help provide them with guidance and feedback.
- I Will Focus on My Goals and Dreams: The Virtuoso path requires an ability to focus many hours each day, for many years. Virtuosos do not allow themselves to be distracted by anything which would interfere with their intense desire to stay focused on their goals and dreams.
- I Will Maintain and Improve my Knowledge-Base Through Writing: Many Knowledge-Based Virtuosos write for industry trade magazines/publications. Some also share their knowledge on blogs and the media. This helps to boost their personal brand and Virtuoso status.
- I Will Maintain and Improve my Knowledge-base Through Speaking: Many Virtuosos are professional speakers. They share their expertise with thousands of people every year at conferences and industry-related events. This helps to boost their personal brand and Virtuoso status.
- I Will Devote 30 Minutes or More to Daily Exercise: Most Skill-Based Virtuosos exercise daily to maintain their physical strength and health, which enables them to perform their skills optimally.
- I Will Control My Words and Emotions Every Day: Virtuosos understand that in order to effectively work with others, including customers/clients, they must control their emotions. No one wants to work with or do business with individuals who lose their temper or are emotionally unstable.
- I Will Seek to Meet or Exceed the Expectations of Others: Virtuosos are Virtuosos because they desire to be the best at what they do. The desire to meet or exceed the expectations of others drives them to grow and improve in their knowledge and/or skills.
- I Will Seek Feedback From Others: Virtuosos seek feedback from supervisors, mentors, customers/clients and others in order to become better at what they do.

- I Will Ask Questions in Order to Learn From Others: Virtuosos ask a lot of questions. They do this in order to learn, grow and improve.
- I Will Seek to Add Value to Others: The very reason Virtuosos are the highest paid within their industry is their desire to add value to the lives of those they serve.

## Path #4 Dreamer-Entrepreneur Path

Pursuing a dream can be the most rewarding thing you ever do, not only in terms of personal fulfillment but also in terms of financial success.

The Dreamer/Entrepreneurs in my study liked or loved what they did for a living and that passion showed up in their bank accounts. This group of self-made millionaires had an average Net Worth of $7.4 million, far more than any other group of millionaires in my study. But that higher wealth came at a cost.

**Requirements**

- Long Work Hours: The Dreamer/Entrepreneurs in my study worked an average of 61 hours a week, for 12 years. Weekend and vacations were almost non-existent. Those long work hours impacted everyone in the Dreamer's immediate orbit. Family and friends are hit the hardest by their absence. Often one spouse must take up the slack and raise their children, almost as if they were a single parent. Close friendships whither on the vine, due to those long work hours.
- Financial Stress: Until the Dream begins to pay off, making ends meet can cause almost intolerable stress. Only the strong can survive that stress and that includes the spouses. In the early going, getting a steady pay cheque is near impossible. Weak marriages will almost certainly fall apart, due to this stress.
- High Risk: Dreamers have to put everything they own on the line. Their homes, retirement plans, and savings become the assets that breathes life into their Dream. When a Dreamer runs out of assets, they have no choice but to turn to debt to continue to finance their Dream.

The lucky ones can secure Lines of Credit to keep them afloat. The unlucky ones are forced to rely on credit cards or loans from family and friends to survive until they thrive. If they thrive. Pursuing a Dream is a gamble. There's absolutely no guarantee that the Dream will every pay off.

Many fail. In fact, 27% in my Rich Habits Study failed at least once. Failure can mean bankruptcy. Sometimes that bankruptcy is followed by divorce.

**Personality Traits of Dreamer-Entrepreneurs**

- High Risk Tolerance: Entrepreneurs are willing to take risks most would run away from. They develop this risk-fearlessness by taking calculated risks, which are well thought-out risks. They also develop this risk-fearlessness by surviving risks taken. Taking risks forces growth. This growth gives Entrepreneurs valuable knowledge and insight as to what works and what doesn't work.

- Highly Competitive: Entrepreneurs thrive in competitive environments. They have a winner-takes-all mindset.

- High Stress Tolerance: Entrepreneurs have an either innate or highly developed ability to shoulder great stress.

- Strong Work Ethic: Entrepreneurs are willing to work oppressive work hours in an effort to succeed in realising their dreams. They are willing to travel often on company business, which takes them away from family and friends. They prioritise work over family and friends. Work comes first for Entrepreneurs.

- Good Multi-Taskers: They have an either innate or highly developed ability to juggle many things at one time. They are very good at switching from one task to another, almost seamlessly.

- Creative: Entrepreneurs are highly creative. This creativity allows them to solve numerous problems and overcome many obstacles.

**Common Rich Habits of Dreamers/Entrepreneurs**

- I Will Forge Success Habits: As a general rule, Entrepreneurs forge good habits. Their dreams and goals force them to acquire specific habits that enable them to grow, stay healthy, build relationships and acquire knowledge and/or skills that help them to succeed.
- I Will Build Strong Powerful Relationships with Influencers: They devote more time to building and maintaining relationships with powerful influencers than any other category of self-made millionaire. For Entrepreneurs, power relationships are their currency. Forging and maintaining power relationships is, second only to persistence, one of the main drivers of their success.
- I Will Dream-Set: Entrepreneurs follow a clear vision that they mapped out long before becoming wealthy. Through that vision, they pursue success, relentlessly. Their vision gives them the passion and persistence to keep going when the going gets tough, which is often, especially in the early stages of their entrepreneurial journey.
- I Will Do Work That I Like or Love: They become Entrepreneurs because they are pursuing a dream they are passionate about. Because they like or love their work, they are willing to walk through Hell in achieving their dreams and goals.
- I Will Forge Daily Goal Habits: Entrepreneurs pursue their goals every day. The pursuit of these goals is part of their daily Priority List. They continuously tweak their goals as they are forced to navigate around unexpected problems, mistakes, failures and obstacles.
- I Will Forge Good Health Habits: Most Entrepreneurs in my Rich Habits Study were avid exercisers. They understood that exercise, especially aerobic exercise, helped boost brain performance and energy levels, allowing them to weather those long work days.
- I Will Maintain a Positive Mental Outlook: More than any class of self-made millionaire, Entrepreneurs depend on their positive mental outlook for success. Their upbeat, never-quit attitude enables them to: weather the entrepreneurial rollercoaster ride, find solutions to problems and see opportunities that are invisible to others.

- I Will Control My Words and Emotions: Because the entrepreneurial journey is such a rollercoaster ride, it is imperative that they are in full command of their emotions. They do not have the luxury to lose their cool or get depressed – such things could quickly sink them, especially in the early stages of their journey.

- I Will Never Quit on My Dreams: Successful Entrepreneurs become successful because they simply refuse to quit on their dreams, no matter how difficult the journey becomes.

- I will Forge Positive Beliefs and Eliminate Negative Beliefs: Entrepreneurs eliminate any negative, limiting beliefs they might have and forge positive beliefs. They understand that negative beliefs are like stop signs on the journey to success and those stop signs must be removed if they are to succeed.

- I Will Seek Out Success Mentors: Mentors are the fast-track to success. Entrepreneurs seek out mentors within their industry, to help them figure out what works and what does not work. This saves them time and, more importantly, money, which is often a scarce commodity, especially during the early stages of their entrepreneurial journey. Mentors also infect Entrepreneurs with their good habits.

- I Will Take Calculated Risks in the Pursuit of my Dreams and Goals: Successful Entrepreneurs make a habit of doing their homework before making any investment of time or money. This significantly reduces their investment risk.

- I Will Create Multiple Streams of Income: Most successful Entrepreneurs devote a minimum of 12 years in turning a dream into a profitable business. They then use their core business to help launch other related side businesses which generate additional, separate streams of income. The average Entrepreneur in my Rich Habits Study had three revenue streams that they created. These multiple revenue streams were instrumental in helping them grow their wealth.

- I Will Use the Power of Leverage to help Me Achieve My Goals and Realise My Dreams: Entrepreneurs leverage existing assets, cash flow, their Power Relationships with Influencers, knowledge, skills and their brand to help them succeed in achieving their goals and realising their dreams.

- I Will Not Let Fear and Doubt Prevent Me from Taking Action on My Goals and Dreams: Entrepreneurs develop the habit of being courageous. While they have fears, they do not let their fears stop them from acting on their goals and dreams. Taking action despite their fears, and surviving, helps boost their confidence.

- I Will Seek Feedback from Others: Entrepreneurs learn, grow and improve by seeking feedback from others. This feedback helps them become better at what they do.

- I Will Ask for What I Want or Need: Entrepreneurs make a habit of asking for help from others in order to get what they want or need.

- I Will Create Priority Lists and To Don't Lists: Because Entrepreneurs put in the most hours out of any group of self-made millionaires in my Rich Habits Study, their time is valuable to them. To help them manage their time, they used Priority Lists and To Don't Lists in order to be able to focus on the most important things they need to do to keep moving ahead.

- I Will Ask Questions in Order to Learn from Others: Entrepreneurs boost their knowledge and improve their skills by asking many questions. They have a close-knit group of insiders they make a habit of bouncing questions off. These insiders are experts, other entrepreneurs and other successful people.

- I Will Seek to Add Value to the Lives of Others: Entrepreneurs succeed when they are able to add value to the lives of others. People and organisations are willing to pay them for their products or services because those products and services improve their lives in some way.

So, the good news is that there is more than one way to skin a cat. You can become rich no matter your personality type. You just have to know which path to wealth is right for you, based upon your individual personality.

SECTION FOUR

# WHY RICH ASSOCIATIONS AND RICH THINKING MATTER

*Michael Yardney and Tom Corley*

# CHAPTER 46
# MODELS, MENTORS AND MASTERMINDS

In this final section of our book we're going to explore the importance of models, mentors and masterminds in the lives of the rich and successful.

First up, we'll spend some time explaining how our decisions — good and bad — are based on our internal subconscious mindset and this is in turn is based on what we call "models".

## What is a model?

Your model is your own internal construction that encompasses the way your brain helps you to make sense of the world. Some of your models will be positive and others negative, some are supportive and others are obstructive.

What's important to understand is the power these can have; once you believe in a model, whether it helps you or harms you, as soon as you accept it to be true it will become your mind's reality and you'll no longer even think about it. It enters into your subconscious, and continues to impact on the way you deal with the world.

The problem is we completely ignore that the model is there, running in the background, manipulating our inner dialogue — for better or worse. As much as we try to stick to the facts, ***we look at the world through our tinted glasses*** and perceive things only according to the manner in which our mind allows us to think about them.

Our perception is our reality.

That's why it's important to have an effective wealth model; because the amount of wealth you create will depend on exactly how much your model will enable you to have.

## Modelling

And even though most of us were never taught money skills, we can learn them by modelling somebody who already possesses sound money habits.

In the early 1970s, when Michael stared investing in property and wanted to become successful at it, he discovered that his own learning and experience wasn't enough. So he started to look elsewhere and turned to books, teachers, mentors and even consultants for advice. And they all seemed to point to the one common denominator — one of your best educational tools is to learn from others; people who have gone before you and done what you want to do.

What this meant was that he didn't have to start from the beginning and learn from his own mistakes. In fact, he could start where someone else had left off, he could give up his need to "do" in order to learn. In fact, he could learn faster.

You see... when Michael first started investing he wanted to do it all himself.

There were probably two reasons behind this — one was he thought it was the best way to learn. The second reason (and he's prepared to admit it) was that he had Poor Habits — he was "cheap". He thought it would save him money doing it all myself, when in fact it cost him much more. ***Experience is an expensive teacher.***

When Michael recognised he didn't have to do it all himself or make countless mistakes — it was one of his biggest "a-ha" moments. In fact, now he jokingly says that some of his best thinking was done by other people.

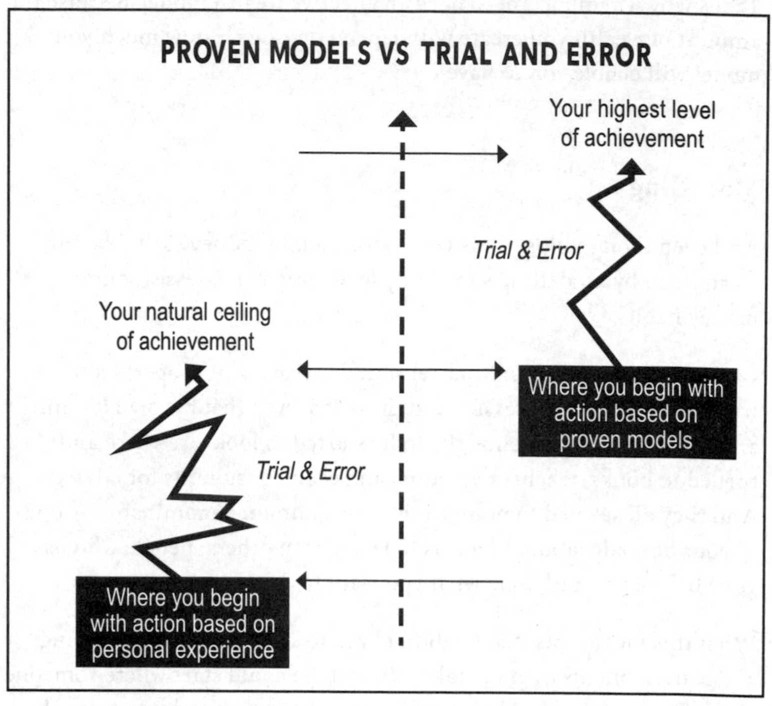


Michael remembers reading a great book by Tony Robbins many years ago — *Unlimited Power* — who put a name to what he was looking for, which was **modelling**. In his book he explained the process for finding these proven models. He suggested that you should look at the very best people in a field and study what they do, how they behave and how they think and then do the same.

And guess what? By taking this approach you can often repeat their success.

The key is to learn how they achieved their goals and then understand why they did it the way they did. When you grasp these two things, you can start your own journey where they left off.

When Michael realised this years ago he started to become an avid reader of success stories, searching for models to base his growth on.

He looked for people who had already achieved what he wanted to achieve and then studied how they did it. This led him to the point now, where he has been a mentor for others and runs a 12-month Mentorship Program: www.MichaelYardney.com.au.

One of the basic themes of the program is that your wealth, your external life and your relationships can only grow to the extent that you do. So one of the program's aims is to enable participants to grow to a place where they can overcome all of the obstacles and problems that get in the way of creating the life they deserve and creating the wealth they want.

But it's not just about getting the money; it's not just about attaining the wealth; once you have it you need to maintain it. And to in order to maintain wealth most people are going to have to upgrade those files in their mind — their financial blueprint.

An analogy we've heard people use is to think of yourself as a cup. If your cup is small but your wealth is abundant, it will spill over and you will lose it. You simply cannot have more money than your cup will accommodate.

So does this mean you should accept having less money?

Not at all; you must grow yourself into a bigger cup so that you can not only obtain more wealth but attract more wealth — by changing your mindset.

As you know, the universe hates a vacuum. This means that if you have a large money container, wealth will rush in to fill in the space. In other words, upgrade your way of thinking, become a bigger person and you will attract more wealth.

Most people want to grow, want to improve and want to lift their personal ceilings of achievement, and they think they can do this through trial and error — they are prepared to learn from their mistakes. Yes, you can learn and improve this way — but only so far and so fast. ***Learning from your mistakes is a slow and demoralising way of growing yourself.***

In contrast, seeking out mentors and learning from those who have achieved what you want to achieve can help raise your level of accomplishment dramatically, and in a relatively short period of time. Of course, it's not a guarantee of success, but a proven model built on the practices of people who have already achieved what you want to achieve that will maximise your chances of success.

Models aren't really new — they are everywhere. Everyone follows them — most people just aren't aware of these repeatable processes they have developed, like how to tie your shoelaces or brush your teeth. Apart from models rich people also have teams around them…

## What's the secret to being rich and successful?

If you were planning to scale Mount Kilimanjaro next year, wouldn't you want to speak with someone who had survived the journey to the top? You'd be surprised how many people, starting the climb up their own financial mountains, ask the advice of people who are floundering below sea level.

There is no way most people would be multi-millionaires today without their team. ***Having a good team reduces your risk***, increases your knowledge and gives you access to ideas, opportunities and funds you would never have on your own. We have found that collective knowledge and experience lowers risk when investing.

When first starting your journey into wealth creation, you will very likely be working alone. You'll be flying solo in learning, researching and finding investment opportunities.

That's fine, you've got to start somewhere.

However, putting the right team together will accelerate your learning and, more importantly, it will accelerate your wealth accumulation. It's going to take you time and energy to put the right team together, but it's a necessary part of learning and growing. What might take the typical investor 10 years or more to learn, you can learn in one or two years with the right team in place.

There are two aspects to having a wealth team on your side:

1. *Building your team.* You'll have to find the right team members and sometimes that means spending a little more money than you want.

2. *Leading your team.* It's up to you to be in control of your wealth and that means leading your team.

## Who's on your wealth team?

This will vary for everyone, but here's a general list of the kinds of people you'll want to consider:

***The Leader***

That's you! It's your job to find the team members and then lead them by directing them towards your goals. Even while you're in the steep learning curve of Level 3 investing, you have to maintain control. In other words, although at times you may want to abdicate control to "more experienced" team members, you'll have to push yourself to maintain control. You drive your wealth; you are responsible and accountable for everything.

***Advisors***

Get the best team you can around you — if you are the smartest person in your team, you are in trouble. You need to surround yourself with a team of professionals including a tax-savvy accountant, a smart lawyer who can help you with asset protection, a proficient mortgage broker and an independent property investment strategist — not one who sells property or has a vested interest in helping the vendor or project developer, but someone who is independent and truly on your side.

At first you may be reluctant to pay for advice, because there seems to be so much "free" advice available in books, on the Internet, in chat forums, etc. Here's the best piece of free advice you will receive — ***free advice is very expensive.*** We've heard someone call the cost of the mistakes most investors make trying to do it on their own a "stupid tax".

You won't ever get to Level 3 or 4 on the Wealth Pyramid and develop financial independence without a team of professionals who appreciate what you're creating and understand the principles of wealth creation.

***Mentors***
We've always had mentors, who eventually become peers and associates. Then, we look for new mentors. These are people who know more, have done more, and are skilled and successful in the areas in which you're currently learning.

***Utility Players***
Growing your wealth takes time and effort and as your investment portfolio grows, your time becomes more valuable.

What if you hired people at $15 to $20 an hour to handle all the mundane tasks that take time away from you earning 10 times that amount? You could hire someone to clean your home, mow your lawn, pay your bills and handle your bookkeeping and correspondence. Even to run your errands. An errand that takes you a couple of hours to complete keeps you from spending that time learning, researching or finding a deal that could net you thousands of dollars. Remember that ***millionaires don't clean their own homes or run their own errands.***

Growing your wealth requires time, patience and your leadership. If you truly want to be wealthy, then you will build a team and you will lead that team. There is no other way.

## Mentors matter

People at Level 3 and 4 on the Wealth Pyramid recognise the need for mentors; people they can look up to and from whom they can seek guidance and inspiration. These are people who have been successful and achieved many of the things that they are still aiming to accomplish in life.

Mentors have been critical in Michael's success — they have helped him see things that he couldn't see. He says they identified his blind spots, encouraged him to think differently and made him accountable for his decisions.

We've heard it said that by seeking the advice of a mentor; "somebody's hindsight can become your foresight". All of the successful people we know have benefited from having a mentor.

The rich employ mentors who have already done what they want to do and are successful at doing it. On the other hand, the poor take counsel from advisors who tell them how to do it, but have not personally done it.

By the way… we all have mentors.

You will already have people you model. Sometimes you pick them consciously, sometimes you pick them unconsciously. Some people (unconsciously) pick the people from the Kardashians, Desperate Housewives or The Bold and the Beautiful as their models — interesting isn't it?

## How mentors can help you

Mentors can help you to become rich by contributing to your wealth creation in the following ways:

1. Imparting knowledge: a mentor can bring a wider range of experience to the table and offer you the opportunity to gain years of knowledge in a short space of time. This could be a personal mentor or you could learn from someone who has done it before through a book, a DVD or seminar.

2. Sharing experience: we are all taught to learn by trial and error, but you should learn from somebody else's mistakes, rather than make costly errors yourself. A good mentor will have a thorough understanding of the dos and don'ts to help prevent you making your own mistakes.

3. Mentors make you present your ideas and then make you think long and hard about your ideas and what you're planning to do make you justify what you are planning to do.

4. Providing contacts: ***a good mentor will have contacts that can help you*** to seek out and identify opportunities you wouldn't have found yourself. In this world, it's not who you know, but who you know knows. Having a wide range of contacts will help you enormously.

5. Mentors can motivate you and help you achieve in different areas that you may not have thought you could find success in.

6. Mentors can save you time: having done it before, they can show you the shortcuts and teach you the potholes to avoid, helping you to navigate and take the right turns on your road to riches.

7. ***Mentors are independent and won't have a vested interest in what you do***, so they can offer you support. They'll understand when you're feeling high and why you're feeling low at times and they can relate to the challenges you will go through on your climb up the ladder to being rich and successful.

## Surround yourself with support

One of the keys to success of those who climb the Wealth Pyramid is surrounding themselves with supportive people and recognising the right friends and network of people who can provide support and encouragement along the way.

You see… our peers, the people we associate with, have a great deal of influence over us because they make up our group affiliations. As humans we are innately social beings; we like to form groups for comfort, support and security. Over time these groups develop their own set of values and morals, which become our reference model for how we interact with the wider world. These groups can consist of our families, friends, churches, clubs, golfing partners or whatever.

Many of us crave these informal group associations because they give us a sense of identity and companionship as we move through life. We like to belong to groups and if you think about it, since our group affiliations have such a profound impact on our personal values and priorities, it's important that we associate with supportive and optimistic people as we strive for a better life.

Unfortunately, our world is filled with pessimistic people who often keep us from moving forward and finding the success and joys that we desire in life. One of the tragic mistakes we've seen too many people make on their road to success is listening to all the critics along the way. Too many people put too much emphasis on the silly advice of unsuccessful people. This is particularly evident when people are feeling nervous after hearing or reading all the negative messages the media keeps feeding us.

So why is it that some people are so critical and unsupportive?

Obviously there's not one clear answer, but let's explore this for a moment.

Some people are naturally critical of people who try to succeed because they don't want to admit that they are unhappy with their own circumstances. It boils down to this: for many, another's success merely highlights their own personal failures. Of course, this even happens with family or friends.

Another reason people are unsupportive is because they are jealous or envious. Envy is just an advanced degree of the old green-eyed envy monster, but what we really mean is when some people wish that they had what their friends already possess — they covet their friends' success rather than celebrate it. And since the envious person doesn't have what his friend already has, they wish their friend didn't have it either.

Maybe we can explain that a bit better… jealousy causes a person to wish for something he or she doesn't have; envy causes them to wish the other person didn't have what they don't have.

Unfortunately, the only taste of success some people ever get is when they take a bite of you!

Another reason that you may find some people are unsupportive is because of your own unrealistic expectations. It's important to understand that as you move towards your success you will encounter people who aren't as excited about your own personal growth as you are.

In some ways, it's unrealistic to expect everyone around you to feel the same intense passion about your progress as you do. Don't get too disappointed by an indifferent response; simply realise that ***no one will be as excited about your own personal achievements as you are.***

The antidote to this lack of support from some of the people you have come to know and love throughout your life is to have a handful of supportive people; people who encourage and inspire you.

That's one of the reasons Michael conducts his Mentorship Program and encourages members to have mentorship buddies and form a MasterMind Group. It's important to surround yourself with safe and supportive people, because one of the ways we process information while undertaking the act of changing our financial mindset is by talking about what we're experiencing.

Without the right people around you, you won't have anyone to bounce your ideas off. Surrounding yourself with safe and supportive people is vital when it comes to making significant changes in your life. Peer pressure is a powerful influence — it can encourage us to step out in faith towards a better future, or it can shame us into settling for the status quo.

The influence of encouraging people who spur us on to believe in ourselves and take positive steps can make all the difference to help us transform our lives for the better. One of the best ways to achieve this is to...

## Be part of a Mastermind Group

One of the most powerful tools ever used by successful people — whether they were rich industrialists in the early 20th century or today's super achievers — is that they were part of a MasterMind Group. Napoleon Hill discovered the power of a MasterMind Group and wrote about it in his acclaimed book — *Think and Grow Rich* — almost 100 years ago.

Just to make it clear, this is an alliance of two or more people who work together for the achievement of a definite purpose in a spirit of mutual harmony and cooperation.

When you form a MasterMind Group, we're not talking about positive thinking or affirmations, it's another easy way of reprogramming yourself for success. While you must always do the work of becoming a success, a MasterMind Group can harness and maximise the focus behind your success.

The ideal size of a mastermind group is five to six people. If it is too small, it loses its dynamics. If it's bigger, it gets unwieldy — meetings take longer, some needs go unmet and personal sharing is minimised.

Ideally, each mastermind meeting should be conducted weekly, for about one hour, preferably in person but can be over Skype with all members of the group in attendance.

Some of the benefits you can experience as a member of a MasterMind Group include:

- Being held accountable
- Being questioned and challenged
- Being listened to
- Being recognised for my achievements
- Being accepted
- Being motivated

Understanding how models, mentors and masterminds can help you develop Rich Habits and kick-start you along the path to success is one of the fundamental skills that you need to master if you're serious about changing your life.

# CHAPTER 47
# WHAT EVERY PARENT SHOULD TEACH THEIR CHILDREN ABOUT GETTING RICH

You've now reached the penultimate chapter of our book. Well done for persevering and for learning which Poor Habits you might have and which Rich Habits you need to adopt sooner rather than later.

In this chapter, we'll both give you our thoughts on some of the most important factors which determine whether a child is going to grow up rich or poor.

According to a Duke University Study (2006) 40 per cent or more of our daily activities, thinking and the choices we make are habits. And most of the habits we take with us into our adults lives, we learned from our parents, our teachers or our environment.

This is a good thing if kids are learning good success habits, what we call Rich Habits, but this is a very bad thing if kids are learning bad failure habits, what we call Poor Habits.

Unfortunately, most kids are not being taught good habits at home. Worse, our schools are not stepping up to the plate to teach in school what is not being taught at home.

We've just explained the importance of mentors and role models. The fact is that as parents we are the most important mentors and models for our children. What this means is we teach our children to be either rich or poor.

But with some insight can change your habits so your children have a better chance of a successful and rich life.

While Tom is writing his thoughts about the United States and Michael is including an Australian point of view to this discussion, the principles we're teaching are universal. They apply to anyone in any country.

## Michael's Insights

Will your children be rich or poor?

You have a big say in it, so if you've got children or are planning to have children at some stage in your life, this chapter is a must-read for you.

Let me start by posing two questions: What messages are you giving your children about money?

What lessons are you teaching your children about money, wealth and rich people?

Unfortunately, ***most of us are setting up our children to fail financially in life.***

In his study Tom found poor parents teach their children their Poverty Habits and wealthy parents teach their children their Rich Habits.

My children are grown up now, having children of their own. But if I had my time over again here are 12 lessons we would have taught them when they were young.

1. **The sooner you save, the faster your money can grow through compounding**

It takes money to make money so teach your kids the importance of spending less than they earn, saving the difference until they have sufficient money to buy appreciating assets.

Part of this is learning how to budget. You can start by teaching your children the art of saving for "big ticket" items once they're old enough to earn a few bucks for washing the car or bathing the dog.

### 2. You may have to wait to buy something you want

This is a hard concept for people of all ages to learn, however the ability to delay gratification can also predict how successful one will be as a grown-up. I talked about this concept in detail in a previous chapter. Children need to learn that if they really want something, they should wait and save to buy it.

The problem is we all want the best for our children, which is why a common trap for parents is giving their kids everything they feel they missed out on growing up. Trampoline in the backyard? Check. Brand new clothes each season? Check. Entitled, impatient attitude geared towards instant gratification? Check!

It may make you feel good to give your child all the toys and gadgets they desire, but in doing so you're not doing them any favours. The lesson you want to demonstrate is not one of instant gratification, but one that shows how much reward comes from putting in incremental amounts of effort.

If your child patiently saves $2 per week for a few months to buy a $20 toy, how much do you think they're going to love their new prize? And more importantly, when lessons like this are learned young, it will encourage them to manage their money more smartly as they get older.

### 3. You need to make choices about how to spend money

It's important to explain to your child that ***money is finite and it's important to make wise choices,*** because once you've spent it, you don't have more to spend!

### 4. Today's debt equals tomorrow's slavery

When we're younger we tend to think in very narrow time increments, seek immediate gratification and don't like delaying the purchase of something that we really want.

Unfortunately, this leads many to fall into the credit card trap we've spoken about. But ***today's debt will rob them of tomorrow's earnings*** because they're sacrificing money they don't yet have.

Limiting debt obligations when you're younger will mean having more control over your personal finances later in life.

**5. He or she who dies with the most toys is not the victor**

We all like our toys. Well… I know I do. But expectation is a dreadful enemy of money management.

We see so much of how "the other half live" in glossy magazines and on television these days; glorified as something to aspire to, making many of us think life is all about working just so you can be one of the "have mores" of the world.

Consumerism is the "new black".

The truth is possessions don't make for a rich life; it's the experiences and people — the things that money can't buy — that make you truly wealthy. In my mind "true wealth" is what you're left with if you lose all your money and possessions.

**6. Taking responsibility makes you the master of your own destiny**

Fact is: there are no rich victims.

Yet unfortunately people are too quick to blame others for their own failings in life. We have become a society of litigious finger pointers and, as a result, many people feel they've been unjustly dealt a "bad hand".

The truth is, if you're courageous enough to cast a critical eye over your life, recognise you are where you are as a direct result of your own choices and take ownership of your decisions, you build confidence, self esteem and self respect.

In turn, you'll feel an inner strength in knowing you are master of your own destiny, rather than handing your power and control over to someone else who, let's face it, won't have your best interests at heart the way you do.

**7. Patience and waiting is...**

When you fly the family coop, no doubt you'll want everything yesterday — the flashy car, new furniture and the biggest TV money can buy. But in all likelihood you'll have to work your way up the food chain, learning to prioritise how to make the best use of your fortnightly pay as you go.

***Understand the difference between wants and needs*** and recognise that all the money you spend on those material items you just "had to have" today, is less that you'll have to fund your retirement with tomorrow.

It's that delayed gratification thing again isn't it, knowing that if you work hard and invest even harder, your purchasing power will increase over time!

**8. Luck is made through hard work**

Many of us like to attribute the success of others all to "good fortune". Perhaps they were in "the right place at the right time" or knew "the right person". While a handful of people have lucked out by winning the lottery, truly successful people do the hard yards to reach the pinnacle of their chosen field or endeavour.

If you can find something that you're passionate about and make a living doing it, you'll be far more likely to achieve great things because you'll work harder to reach your goals... and every day won't be a struggle.

**9. You don't need millions to achieve financial freedom**

Plenty of millionaires are up to their eyeballs in debt and that's the truth of it. Many of society's rich power players are asset-rich, but cash poor. Other people who earn $50,000 a year are without debt and have more financial freedom.

Financial freedom is not dependent on money itself, but on your relationship to it and the level of personal responsibility and fiscal discipline you're prepared to exercise throughout life.

**10. Only use a credit card if you can pay the balance off in full each month**

Buy now — interest free! No repayments for 24 months! It's all too easy to slide into credit card debt, which gives your child the burden of paying off credit card debt at exorbitant interest rates. Plus a default could affect their credit history, which could make it difficult to, say, buy a car or a home.

**11. You're youth won't last forever, so use it wisely**

Compounding to grow your wealth relies on more than money — it relies on time.

In fact, given enough time, compound interest — that is the interest earned on the interest earned on your high growth assets — is so effective that Albert Einstein called it the most powerful force in the universe.

***Start saving and investing early in life*** and you're likely to secure your financial future.

**12. Spend less than you earn and invest the rest**

If you follow this one golden rule above all else, you will quickly establish yourself on the path to financial freedom.

Aim to invest at least 10 per cent of your earnings and the power of compounding will take care of the rest. And speaking of the power of compounding…

## The bottom line

I'm trying to show you that the rich have good daily success habits that they learned from their parents. These daily habits are the real reason for the wealth gap in our country and the real reason why the rich keep getting richer.

We are likely to be the only mentors, and we're definitely likely to be the most influential mentors, our children ever have. Unless we teach our children good daily success habits, and level the playing field, the rich will continue to get richer and the poor will continue to get poorer.

So it just might pay (literally) to give them a bit of your time.

## Tom's insights

### *Why is there so much unrest in America's inner cities?*

The experts are quick to point the finger of blame at a variety of causes: low wages, racial discrimination, police gone wild, America's shrinking manufacturing base, US companies moving oversees, China stealing our jobs, illegal immigrants stealing our jobs, poor education system, the rich exploiting the poor, insufficient taxation of the rich, etc.

But none of these pundits ever address the real source of this unrest — ***bad parenting***.

America's growing discontent among the poor of the inner cities and the growing disparity nationwide between the rich and the poor is a reflection of how America's "haves" and "have-nots" were raised by their parents.

As you know by now, I spent five years conducting my Rich Habits

Study. And then I detailed many of the habits that separate the rich and the poor in my books *Rich Habits, Rich Kids* and *Change Your Habits, Change Your Life* and of course this book.

## What I learned from my five-year study was that habits are contagious

Almost all of the self-made millionaires in my study picked up specific habits from their parents that gave them a leg up and enabled them to build a successful, happy and fulfilled life.

And almost all of the poor in my study picked up habits from their parents that contributed to a generational cycle of poverty, misery and discontent.

***Nicolas Christakis, a Yale University professor and leading researcher on socially contagious behaviours agrees.*** In his research, he found that ***habits are contagious, passed from parents to children, good or bad.***

There are a number of examples of contagious habits which you may recognise:

- If parents eat healthy, their children will eat healthy. If parents are overweight, their children will be overweight.
- If parents smoke cigarettes, their children are more likely to smoke cigarettes.
- If parents exercise regularly, their children will exercise regularly. If they don't exercise, their children will not exercise.
- If parents value education and learning, their children will value education and learning. If they don't, their children will not.
- If parents are law-abiding, their children will be law-abiding. If parents are lawbreakers, their children will become lawbreakers.
- If parents are violent, they will raise violent children.
- If parents have an optimistic, positive outlook, their children will have an optimistic, positive outlook. If parents are pessimistic and negative, their children will be pessimistic and negative.

## Habits spread like a virus

The habits you learn from your parents shape the life you lead. They will either lift you up or tear you down.

In my study I found a number of habits which successful people picked up from their parents which helped them to succeed later in life. These include:

1. **You Create Your Life.** The self-made individuals in my study were taught that they were the architects of their lives. You and you alone create the circumstances that make you rich or poor.

2. **Individual Responsibility.** Self-made individuals were not allowed to play the victim. ***They were taught to take personal responsibility for the good and bad in life*** and were not allowed to blame anyone but themselves when things went wrong because things always go wrong in life.

3. **Respect for the Law.** They learned from their parents to respect police and law enforcement officials. If they broke the law their parents punished them severely.

4. **Pursue Your Main Purpose.** They were exposed to numerous novel activities. The purpose of this was to help their kids discover their in-born talents.

   About 93 per cent either liked or loved their jobs. When you find and use your innate talents to make money that leads to happiness and financial success because you will want to devote more time to anything you love doing.

   When you can make money doing what you love this leads you to your true calling in life. Most parents don't do this. Most lock their kids into one or two activities for 10 years or more. As a result, kids never have an opportunity to explore different activities. There's just not enough time to learn something new when you spend most of that time on travel teams.

5. **Pursue Dreams and Goals.** About 61 per cent were required to Dream-Set which is the process of writing out a script of your ideal perfect life. This script then became a blueprint for their lives. Some 80 per cent were taught to focus on one stretch goal (long-term goal) until they achieved it. About 97 per cent were taught a very different definition of a goal, which is: all goals require physical action and all goals must be 100 per cent achievable, meaning you have the knowledge and skills to pursue the goal.

   Most failed at achieving goals because they were taught the wrong definition of a goal, which is: goals are broad objectives, like making $100,000 a year. That's a dream, not a goal. Goals and dreams are not the same thing. You create goals around each dream and when you realise all of the goals, you realise your dream.

6. **Pursuing Wealth is a Good Thing.** About 97 per cent were taught that wealthy people were good, honest and hardworking. They were not evil or greedy.

7. **Hard Work Ethic.** The self-made individuals were not given things by their parents. ***They were required to work for the things they wanted.*** At an early age (nine or 10) they had to work to buy things they wanted. About 55 per cent were forced to work 10 or more hours per month, at a minimum.

8. **Respect Property of Others.** They were taught by their parents to respect the hard-earned property of others.

9. **Daily Self-Improvement.** Some 88 per cent were required to read educational books a minimum of 30 minutes or more every day. About 54 per cent were required to learn new words to expand their vocabulary and 68 per cent were programmed for college — they were indoctrinated with the idea at an early age that they would be going to college.

10. **Use Time Productively.** Finally, they don't allow their kids to waste time on TV, video games, social media, internet, etc.

Of course I also studied the poor and found some common habits that they picked up from their parents, which set them on a path to poverty in their life.

1. **Dependence on Government and Handouts.** Poor people were taught to rely on government benefits and the handouts from others. This created a dependency mindset that stayed with them their entire adult lives.

2. **Defiance of the Law.** They were taught that because the cards were stacked against them, the police and law enforcement were their enemies and were intent to keep them down and out. This mindset puts many of the poor in prison, which only keeps them poor.

3. **Resenting the Rich.** They were taught to despise those who were successful because the rich were evil, greedy and responsible for poverty because they paid low wages.

4. **Poor Work Ethic.** They were taught, by example, to seek out free government benefits in order to help them survive. ***Dependency results in a poor work ethic.*** Why work if you can get what you need without working?

5. **Entitlement Thinking.** They instilled in their kids the belief that the poor were unfairly persecuted and taken advantage of by the rich. Therefore, they were entitled to the property of rich people. About 87 per cent of the poor believed rich people should be taxed more so that government would have more money to give back to poor people.

6. **Gambling.** They learned from their parents that gambling was one of the only ways out of poverty. As a result, 77 per cent of the poor gambled on the lottery every week.

7. **Drugs.** They learned by watching their parents that drugs were their only escape from their hellish existence. About 60 per cent of the poor admitted to getting drunk frequently.

8. **Over Eating.** They picked up the bad eating habits of their parents so 66 per cent of the poor were 30 pounds or more overweight

9. **Waste Time.** They watched their parents spend hours in front of a TV and that habit became contagious. About 77 per cent admitted that they watched more than an hour of TV every night, while 78 per cent admitted to watching a lot of reality TV. This time-wasting habit infected their own kids. The poor in my study said that their own kids spend many hours every day watching TV, playing video games or spending their time on social media, the internet, etc.

## The buck stops with parents

***Children mimic the habits of their parents.***

Parents are the only shot most have at a mentor in life.

When parents are poor mentors, their kids suffer and this often leads to poverty; a cycle of poverty that extends to multiple generations and causes discontent, dragging society down along with them.

# CHAPTER 48
# SOME FINAL THOUGHTS

One of our assumptions behind writing this book was that the big question on many people's minds today is "How do I get rich?" And we wanted to provide readers with some answers.

And while Michael has provided a few financial concepts at the beginning of the book, our main goal was to teach you about the way rich people feel, think and behave — we wanted to teach you their Rich Habits.

While there are many books on money and investing, and there is plenty of content on the internet about how to get rich, we believe the fastest way for you to become financially successful is to adopt the thoughts, behaviours and habits of people who are already rich.

You see… all successful people have successful habits and ***all rich people have Rich Habits*** — habits that they have created and refined over time because they help them reach their goals and we've shared them with you in this book.

So now it is your turn to ask yourself which of these habits will help you achieve your goals?

## Where do you start?

There are four steps involved in the formula of developing these Rich Habits.

### 1. Develop Awareness

The first step is to evaluate your current position. How are you going financially?

Become aware of what's working — the thoughts, actions and habits you want to keep.

Then clearly identify your Poor Habits — your unproductive and disempowering habits. It's also important for you to think about the future consequences of your bad habits.

The problem is, as you look at your Poor Habits one day at a time, they may not seem so bad, but compounding these into the future, a month, a year, a decade ahead — then the consequences can be devastating.

### 2. Discard your Poor Habits

Now that you understand that some habits are holding you back it's time to discard your Poor Habits.

### 3. Develop new Rich Habits

You then need to adopt the belief systems and habits of rich and successful people.

Model yourself on other successful people — people who have already achieved what you want to achieve.
Define the Rich Habits that you want to adopt. Often these are the exact opposite of the Poor Habits you want to drop. Ask yourself what you're going to need to do and to motivate yourself, think about all the benefits and rewards to you and your family are going to achieve if you adopt these new Rich Habits.

The more vividly you describe the benefits, the more likely you are to take the actions.

### 4. Take Action

Write down which actions you are going to take and then take action!

It's called Be, Do, Have. You become the person you want to be as soon as you start thinking and acting like that person.

If you want to become wealthy, become wealthy in your mind first (be that person). Then ***do what wealthy people do*** — act wealthy and practice Rich Habits. In turn you will have what wealthy people have.

That's because wealth is a result. It's a result of your thoughts beliefs and habits, which lead to your actions.

We've said it before, but it's so important we'll say it again… Nothing will change until you change. If things aren't working out the way you want them to, you need to stop taking the easy way out and blaming outside factors.

It's not your boss's fault, nor is it the government's fault or the market's fault. It's not even a lack of information. You need to stop justifying why you are not financially successful.

Most of what you have today you have attracted by becoming the person you are. If you want things to change in your life financially, you must change first.

It is important for you to understand that you are fully responsible for your financial results.

The good news is that your life can change because you can change.

Once we throw out our blame list and start becoming more of ourselves — interestingly everything will begin to change around us.

## What now?

The trouble with so many books is that when you've finished them, you're finished with what they have to tell you. What happens after that? Readers are often left to their own devices to try to take the next step and put the theory they have learned into action. This book is going to be a little bit different.

We are eager for the ideas in this book to work for you, so we have assembled a "tool-kit" of resources for you to help you in your climb up the investment ladder — just go to www.RichHabitsPoorHabits.com and collect them now. There's special reports, spreadsheets, the results of Tom's study and much more.

We also recommend you subscribe to our blogs — Michael's at www.PropertyUpdate.com.au and Tom's at www.RichHabits.net so we can keep you up-to-date with how we're thinking.

And subscribe to The Michael Yardney Podcast on your favourite podcast app — where Michael and Tom regularly chat about Rich Habits and Poor Habits.

So thank you for reading this book — now it's up to you!

You now have the knowledge to take the next steps and develop Rich Habits. You are now ready to join the ranks of the financially free. When you do, please email us and let us know about your success. We love getting emails from readers of our books who have successfully put our strategies to work.

Spend your time… wisely.

Michael Yardney — michael@metropole.com.au

Tom Corley — tom@RichHabits.net